# The Colonialism of Human Rights

# The Colonialism of Human Rights

## Ongoing Hypocrisies of Western Liberalism

## Colin Samson

polity

First published in 2020 by Polity Press

2

Polity Press
65 Bridge Street
Cambridge CB2 1UR, UK

Polity Press
101 Station Landing
Suite 300
Medford, MA 02155, USA

ISBN-13: 978-1-5095-2997-1
ISBN-13: 978-1-5095-2998-8 (pb)

A catalogue record for this book is available from the British Library.

Library of Congress Cataloging-in-Publication Data

Names: Samson, Colin, author.
Title: The colonialism of human rights : ongoing hypocrisies of western
    liberalism / Colin Samson.
Description: Cambridge, UK ; Medford, MA : Polity, 2020. | Includes
    bibliographical references and index. | Summary: "Human rights have
    never been universal and the costs are still being unequally paid
    today"-- Provided by publisher.
Identifiers: LCCN 2020000112 (print) | LCCN 2020000113 (ebook) | ISBN
    9781509529971 (hardback) | ISBN 9781509529988 (paperback) | ISBN
    9781509530007 (epub)
Subjects: LCSH: Human rights--Developing countries. | Imperialism--History.
    | Slavery--History. | Indigenous peoples--Colonization. | Indigenous
    peoples--Civil rights. | North and south.
Classification: LCC JC599.D44 S26 2020  (print) | LCC JC599.D44  (ebook) |
    DDC 323.09172/4--dc23
LC record available at https://lccn.loc.gov/2020000112
LC ebook record available at https://lccn.loc.gov/2020000113

Typeset in 10 on 12pt Sabon
by Fakenham Prepress Solutions, Fakenham, Norfolk NR21 8NL
Printed and bound in Great Britain by TJ International Limited

For further information on Polity, visit our website:
politybooks.com

# Contents

# Figures

# Acknowledgements

Exchanges with many people have seeped into my thinking and writing.

For twenty-five years, I have researched and worked with indigenous groups in many places, and these experiences sensitized me to the ongoing nature of colonialism. Seeing how indigenous peoples struggle to maintain their lands and ways of life against the power of national governments to dispossess and assimilate them made me aware of parallels with formerly colonized and enslaved peoples. I saw such parallels while working with the Innu of the Labrador-Quebec Peninsula, joining families in hunting camps on lands officially earmarked as 'Crown land', and attending meetings between Innu and the Canadian government. Among many, I would like to thank Napes Ashini, Marcel Ashini, George Rich and Tony Jenkinson. As a volunteer at the Oceti Sakowin camp in 2016, I participated in the Water Protectors movement at Standing Rock to contest an oil pipeline driving through Sioux lands and sacred places. I would like to thank all those who educated me and took me to Standing Rock while I was at the University of Wyoming, as a visiting professor in 2015–16. These include Caskey Russell, Reinette Tendore and Giz Tendore, and also Tory Fodder, who wasn't at Standing Rock, but was a great source of wisdom.

Some people have read whole chapters of my book, and I owe much to the insights they provided me. Øyvind Ravna of the University of Tromsø not only taught me a lot about treaties and international law, but also read Chapter 5 and gave me valuable feedback. Nawel Hamidi, a Ph.D. student at the University of Essex, read Chapter 4, providing expert guidance on the continuous histories of colonialism in Algeria. Stephen Small of the University of California at Berkeley thoroughly read, commented on and gave me new ideas on Chapter 3. Conversations with Lydia Morris, my colleague at Essex, helped a lot with understanding and applying the concept of civic stratification. Exchanges with many others were equally valuable: Andrew Fagan, Director of Human Rights at Essex, on the political positions in the human rights community; Rob Schehr of Northern Arizona University on social justice in the USA; my colleague Carlos Gigoux on US intervention in Latin American politics; my former Ph.D. student Liz Cassell, on colonial law; my colleagues Jason Sumich and Afia Afenah on the democracy – economic growth links in Africa; Pierrot Ross-Tremblay of the University of Ottawa on the concept of cultural obliteration; and my partner, Nicola Gray, on the contemporary arts and colonialism.

For almost twenty years, I have taught a module called 'Colonialism, Cultural Diversity and Human Rights'. The students taking it have motivated and encouraged me, and all have contributed something to this book. I would like specially to thank Passent Moussa and Malika Irshad for showing me how pervasive colonial laws are in formerly colonized territories. The University of Essex Sociology department gave me time, space and support to complete the book. Lastly, librarian Sandy Macmillan ordered every single book I needed, and even came up with many that I hadn't thought of.

# Introduction

As a white person, I have been privileged. This is so although I had no privileged upbringing in any conventional sense of the word. Born of an unknown US enlisted serviceman and the teenage daughter of an elderly farm-labouring couple, mine was not a childhood for which there were many templates. I remember the Americans who came up our lonely stretch of road lined with Scotch pines on the edge of the Norfolk Fens to see my mother. They drove their Chevvies and Fords to a cottage without electricity or plumbing, and then later when the landowner got my grandparents on the housing list, they came to see my mother in our council house in a nearby village. Many visitors were brown and black, friends to my mother's various white boyfriends. To a child grappling to understand the world, they were friendly and fun and I soon got used to the fact that Americans all looked different.

One day, a great-uncle known for his sporting and ribald humour was in conversation with a black airman in our living room. What he said to the airman stopped the talking just for a second. There was a pause after the short, nasal-voiced elderly man exclaimed: 'Of course, a 100 year ago, you buggers were all slaves.' It must have been hurtful to the airman, even though he had probably heard similar in his life. As a child of about 7, I didn't know what he meant. It was probably a digression in a story, which was the main form of communication among older East Anglians. Over the years, my grandmother would remember it to me as she relayed episodes of her life with each visit I made back to the village. I laughed with her, but didn't know whether it was the great-uncle or the airman or the sentiments that we were laughing at.

Some years later, I got a US military loan to attend the London School of Economics (LSE) for a Master's degree. On weekends, I returned to the village to stay with my grandmother. She virtuously made vegetarian adaptations of meals that I remembered as a child before my adolescence had been punctuated by migration. My mother, sister, Texan stepfather and I went off in 1969 to an air base in California, and then to apartment complexes in Arizona populated by white drifters like we had become. When I saved money to return to England several years later, I liked the contrast of being around my grandmother and childhood friends in the village. They made me think that, despite years outside the desert city of Phoenix, and despite being unplaceable within British class taxonomy, I was still somehow English. In those days, I used to go to the pub my grandfather once frequented and got into conversations about politics with a wealthy landowner. When I defended decolonization – it was 1981 and the time of the transition to African majority rule in Southern Rhodesia – the dapper, well-mannered man some twenty years my senior calmly asked me which African countries were better-off now that the British had withdrawn. Having the bulk of my education in Arizona, and not being exposed to regular international news bulletins like my more solidly British and middle-class fellow students at the LSE, I had no answer. I had no facts on which to pin any kind of response. I did not immediately connect the corruption and strife in much of Africa with what the colonists had left behind. The virtue of the British just hung there.

Conversations with the jocular great-uncle and the snappily dressed landowner were just two of the incidents I remember that made me question who I am and with whom I stand aligned in the unequal world I was born into. The sense of moral integrity of white people who must in some way reckon with slavery and colonialism puzzled me. Thinking about it now, it seemed that my great-uncle was saying that slavery was nothing to be ashamed of. In fact, it was the black airman who should feel shame. Similarly, colonial rule, whether under Ian Smith's Rhodesian apartheid government or otherwise, was not just benign but it improved the lot of Africans. Their subsequent descents *en masse* into poverty, war and corruption were an inevitable consequence of their own failings. Africans should be grateful to the British, and perhaps even petition for the return of an Empire that once controlled about a quarter of the globe. The credit for unselfish progress is borne by the nation itself, and the insults to others, the presumed beneficiaries, is merely the reverse side of the same coin. White privilege is – or at least it has been until recently – the ability to be cocooned in a virtue so unquestioned that others can be condescendingly dismissed, denounced and despised without repercussion.

Over the centuries, national pride and moral authority have been derived from the equation of Western civilization with liberal virtues such as human rights. Despite the many situations in everyday life in which white privilege – or, more properly, white dominance – is manifest,[1] original rectitude has remained a deeper underlying sensibility of many white people. Until recently the privileges, which often translate into differences in how people are treated, have been submerged by a discourse in which 'progressive' Western principles are globalized, administered by governments and declared to apply equally to all. Many of those adhering to liberalism have refrained from insults to those regarded as their beneficiaries – now, these are only the preserve of populists – and have envisioned a world of rights scraped clean of slavery and colonialism. This perspective is displayed in human rights discussions, scholarly and official. According to Karima Bennoune, UN Special Rapporteur on Cultural Rights, universal human rights are a 'basic tenet of international law'. This is so fundamental that there can be 'no second-class citizens' she said.[2]

While the UN is outwardly unambiguous about universal human rights, it has of course committed human rights offences, among them the 1999 bombing of Yugoslavia causing 500 'second-class' civilian deaths.[3] By contrast, states that are charged with enforcing human rights are more equivocal, proclaiming rights that their actions often deny. American Defense Secretary General James Mattis spoke of 'the unwavering respect for human rights' of the USA and larger international community in relation to the state-authorized murder and dismemberment of journalist Jamal Khashoggi in the Saudi Arabian consulate in Istanbul.[4] Mattis made these commitments in Bahrain where, a year earlier, the leading human rights advocate in the country had been jailed, the only independent newspaper was closed by the government, death penalties had been meted out after forced confessions, and access to the country had been denied to the Office of the UN High Commissioner for Human Rights and the UN Special Rapporteur for Torture.[5] A few months later, the President whom Mattis served reiterated his support for the Saudi regime that ordered the killing of Khashoggi, a US resident and critic of the Saudi autocracy, citing billions of dollars in Saudi investments in US companies as a rationale.[6] Since this time, the US Congress has blocked the sending of arms to Saudi Arabia and the Gulf autocracies, but this was easily sidestepped through a Presidential veto in July 2019.

The British government's confusion over human rights is equally profound. In 2018, on the seventieth anniversary of the United Nations (UN) Universal Declaration on Human Rights (UDHR), UK Foreign Office minister Lord Ahmad of Wimbledon declared that 'Britain is a global defender of human rights, fundamental freedoms, and democratic values, and has championed campaigns to end modern slavery and human trafficking, to prevent sexual violence in conflict, and to ensure at least 12 years of quality education for girls.'[7] A few months later, the International Court of Justice (ICJ) ruled that Britain had violated the human rights of approximately 2,000 residents of the Chagos Islands, whom it deported to Mauritius to lease out their lands to the US military in 1965. That same day, Lord Ahmad announced that the UK would be seeking re-election to the UN Human Rights Council (HRC) in view of, among other things, a 'rising tide of impunity' around the world.[8] No reference was made to the ICJ ruling, and no apology to the Chagossians has been forthcoming. Indeed, the British government ignored the demand to end its colonial control over the islands as soon as possible, and when the UN General Assembly voted by a margin of 116–6 on a resolution for Britain to surrender the Chagos archipelago to Mauritius so that the Chagossians could return to their lands, the Foreign Office could only register its disappointment and underline that the US base on the Chagos Islands keeps the world safe from terrorism.[9] Ensuring safety has meant that the islands were used, contrary to basic human rights standards enshrined in the UDHR and many other instruments, for secret renditions of terrorist suspects to detention camps or military ships there.[10] Retaining control of the islands as a leased-out military colony further violated UN Resolution 1514 which prevented the breaking up of colonies before independence. Britain's impunity co-exists with its enthusiasm for human rights.

Expressed in many ways today,[11] human rights call for universal application through national and international institutions recognizing specific, sometimes 'inalienable', rights that accord to people either as individuals or as collectives. Broad rights to equality, liberty, freedom, legal protections and private property decreed in the Enlightenment, but having antecedents in Roman, Greek and early modern European thought, were believed to be fortified by the French and American Revolutionary declarations as well as nineteenth-century British liberalism. According to Lynn Hunt, these declarations 'gave birth to an idea that would make slow and steady progress in Europe and the rest of the world during the nineteenth and twentieth centuries'.[12] These rights were integrated into state constitutions, jurisprudence and other written laws, especially after the 1948 Declaration. Although most chroniclers of human rights rarely venture outside the European orbit, some argue that the sources of human rights can also be traced to declarations, activism and legal argument emanating from the Global South.[13] However, these are not the product of epistemologically distinct indigenous cosmologies that might consider the issues at stake very differently, something I shall consider in chapter 6. Human rights were given international expression through the UDHR in 1948, the Geneva Convention in 1951, further

UN Covenants and international jurisprudence in international and regional courts. These may be called human rights, but they are also civil rights, citizenship rights or just 'rights'. Indeed, many of the great social movements placed all such rights under the same umbrella, and have called for equal and universal application.

Nevertheless, denial of human rights, and rationalizations of such denials based either in law or in exceptions to the law, often occur alongside assertions of virtues that are held to reside largely with, and derive from, Europe and its North American diaspora. This paradox – or, to use a harsh word, hypocrisy – is incarnated in the colonial dimensions of human rights pronunciations, and is a component of ongoing white privilege and asserted moral rectitude. A Janus-faced orientation to the world recalls European writers struggling with Empire, such as George Orwell. As an English person commenting on a world in which the British state and society had such profound influence, Orwell was exercised about the imperial subordination of others regarded as inferior. In *Burmese Days*, and essays such as 'England Your England', he illustrated how the British Empire was presented as a triumph of civilization, exposing contradictions between this and the numerous abominations committed in Britain's name.[14]

It is something of this that attaches to discussions of human rights. Rights which were rhetorically associated with Western civilization, and often held to be universally valid, were explicitly denied to colonial subjects, indigenous peoples and the enslaved. The denial of equal rights – or, sometimes, any rights – to these populations was justified by their imputed savagery, backwardness and inferiority. Indeed, the claim to be acting on behalf of humanity was a convenient justification for colonialism. General Mattis and Lord Ahmad of Wimbledon are emblematic of a longer history in which the practice and endorsement of non-universal human rights corresponds with claims to allegiance to universal human rights. This tension is now manifold, as the exceptions, exclusions and denials of human rights that occurred simultaneously with colonialism and enslavement metastasized into new realms of *de facto* non-universality.

Contemporary human rights conflicts are layered onto this uncompleted history of racial domination. Consequently, my focus is on past and ongoing practices of Western colonial powers and settler colonial states and their relevance to selectivity and differentiation in human rights today. My task is not to follow the footsteps of numerous human rights scholars who trace genealogies of international human rights, or to advocate a system of apolitical and fully universal human rights. This is not so much a study of human rights, but of uncompleted histories of exception, differentiation and rightlessness which cannot be entirely extricated from the study of human rights.

As I hope to show, the official treatment of particular populations is linked to colonial domination and its enduring social, political and economic expressions. Human rights recognition and implementation can be roughly mapped onto ongoing histories. Following Chantal Mouffe's agonistic politics,[15] we may say that Western colonial domination as a 'social division' is constitutive of a colonialism *of* human rights. States which administer human rights are represented by institutions and personnel that embraced ideas affirming the inferior status of indigenous and enslaved persons. Because states are dedicated to the perpetuation of hegemony, neither they nor the official human rights they oversee can hold great potential for social change.

## Where I Am Coming From and What Follows ...

I would like to think that Orwell's spirit attaches in some small way to the following chapters linking human rights to colonialism. While what follows is not autobiographical or ethnographic, it is connected to my animation onto these pages. A large part of this emerges from experiences, both in my personal life and working with indigenous peoples, and in seeing at first hand the many futilities of claiming rights within alien systems of law that perpetually situate indigenous peoples as petitioners in inferior relationships to the state and other third parties.[16] The book also emerges from my work as a teacher, and insight accrues from collaborations with students, texts and sources in university contexts. I have often asked myself whether there can be a dividing line where research somehow legitimates itself by crossing into being impersonal and devoid of the feelings that come from interacting with each other.

But there is no neutral place to stand. As a writer and educator, I feel compelled to comment critically on human rights. As Lydia Morris observes, human rights are mediated by social processes, rather than emanating from primordial 'natural' principles.[17] This social mediation includes their embedding in – and, I would add, exclusion from – law. Underlined much earlier in Émile Durkheim's essay on the French Revolution, the distinction between the Declaration of the Rights of Man as a type of sociology and as a historical event is salutary.[18] The context-laden human authorship of the Declaration and, by extension, other statements of human rights have often been assumed to be clear propositions about the characteristics of a society human rights, springing from certain elemental sources. They have, therefore, become elevated to a type of sociology, but without context. Earlier, Jeremy Bentham had, almost line by line, debunked the French Declaration of Rights. Calling it 'nonsense upon stilts', Bentham showed that the Declaration amounted to a number of assertions about rights which were both metaphysical in terms of their origins, and meaningless in terms of their realization since they lacked any concrete context.[19] Following Durkheim and Bentham, iterations of human rights should be situated as social constructions, and we could add that the study of human rights needs to include prominently the differentiation of rights, rightlessness and states of exception.

My bias then is towards seeing human rights sociologically, but I believe that singular devotion to any academic discipline and the associated exploration of subjects through a prism called 'the literature' is limiting. Encasing one's ideas within professionally approved formats curtails the imaginative possibilities inherent in the plurality of methods, genres and sources. This means that, whereas I cite a wide array of writings, I do not systematically trek through standard, popular or academic opinions pertinent to the subjects I cover in this book. While a vast number of scholars are mentioned, I am reluctant to fatigue readers with reviews, or debates with authors whose perspectives might agree or differ from mine. What follows is also not the product of specialism. Readers seeking more detail on some of the historical and contemporary issues discussed here will need to consult specialist works.

Consequently, this book is about the connections between elements of colonialism in particular places and times and human rights. I consider the intersections of colonialism and human rights not just through their empirical, theoretical and, importantly, political dimensions, which are manifold, but also through the lenses of art, literature, film and creative non-fiction. Visual, literary and imaginative works can help us understand sociological processes and historical events in more visceral ways. While I am aware that I write as a social scientist, creative works provide subtlety, perspective and immediacy often lacking in purely expository writings, concerned as they are with argument, theory and methodology. Imaginative works, although only appearing in cameos, are imperative to the writing of essays.

Chapter 1, 'Non-universal Human Rights and Rightlessness', introduces the contexts for the major concerns of the book. Here, I discuss the multiple articulations of differential human rights occurring through racial, rather than social, contracts and internal civic stratification of populations. I identify various practices that produced categories of people who, in Hannah Arendt's famous phrase, lacked the right to have rights. Given the histories and ongoing consequences of colonialism and slavery, rightlessness and variegated human rights, it is suggested, are crucial arenas for study.

One of the reasons prompting such study is the recent interest in colonialism, apparent in concerns among activists, artists, scholars and journalists over public memorials, museums and cultural forms linked to colonialism and slavery. Chapter 2, 'The Uneasy Present of Colonialism', looks at these contemporary efforts to know about the activities of colonial and slave states, but also how they are rebuffed by governments concealing records and trying to shape knowledge of history. The chapter also considers the tenuous link between democracy and human rights, both inside Western democracies and in former colonized states that have retained colonial laws inimical to human rights. Finally, the chapter considers the reactions of colonized peoples to articulations of Western virtue by invoking Frantz Fanon's 'muscular lockjaw', and speculates that the acts of colonizing itself produced a kind of amoral sensibility that survives in the current selective attention to human rights.

I proceed by examining several concrete examples that link colonizing and human rights. These bias heavily towards discussions of the United States and France, partly because these are the states whose various revolutionary declarations are seen to have operationalized Enlightenment notions of the 'rights of man' in laws and constitutions.[19] Discussions involve three broad categories of colonial practice. These will be considered not as the snapshots or discrete contemporary episodes so common to legal human rights focuses, but as enduring violations with past and contemporary manifestations in Western countries. The forced extraction of labour, colonial occupation and assimilation programmes, and expropriation of land will be considered. While it is true that human rights offences occur everywhere and many of them are not connected to colonialism or Western powers but to local forces, histories and exertions of power, these will not be a specific concern of this book. Likewise, space does not permit analysing all the human rights violations occurring in contexts of inequality, corruption, violence and autocracy which may be directly related to Western foreign policies and blowback from military invasions that have distinct colonial dimensions.

I understand colonized peoples as divided into various groups that were subject to one form of colonization or another. Memberships sometimes overlap, but principally my focus is on: (1) the Afro-descended peoples of the Americas and the larger Black Diaspora whose ancestors were captured, bought and transported from Africa as slaves from the seventeenth to the nineteenth centuries; (2) those who came under formal European colonial rule in Africa and Asia during the occupation of their lands, including the North African and Middle Eastern territories within the Mandatory system implemented after World War I to divide up the Ottoman Empire between Britain and France; (3) indigenous peoples of the Americas, whose lands have been appropriated, and over whom an external European-style state authority has been imposed. Chapters 3, 4 and 5 will roughly correspond to these divisions.

Although not formally within the remit of this book, another category consists of those under legal, military and economic occupation who are subject to similarly differential, largely inferior, rights from those who form part of the occupying society. This would prominently include Israel, where a chiefly settler Jewish population supplanted a pre-existing Palestinian Arab population, and whose Basic Laws assert that it is a Jewish and democratic state. This gives primacy of citizenship rights to one ethno-religious group. In 2018, this was embedded further by making self-determination a unique power of Jewish people. In a policy of 'juridical erasure' deriving originally from exceptions within the British Mandate,[20] Palestinians have no such rights. Additionally, Israel imposes military occupation and martial law over the Occupied Palestinian West Bank and, to a lesser extent, Gaza, territories which are to be the basis for a future Palestinian state. Large parts of the West Bank have been annexed for Jewish-only settlements. The 2018 addition to the Basic Laws formalize the primacy of Jewish institutions, the Hebrew language and the unfettered unique rights of Jews to migrate to Israel.[21] Another instance is the Moroccan-occupied Western Sahara, where a settler population has displaced indigenous Sahrawi peoples. Despite an ICJ ruling in 1975 that denied Moroccan sovereignty over the territories, the region has been occupied by the Moroccan military, settled by Moroccan civilians, and laws denying all forms of Sahrawi self-determination have been imposed. Mass imprisonment of Sahrawi civil rights activists, banishment to refugee camps in Algeria, and suppression of the press and local Sahrawi culture have been common.[22]

Chapter 3 is the first of these more focused chapters. Entitled 'Slavery and Its Afterlives', it examines the human rights implications of enslaving Africans, particularly in the USA, a nation that has been referred to as the 'Applied Enlightenment'. While six European countries all had major slave plantations in their colonies in the Americas, I spotlight the USA, in part, because its enslavement of Africans, and human rights enunciated by the Declaration of Independence and the Constitution, are simultaneous and related. In this chapter, I will articulate how this contradiction, incarnated especially in the life and thought of Thomas Jefferson, was destined to be played out through later policies that created differential rights for African-Americans. This was recognized early by numerous black scholars, orators and creative artists who, from Frederick Douglass onwards, realized that the country designed for them was anything but enlightened. Federally enforced segregation, discrimination and racialized concepts of rights after slavery set the precedent for ongoing police violence against black people and suppression of basic civil and human rights.

Chapter 4, 'The Less Than Human', considers how liberal Republican principles incarnated in the French Revolution co-existed with the colonization of Algeria and its aftermath. From 1830 to 1962, France's North

African colony was governed by decrees and policies that inferiorized Muslims, renamed their lands, and humiliated them through aggressive assimilation campaigns, including the ritual unveiling of Muslim women. The means to pacify Algerians, especially when they took up organized resistance, was often through violence and torture, and part of this will be analysed through the writings of Frantz Fanon. I argue that these contradictions continue and can be seen in the perpetuation of racial ideas that stigmatize entire populations, such as those expressed by Presidents Sarközy and Macron and the persistent discrimination against Algerians in France today. The violent and autocratic aspects of French rule have also continued in Algeria, evident in the Arabization movement, suppression of minorities and persecution of migrants. Some of these tensions will be explored through historical analysis, as well as works such as Gillo Pontecorvo's film *The Battle of Algiers*, and Kamel Daoud's novel *The Meursault Investigation*.

Chapter 5, 'The Impossibility of Indigenous Human Rights', deals with the contradictions between the desire of indigenous peoples to retain their rights as autonomous peoples on their own lands and the positioning of the colonizing state as maintaining its sovereignty through mere assertion. In this chapter, I will consider the American treaty system and the Constitutional and legal position of Native Americans, indicating that the formulation, implementation and enforcement of laws operate through the construct of Native peoples as subordinate populations. I then move to the recent conflict at Standing Rock Indian Reservation over the positioning of the Dakota Access Pipeline (DAPL) adjacent to the reservation and traversing sacred sites, burial sites and lands guaranteed by treaty. The pipeline, approved through President Trump's 2017 Executive Order, effectively underscores a state of exception, enabling the state to build on prior violations of its own policies and laws and initiate new violations of indigenous rights.

Chapter 6, 'Decolonizing Human Rights', concludes by looking at where the hypocrisies of Western liberalism have led. It examines the disorienting colonial situations in which non-universal rights emerge, the 'titanic inequalities' which form their current context, and active disavowal of human rights in Western democracies. It ends by discussing ways through the morass of contradictions in which human rights stand: reparations for wrongdoing in colonialism and slavery, and indigenizing the law to resolve disputes over land, culture and sovereignty between indigenous peoples and states. These measures would help bring the present into conversation with the past, connecting the wrongdoings of colonialism and slavery with the differential human rights accorded Afro-descended, formerly colonized and indigenous peoples. I suggest that making these connections could help decolonize human rights by addressing the original and ongoing racial exceptions to human rights.

# 1

# Non-universal Human Rights and Rightlessness

... the rights of man [are] narrow and fragmentary, incomplete and biased and, all things considered, sordidly racist.[1]

Aimé Césaire

## Racial Contracts

While white privilege is often about substantial social, political and economic advantages that white people in various societies are said to benefit from, and to which their identities are connected, it is made possible by multiple articulations of the basic inferiority of others. This may have to do with their ancestry, as in the case of my great-uncle's remark at the expense of the black airman, or their basic unsuitability to make independent decisions over their own lands and affairs, as with the claim that African countries were 'better-off' under British rule. White privilege fits a view of the world as socially and culturally graded, where differences translate into exceptions to general principles, and where equal consideration or treatment of different types of person is always discretionary.

This discretion, coupled with selective outrage towards violation, is why Aimé Césaire bluntly described human rights as racist. In his *Discourse on Colonialism*, Césaire observed that Europe's wars which prompted the UDHR were only seen as a disgrace because the corpses were primarily white. No such extensions of soul searching or appeals to international regulation and human rights were made when the

bodies were not white. Moreover, the mid-twentieth-century deliberations on the founding of the United Nations were not characterized by
any sorrow over colonialism and slavery, but by an attempt to prolong
the self-appointed civilizing mission of the British Empire. This was
especially apparent in the views of the South African apartheid leader
Jan Smuts, who took a prominent role in founding the UN, and believed
that rights should match the evolutionary stage of different races.[2] Smuts
drafted the Preamble to the UN Charter.

But how do rejections of the equality of human worth and dignity
relate to the guarantees of equal human rights within liberal democracies? What happens when a hierarchically ordered expansionist
culture, filtered through its extensions of colonialism and slavery,
considers human rights? How are the precedents of slavery and colonialism relevant to a consideration of contemporary human rights? What
happens when human rights are mapped onto national societies and a
global order that contain massive inequalities and imbalances of power?

Universal human rights seemingly sit uncomfortably in a world of
white privilege, and consequently, as Charles Mills points out, it is rare
that legal and philosophic disquisitions on rights are brought into conversation with topics such as colonialism, slavery and racism.[3] Meaningful
dialogue about universal human rights today is therefore uneasy, and
much of it currently revolves around outwardly raceless legal prose and
official pronouncements. Western inheritances of Enlightenment thought,
the principles of popular sovereignty emerging out of the American and
French Revolutions, nineteenth-century liberalism, the 1948 UDHR
and the various official proclamations of human rights since then are
often taken as emblematic of some primordial quality of 'civilized
societies'. Consequently, it might be understandable that Europeans and
Euro-Americans are proud of the principles of rights and democratic
government that they believe they have inherited and disseminated
because these emerged after long periods of sacrifice, war and social and
intellectual struggle against class oppression and despotism in Europe. So
powerful is this pride that abstract conceptions of rights within representative government are central to Europe's political thinking. From the
franchise to impartial social justice, freedom of expression to the right to
the fundamentals of life, human rights are a key indicator of the inevitable movement of global history in Western thought.

This universalism does not mean that either the early theorists of
rights or their colonizing compatriots acted without reference to cultural
variation, but that universalizing occurred within a hegemonic process
that delegitimizes other renderings of history and rights.[4] Nevertheless,
there were many times when colonial administrations had to tolerate,
and even accept, traditional and customary laws[5] – for example, when

they were demographically outnumbered. In India, the British incorporated some indigenous norms within colonial administration, but 'instead of abiding by the local definition, they redefined and invented customs and traditions as per Western ideologies and the aims of British imperialism'.[6] Sen suggests that this was partly because Indian customs were more humane than British laws.

Their sense of cultural superiority largely meant that colonial agents who were adjudicating rights and responsibilities were often dismissive of rival values among those they administered. Although universalism is ostensibly raceless, Enlightenment philosophers of rights used race as an important category to differentiate human qualities along one universal continuum. Prominent, but not alone, among liberal thinkers is Immanuel Kant, who distinguished gradations of personhood and rights based on the premise of white superiority.[7] Georg Wilhelm Friedrich Hegel developed his master–slave dialectic as the Atlantic slave trade and the rebellion of enslaved Africans in Saint-Domingue (which became Haiti) were taking place. He made no reference to these events,[8] possibly because of his evident contempt for Africans in *Dialectics of History*. Indeed, the Haitian Revolution of 1791–1804, which led to the first independent black republic, is largely ignored in scholarly accounts of the origins of human rights.[9] Instead of being praised as an exemplar of universal values and the 'Rights of Man', Haiti quickly became indebted to its former enslavers, and had to pay huge financial compensation to France to obtain international recognition.[10]

Another Enlightenment figure, John Locke, was General Secretary of the Board of Trade and Plantations, which regulated British slave trading. He was also a shareholder in two slave-trading companies, including the Royal Africa Company at a time just before the massive expansion of British slave trading.[11] Locke's idea of representative government through consent to the social contract did not encompass African people. In fact, he argued that slaves cannot be part of the social contract, and hence by default can legitimately be subject to absolute or arbitrary authority. The enslaved Africans that he had such an important role in administering go unmentioned in the 'Of Slavery' chapter of *The Second Treatise on Government*. In parallel, fellow liberal thinker Jean-Jacques Rousseau made explicit that slavery could never be based on consent, the basis for all social contracts, but even he makes no reference to European enslavement of Africans in the 'Of Slavery' chapter of *The Social Contract* of 1791.[12] Likewise, other French *philosophes* were either indifferent to the enslavement of Africans or took many years to pronounce against it.[13]

Thus, it must be, as Mills argues through the concept of the racial contract,[14] that race is a shaping constituent of Western liberal ideals, prominently including those involving rights as well as duties and government responsibilities. Mills' racial contract is intended to critique and replace the social contract, the mythical transaction whereby individuals in a perilous, insecure 'state of nature' are asserted to forgo voluntarily natural rights to autonomy in return for protections and legal and police powers of the state. Under Locke's social contract, the state is therefore legitimated by popular consent, thus establishing firm links between the state, rights and democracy. The social contract individuates people, removing them from formerly autonomous cultural communities that are depicted as primitive and lacking protections. Following Mills, we could say that if a real social contract were to exist, it would be an arrangement leading to racially differentiated relationships to the state, and, via colonialism and slavery, these would be cemented together through compulsion and violence.

An example in which particular attributions about specific groups get translated into structurally embedded denials of supposedly universal rights is contained in Locke's 'Of Property'.[15] The outwardly secular Locke held that rights to property could only be claimed by farmers who worked as God intended. This seemingly random assumption meant, above all, labouring and improving the soil. Such a stipulation conveniently invalidated land rights for American Indians in North America since, in Locke's erroneous view, Indians were simply wandering hunters. Their property was therefore vested only in the animals they killed. Through this contrivance, indigenous people could – and were – deprived of their lands by English colonists, who often took land on this basis.[16] In formulating a 'principle' for property ownership, Locke misrepresented both indigenous societies who often 'improved' soil by alternating hunting and farming practices, and English farmer colonists whose agriculture often exhausted the soil and depleted the natural environment. Therefore, because such a fundamental right as that to land was made to apply differentially under settler colonialism, the liberal social contract became a lever of dispossession. Likewise, the absence of any mention of African slaves in relation to the social contract by liberal formulators of rights such as Locke and Rousseau makes racially segmented rights the default position.

Nevertheless, philosophies allied to the French and American Revolutions and Enlightenment have featured in genealogies of human rights. Todorov's affirmative interpretation of the inextricable Enlightenment linkages to democracy and human rights illustrates such claims:

> Our knowledge of the world has progressed freely, without ideological prohibitions causing too much concern. Individuals do not fear the

authority of tradition as much any more and try to manage their private space by themselves, enjoying all the while great freedom of expression. Democracy, where popular sovereignty is exercised with respect for individual liberties, has become a model cherished or desired everywhere. Universal human rights are considered a common ideal and equality before the law is the rule in any legitimate state. Pursuing personal happiness or common welfare are personal choices that no longer shock anyone.[17]

Despite this flattering assessment, both the French and American Revolutions granted rights of franchise and property only to white males. Unequal rights were further necessary because colonial states were concerned with control of land, and, to justify this, a discourse representing the peoples who inhabited these lands as unqualified to hold on to it was invoked. Colonial subjects, therefore, were treated under exceptional measures. Denial of the rights celebrated in the Enlightenment was often justified under colonialism as part of the necessary tutelage of backward peoples. As Alice Conklin argues, regarding the early French Third Republic and its colonial occupation of West Africa, the *mission civilisatrice*, while attempting to destroy local customs and 'feudal' economies at variance with liberal Republicanism and to instil liberal values and market capitalism, crushed rights that would have been extended to Europeans.[18] The French may have built railways, schools, roads and hospitals, but 'with disastrous consequences for Africans: forced integration into the world market on unfavorable economic terms, suspension of political rights, corvée labor, as well as the denial of full legal protection'.[19]

As Benton and Slater observe, 'the world that launched notions of civic rights, was a world not of nations but of empires'.[20] As empires, European states necessarily introduced laws, codes and institutions that embedded differential rights between the categories of people configured under their dominion, and these were often supported by powerful currents of political thought. Furthermore, the sensibilities, convictions and racial dominance, as well as the institutional dynamics, that sustained colonialism and slavery have not expired along with formal empires and trans-Atlantic slavery.

## Non-universal Human Rights

While contemporary liberalism often associates human rights with the legacies of classical thinkers, law is frequently invoked as the key to current understandings of human rights. There exists a pervasive legalism that sees human rights as apolitical and ahistorical sets of events in which lawyers call witnesses, ascertain intent, and measure evidence of violation against the growing body of national and international laws. This is not to say that national and international laws are irrelevant, but undue emphasis on them and the legal scholarship surrounding them obscure how the definition and interpretation of human rights are enmeshed in broader social, spatial and temporal processes. Instead of being seen purely as an instrument to assess human rights, law, especially that pertaining to rights, was also an enabler of colonialism and maintains this role in administering the ongoing consequences of it. As mentioned earlier, colonial judiciaries may have in some places and in some respects borrowed from indigenous traditions, but they ultimately served the cause of colonial domination over lands and peoples.

States, no matter how they acquired their powers, are unique in having what is depicted as *legitimate* authority to interpret and administer rights of populations. They are protected through the construct of political sovereignty, which enables states to ignore, contradict or violate law. This is significant for European powers, which are largely immune from formally being charged with legally defined human rights abuses related to colonialism and enslavement since the crimes took place before the instruments, and courts such as the ICJ, the International Criminal Court (ICC) and regional bodies like the Inter American Court of Human Rights or the European Court of Human Rights (ECHR), were established. Although there is in law a concept of continuing violation, courts in Europe have been reluctant to hear such cases because they 'have usually a political aspect with which tribunals are, in principle, hesitant to deal and, secondly, because of the fear that the examination of such cases will increase considerably the workload of the organs with competence to deal with complaints for violations of human rights'.[21] That the principle of continuing violation does not extend to colonial situations was recently affirmed by the ECHR in a case brought by descendants of the twenty-four Chinese rubber-plantation workers executed by British soldiers in 1948 at Batang Kali, Malaysia. The judges reasoned that the killings that the troops were accused of carrying out in the colony occurred before the Court was established.[22] Other means to hold Britain accountable through a Public Inquiry were rejected by the Cameron government in 2015. As this case illustrates, in its caution regarding retroactive application to the colonial past, the law permits, even embraces, selectivity in what violations are justiciable. German atrocities in Europe before and during World War II, for example, were not exempt from retroactive law.

It is no doubt true, as Max Weber argued, that impartial and rational law is simply the latest phase in the history of authority.[23] To be legitimate, it must follow prescribed rules and procedures, and, by doing so, law supplies legitimacy to states, in part through the imagined social contract. But this appearance of legitimacy presupposes both that the law covers all eventualities that states administer, and that politicians, especially executives, work for the public good rather than for a partisan or other cause. It further assumes that the law itself, which states create, interpret and enforce, is impartial. In his classic statement on this, 'Politics as a Vocation', Weber admits that, among the ranks of politicians, lawyers loom large.[24] This means that those who are charged with formulating and interpreting the law also wield powers to manipulate the law in myriad ways. In considering Batang Kali, the lawyers at the ECHR and politicians of the British state each affirmed the selective inapplicability of human rights.

Hence, even Weber's legal rational authority can never be a purely bureaucratic exercise. Drawing on the works of Giorgio Agamben,[25] we could say that it is not an impersonal bureaucracy that formulates and dispenses law and applies it rationally to all individuals, groups and institutions. Rather, although there are some sporadic checks such as judicial reviews in most countries, state sovereignty enables executives to override the checks, making any attempts to separate the legal from illegal a Sisyphean task. While qualifications, differentiations and conditionality can be applied to human rights laws, following the philosopher Carl Schmitt, Agamben argues that a 'state of exception' is vested in sovereignty itself. Indeed, pronouncing exceptions to the general rule is what defines sovereignty. The state is sovereign over citizens and free to make laws to control, categorize, register and document people, as well as to make differentiations within the citizenry and between it and non-citizens. The state can also make new laws or take executive actions to supersede protections of civil liberties and to violate its own laws. In democracies, state officials need not always follow the tortuous legislative processes to implement such differentiations, and can circumvent or ignore the multitudes of laws, conventions and protocols to impose decisive action. The state of exception is increasingly common and has become the 'dominant paradigm of government'.[26] Therefore, if the formal and informal group differentiations of rights are not enough to sustain legally a hegemonic social and economic order, a state of exception is the default position.

However, a state of exception is often unnecessary, because of the existence of social differentiations that rule out exercises of human rights that might be inconvenient to state politicians in one regard or another. Contemporary differentiations in the position of people regarding their human rights in colonial situations are paralleled internally by massive social and economic inequalities in Western countries that have serious implications for the exercise of rights. These were publicized by nineteenth-century reformers in Britain and the USA such as Seebohm Rountree, Charles Booth and Henry Mayhew, as well as their twentieth-century counterparts Jacob Riis, Jack London and George Orwell. These writers vividly described the misery that befell working people as urban industrial capitalism established itself. The wealthiest cities were populated by masses of paupers, homeless people, beggars, and sick and infirm people living on streets or in overcrowded hovels. The exacerbation of inequality coincided with the advent of capitalism, which Karl Marx and Friedrich Engels, jointly and separately, would use as evidence for their commentaries on capitalist society. One dimension of this was the realignment of rights away from those obtained via feudalism – in which mutual obligations between landowners and peasants cemented a stable but exploitative social order – to capitalism, where owners of capital (employers) replaced the paternal bonds with the 'callous cash nexus', the uncertainties of economic cycles, and mechanisms to minimize wages and maximize production.

In the vast arena of social and economic change in which capitalism emerged, Marx and Engels have shown that relations of production dictate the specific types of rights that pertain to workers – and therefore the unhealthy, degrading and dehumanizing conditions in which they lived. The massive inequalities produced and maintained by capitalism therefore meant that, even though the 'rights of man' existed in Marx's time, and today universal human rights exist on paper – for example, through rights to an adequate standard of living in the UDHR and elsewhere – they are compromised because people cannot realize these rights equally. In the Marxian view, this is because the unequal social order is legitimated by an ideology that asserts that wealth and poverty reflect differences in individual merit.

In the wider Marxist view, law is an institution that derives its power from the state, and the state reflects the economic and political interests of those who own the productive institutions within capitalism. In his 1843 essay 'On the Jewish Question', Marx commented on human rights,[27] arguing that Jewish emancipation could not be achieved without Jews emancipating themselves from finance capital (in which they had excelled because they were banned from entering other trades in much of Christian Europe) and promoting broader economic emancipation. Both Jewish emancipation and wider human emancipation depended on rejection of capitalism, which in Marx's view shaped state actions to perpetuate exploitation and inequality.

For Marx, human rights held out little hope for emancipation. This was because the 'Rights of Man' that emerged with the French

Revolution were part of a series of governing principles that also brought about the power of the bourgeoisie who had principal interests in business, money, trade and exchange. While human rights articulated in the French Revolution signified the end of feudal rule and the church power that was used to prop it up, and also represented a victory by peasants in rejecting privilege, tyranny and humiliation, the new order of rights also enabled the functioning of a capitalist society dominated by commercial interests in which peasants would eventually be transformed into an industrial proletariat. French society remained grossly unequal, in what Honoré Balzac called a 'democracy of the rich'.[28] The French Revolution may have led to the abolition of privileges based on birth, rank and education, but it did this only to bring people under the central power of the state representing the bourgeoisie. Furthermore, echoing later critiques of liberalism, the 'Rights of Man' emphasizes individual rights that reorient people towards egoism and the accumulation of capital. The bourgeois concept of freedom, for Marx, is *laissez faire*, and the rights organized around this are those that enable the entire society to function to protect private property and capital accumulation while ensuring the subjugation of working people.

Capitalism – or at least organized profit-seeking – is therefore a major factor influencing human rights. The observations of Hannah Arendt in her essay 'The Political Emancipation of the Bourgeoisie'[29] segue to the contemporary linking of colonialism and human rights. Arendt remarks that the bourgeoisie required colonialism – and, by extension, gross violations of the 'Rights of Man'. This is because capitalism works by investing capital that has been procured from material production, and, to maintain profitability in the face of competition, it must grow. To grow, it needs to travel. Therefore, the Americas, Africa and Asia provided rich sources of expansion for the labour, raw materials and, later, the markets of colonial powers.

Arendt quotes Cecil Rhodes, the British colonist, explorer and founder of the DeBeers mining company in South Africa in 1888, who fell into despair every night looking at the sky and realizing that these stars and planets could not be annexed and commercialized.[30] The constant need to expand capitalism was for Arendt – and many other historians and political analysts since – the preparatory stage for fascism, that great denial of human rights of the twentieth century. Fascism represented a convulsive type of intra-European imperialism in which bankers and industrialists played key roles in supporting Mussolini and Hitler, materially and financially. Germany's main aim was to capture as much territory in Europe as possible for the benefits of German industry and wealth creation, upon which Hitler realized Nazi legitimacy would ultimately rest. Germany was also governed by racial beliefs, as were the imperial and colonial conquests of its enemies, Britain and France. Denial, differentiation and violation of human rights were therefore driven by the central economic dynamic in Western societies.

## Hierarchical Orderings of Rights

Often with little explicit reference to these social contexts, contemporary iterations of human rights such as the UDHR are those relating to liberty, nationality, privacy, property, religion, social security, education, culture, and freedom from slavery, torture and arbitrary detention. The ultimate guarantor of these rights is the state, which in the UN framework is assumed to be amenable to international moral pressure to enact liberal principles. Thus, human rights are most consistent with democratic political orders in which the state is seen to be a product of popular consent and, in turn, guarantees the rights of those that are its subjects. Indeed, advocates for rights of one type or another often frame them as a principle of nation-state democracy.

For example, the rights that Martin Luther King and members of the civil rights movement advocated were workers' rights, fair employment, decent housing, guaranteed incomes and political participation. King's dedication to the fusion of racial and economic justice was underlined by his support for striking sanitation workers in Memphis, the city where, tragically, he was assassinated. His advocacy was not just civil rights for African-Americans but human rights, and they were influenced by understandings of rights declarations that made no reference to racial specificity.[31] The problem the movement addressed was that the state was not regulating the various spheres of civil society in order to allow for the realization of democratic rights. Thus, for King, 'it is not a constitutional right that men have jobs, but it is a human right'.[32] While he may have sensed that human rights were highly contingent, and that they favoured whites and those with property and money, King understandably pleaded for the universal human rights that the American government explicated in its Constitution, jurisprudence and laws. King was simply holding the US government to abide by its own stated liberal principles.

However, the fraught coexistence of assertions of universal human rights with variably applied civic and citizenship rights, which King contested, has endured within the Western history of ideas, as well as in policies and laws. As far back as Athenian democracy, complex laws applied to slaves and citizens differently, but their administration and rule were interlocking.[33] Among the Romans, exemplified in the famous tablets of the Gortyn codes of the Roman Odeion of first-century Crete, laws were inscribed to apply differentially to separate categories of people – men and women, free people and slaves – and punishments for different configurations of transgression depended on the circumstances, and the status of both victims and perpetrators. Amendments were made that coincided with changing social patterns, and these can be interpreted from various inscriptions on the slabs.[34] Hence, as Hanchard shows, democracies of the past relied on legal regimes of exclusion, and these are relevant to the consideration of contemporary democracies. The difference is, however, that contemporary democracies explicitly assert equality,[35] while tolerating and often abetting the ongoing effects of exclusionary mechanisms.

Colonizing and enslaving shaped these exclusions since they were underpinned by ideologies emphasizing cultural hierarchy. This was expressed in the use of the trope 'civilization', which connoted an opposition to be overcome in the barbaric or savage. For Immanuel Kant, if a territory lacks 'rudimentary modern legal and commercial institutions and a centralized coercive authority', it is a threat to civilized states, which have a right to impose order upon the peoples of the territory to set them on the path of modernization.[36] That may mean, as it often did under colonialism, not permitting such peoples equivalent rights to those who considered themselves civilized. Within this foundational liberal ideology, the human rights of non-European peoples under European dominion were often constituted as rights to be 'modernized', and therefore these peoples were denied some of the liberal 'universal' rights articulated by Enlightenment philosophers. The British Empire, for example, incorporated Asian, African and indigenous American peoples into its political and legal order with complex differentiations of rights according to caste, religion and tribe.[37]

Britain's enslaved Africans in the Caribbean and elsewhere, of course, had no such citizenship rights, and the terms of the abolition of slavery dramatically illustrated how rights and privileges were mapped onto ways of thinking about human beings through hierarchy. Despite abolitionist voices, Britain did its utmost to preserve slavery. It was 'the settled policy of England to encourage the slave trade'.[38] The British Parliament intervened to prevent attempts to prohibit slavery or limit the importing of enslaved people in its North American and Caribbean colonies in the eighteenth century.[39] After Britain eventually abolished slavery in its colonies, in 1834 a sum of £20 million, equal to anywhere between £2.57 billion and £76 billion in 2010,[40] was set aside to compensate proprietors of enslaved people through a loan from the City of London that was only paid off in 2015. At the time, there was 'a feeding frenzy amongst members of the British elite over the compensation money, a frenzy which drew thousands of Britons into asserting their ownership of slaves once the state attached specific and immediate monetary value to the claims of ownership'.[41]

By contrast, as Nicholas Draper shows in his analysis of documents relating to the Compensation Commission set up to disburse the monies,[42] neither reparation nor human agency was attached to those enslaved by the British on their Caribbean plantations. Under the Act abolishing slavery, freed people were required to work as unpaid labourers or 'apprentices' for four to six years.[43] The compensation to slave holders and investors in slavery has helped perpetuate privilege and luxury in Britain and elsewhere for the generations of descendants of British enslavers. Including widows, clergymen and many shareholders with financial, trading and other relationships with slavery, those who were compensated for the loss of their property have continued to use this and other monies from slavery to amass wealth, power and advantage. The same is true for various institutions in British society documented by the Legacies of British Slave Ownership project at University College London.[44] Hence, current social and racial hierarchies in Britain are tangibly related to slavery and to the British government's massive rewards to owners of human property.

As this illustrates, hierarchical access to social, political and economic rights was deeply ingrained in British political culture. Similar hierarchies were embedded in the premises of nineteenth-century British thinkers, especially the Utilitarians, whose thought is another important source of liberalism. While advocating constitutional representative government, equality under the law, and freedom of thought, speech and conscience – with only the prominent exception of Jeremy Bentham – they simultaneously provided important sources of guidance for British colonial administration, especially of India. Their support for colonialism meant that these thinkers had to make and justify exceptions to liberal principles. The justifications sprang from the *a priori* position that Europeans in general were superior peoples, and, by the same token, non-Europeans possessed an inferiority often characterized as uncivilized or barbaric. Following the observations of colonial administrators, prominently including the jurist and historian Sir Henry Maine,[45] the idea that non-Europeans were fixed in a prior state of human development became part of the guiding assumptions of liberalism.

Stokes opens his history of Utilitarian thought on India by observing that 'the physical and mental distance separating East and West was to be annihilated by the discoveries of science, by commercial intercourse, and by transplanting the genius of English laws and English education'.[46] To achieve this, James Mill, and his son John Stuart Mill – who spent thirty-five years as a British East India Company official – believed that authoritarian rule would be needed to transform Indians culturally if liberal democracy were to be successful. In 1859 in his introduction to 'On Liberty', John Stuart Mill proclaimed:

> To characterize any conduct whatever towards a barbarous people as a violation of the law of nations only shows that he who speaks has never considered the subject ... Barbarians have no rights as a nation except a right to such treatments as may, at the earliest possible period, fit them for becoming one. Despotism is a legitimate mode of government in dealing with barbarians, provided the end be their improvement, and the means justified by actually effecting that end.[47]

Although most of his writings were meant to apply to Britain, Mill did not think Indians were sufficiently advanced to have liberal democracy extended to them. Because suffrage should not be offered to those who are not 'in the normal condition of a human being'[48] – meaning illiterate and poor people in Britain – it certainly could not be granted to Indians on account of Mill's conviction of their backwardness. Although the British introduced some elements of representative government in India, both Mills opposed it. James Mill's energies were fashioned towards 'a revolution in Indian society carried out solely by the weapon of law'.[49] Much of this was geared towards destroying collective ownership of property, which he regarded as primitive, and introducing individualistic private property relationships. Assuming a Hobbesian version of human nature as egoistic and violent, Mill believed that the individual must be at the centre of all policy, not the collectivity – and certainly not the cultures of those under colonial rule.

France, like Britain, was a colonial power as well as a slave-holding and slave-trading nation. It also necessarily conferred rights differentially. Despite the Republican universality of the French Revolution, exclusions and rightlessness were present in French slave trading, slave owning and the running of Caribbean plantation colonies, with complex gradations of privileges based on racial phenotypes. The Revolution made no decisive break with slavery, and in its zigzag aftermath the state stipulated other categories of inferior rights for women, religious minorities and those without property. In part because of the stark contradiction between the 'Rights of Man' and enslavement, the highly profitable wealth-creating slave trade became a taboo subject which the post-Revolution Constituent and Legislative Assemblies avoided. In the Constituent Assembly, 150 'colonial proprietors' sat as National Deputies. They looked after slave-plantation interests, and this included twice preventing 'mulattoes' from admission as Deputies in a 'storm of protest' so vigorous that the reporter's voice could not be heard.[50] An early post-Revolutionary decree made it a crime to incite unrest in the colonies.[51] Although slave emancipation occurred in 1794 after the Revolution, under pressure from the Société des Amis des Noirs and passionate politicians and intellectuals, it was not meaningfully implemented, and the French slave trade itself reached its peak between 1789 and 1791, with eighty-three slave ships sailing from Nantes and Bordeaux alone in 1790. That same year, over 40,000 Africans were sold in Saint-Domingue, several thousand more than in the pre-Revolutionary era.[52] After seizing power in 1799, Napoleon Bonaparte reinstated slavery in 1802 and denied any political rights to free blacks in the colonies and France.[53] It was therefore the resistance of enslaved people in Saint-Domingue led by Toussaint L'Ouverture that pushed Republican universalist France towards a grudging recognition of 'universal' human rights, rather than liberal French anti-slavery sentiment, as writers such as Aimé Césaire and C. L. R. James have argued.[54]

French enslavement of Africans coexisted with more formal colonialism. Alexis de Tocqueville gave much thought to French colonization in Algeria. His preoccupations were somewhat different from those of John Stuart Mill since he was dealing with a settler colony, and Mill in India was not. When in his 1841 'Essay on Algeria' he turns to looking at rights, he is far more concerned with the rights of the colonists than the colonized, and advocates making life for the former as close as possible to what it would be in France. However, 'our great political institutions' – which Tocqueville lists as elections, freedom of the press and trial by jury – 'are not necessary for the infancy of societies'.[55] He further contends that political liberties need to be suspended due to the necessity of militarily protecting the outnumbered French colonists, whom he believed needed to have their rights to colonize and appropriate land strengthened. He says little about Muslim Algerians rights to their property, and assumes that they will only benefit from French colonization as long as it is carried out thoughtfully. But, in 1848, Louis Napoleon came to power through a *coup d'état*, and then curtailed democratic rights, jailed opponents, set up penal colonies and declared himself Emperor for life. His twenty-year rule coincided with several foreign conquests, including Syria, Indo-China, and the establishing of Maximillian in Mexico, where liberal Republican rights were denied to local populations.

## Civic Stratification

While hierarchies of rights holders were created in British and French colonies and in the home countries in the nineteenth century, as well as in colonial and slave societies such as the USA, such processes are mirrored in contemporary Western countries. The idea of civic stratification, first employed by sociologist David Lockwood to denote how social inequalities could be embedded in citizenship entitlements, differs only from what obtained in colonial situations in that the political setting is notionally non-colonial. For Lydia Morris, who developed Lockwood's civic stratification more widely, the concept is:

> implicitly concerned with the construction of 'moral standing' in society and explores the relations between possession or absence of rights and access to 'moral and material resources'. Briefly put, the argument is that a regime of rights can both shape and be shaped by the moral standing of a given group in society such that an erosion of standing can undermine the enjoyment of, or claim to rights (civic deficit or civic exclusion), while the denial of rights further erodes moral standing. The converse would also apply, in that the accrual of moral standing in society, perhaps through the intervention of civic activists, can lead to an expansion of rights, or to enhanced enjoyment of a right (civic expansion or civic gain).[56]

Morris argues that morality is used to construct hierarchies through which welfare rights can be claimed. Her research showed that the British Conservative government used a moral schema to justify cuts and exclusions, juxtaposing 'hard-working taxpayers' to morally suspect 'dependents'. Indeed, 'class inequality is being written more strongly into citizenship rights'.[57] The way in which this occurs, at least in part, is through increasing conditionality on rights, and limiting the application of international human rights in the UK. The British government has recently conceptualized unworthy citizens and migrants within a similar analytic frame that stresses conditionality, thereby narrowing rights, 'as the treatment of citizens comes more closely to approximate that of migrants'.[58] Regimes similar to the colonial differentiation of rights have simply been imported into domestic British social policy. Civic stratification can be a general feature of government policy, as in Morris' description, or it can be racialized, as with the denial of rights to citizens caught up in the Windrush scandal, as will be discussed in chapter 2.

The results of civic stratification were underlined by UN Special Rapporteur for Extreme Poverty and Human Rights Philip Alston's 2018 report on the human rights implications of UK austerity policies. Alston's report, substantiated by over 300 submissions, depicted Britain's poor as including up to almost 50 per cent of children in the country, and, recalling nineteenth-century British middle-class attitudes towards poverty chronicled by Friedrich Engels, called Britain's social welfare, 'punitive, mean-spirited and often callous'.[59] Public spending per head in England alone is projected to fall by about 18 per cent between 2010 and 2022, and the drastic cuts in public funding for schools, transport and housing will have disproportionately adverse effects on Britain's burgeoning numbers of poor people.[60] The social-welfare benefits and provisions that Britain offers have become more restrictive, through complex rules on eligibility and convoluted digitized access.[61] All this translates into vastly different qualities of life and life expectancies, signalling that certain human rights – such as those to adequate standards of living, housing and schooling – are compromised for vast swathes of the British population. Following shortly after Alston's report, a Human Rights Watch report on food poverty in the UK documented sharp rises in the use of food banks and other indicators of hunger, violating the basic human right to food for vast numbers of Britons.[62]

Alston's parallel report on the USA completed a year earlier was even more critical of the extreme inequality in that country – the highest in the Western world. It urged the US administration to acknowledge the important link between social and economic conditions and human rights. While the report is packed with statistical indices to support its conclusions, Alston's impressions travelling through the USA starkly illustrate the dire situation of the 40 million Americans (12.7 per cent of the population) who meet official definitions of poverty:

> I met with many people barely surviving on Skid Row in Los Angeles, I witnessed a San Francisco police officer telling a group of homeless people to move on but having no answer when asked where they could move to, I heard how thousands of poor people get minor infraction notices which seem to be intentionally designed to quickly explode into unpayable debt, incarceration, and the replenishment of municipal coffers, I saw sewage filled yards in states where govern-ments don't consider sanitation facilities to be their responsibility, I saw people who had lost all of their teeth because adult dental care is not covered by the vast majority of programs available to the very poor, I heard about soaring death rates and family and community destruction wrought by prescription and other drug addiction, and I met with people in the South of Puerto Rico living next to a mountain of completely unprotected coal ash which rains down upon them bringing illness, disability and death.[63]

Alston also details projects, largely from the voluntary sector, that are attempting to address some of these problems, but the overall picture is of a massively wealthy country in which the state presides over the despair and destitution of so many of its citizens. His report was angrily dismissed as biased and 'politically motivated' by Nikki Haley, the US Ambassador to the UN,[64] and in Britain, Theresa May's Home Secretary,

Amber Rudd, brusquely sidestepped Alston's report saying it was of an 'extraordinary political nature'.[65]

These reports and the literature on civic stratification make essential a frame of analysis that centres possession of capital and power as features of human rights. In his essay on the sociological aspects of human rights, Ted Benton summarizes the Marxian position on such rights:

> The general outcome of this line of thought is to emphasise the difference between the juridical allocation and recognition of universal rights, and the very unequal *de facto* ability of individuals to exercise the rights they are formally allocated. Equality under the law is compromised by unequal ability to pay for legal advice and representation, and by the deep cultural gulf between specialised legal profession and many of those who might otherwise benefit from the protection of the law.[66]

Britain's Equality and Human Rights Commission issued a report in 2018 summarizing how these inequalities operate within the criminal justice system in England and Wales: 'defendants from ethnic minorities are more likely to not trust the legal advice they receive and are more likely to plead not guilty than White defendants, owing to a lack of trust in the system. As a result, they are more likely to lose the potential benefits of early guilty pleas in criminal proceedings.'[67] According to the Commission, recent reductions in state funding for courts and legal aid have led to marked disadvantages within the law for those on lower incomes and ethnic minorities. All of this takes place in a social milieu in which hate crimes have increased and the xenophobia associated with the Brexit referendum has not abated. Similar evidence has been presented in the USA, discussed in more detail in chapter 3, indicating that African-Americans have been, and remain, disproportionately represented in the world's largest prison system, and these disparities are attributed in many studies to a lack of information among prosecutors who fall back on racial stereotypes.[68] These are ultimately related to images of black people inherited from slavery, segregation and the history of differential human rights in the USA.

These scenarios also appear in other Western democracies. In France, many people descended from its former colonies live apart in *banlieues*, and 'a legal system … distinguishes between those who should and those who should not have political rights and be eligible for social services'.[69] 'Behind the universal model of the deserving citizen', Fredette argues, lies 'the specter of a particular kind of French citizen'.[70] These differentiations, however, build on fears that human rights would interfere with colonial rule at the time of the drafting of the UDHR and

Geneva Convention. Britain was also against establishing the rights of non-European migrants and asylum seekers in European countries, and European colonial powers and settler states were hostile to the broader institutionalization of human rights for colonized peoples.[71] The current forms of civic stratification clearly relate to the difficulties of maintaining universalism amid systems of historically continuous racial and class discrimination.

Regarding France, discrimination in the application of rights builds on distinctions made in colonial institutions in Algeria (and later West Africa) which reinforced differences between French settlers who were citizens and indigenous Algerians who were subjects.[72] In the period leading up to the Algerian war of independence – covered more extensively in chapter 4 – the complicated double electoral college system gave 1 million European settlers equivalent voting power to over 8 million indigenous Algerians.[73] Although, as Cooper argues, these inequalities were always malleable and subject to 'claim-making from below',[74] they underline the necessity for the colonial state of creating different citizenship regimes and also of modifying access to rights occasionally to placate indigenous populations. But, equal voting rights could never have been built into colonialism, since such rights could undermine colonialism itself. By the 1970s, at the close of the formal colonial era, however, there was a change from dealing with subjects under French dominion, with at least some rights, in France to dealing with immigrants or refugees with a whole different set of rights and exclusions.

The paradox and problem here is that, while nation-states can be charged by individuals, groups and other states with human rights violations, only individuals can be held to account through the various tribunals, courts and reconciliation efforts. Migrants rights advocates in Britain and civil rights activists in the USA might petition for recognition of their clients' human rights, but all channels of appeal are part of the state that ultimately adjudicates all grievances, including those against its own institutions. Some of these institutions, of course, are responsible for formulating, implementing and enforcing rights that may well discriminate between different categories of humanity. In the context of this 'statist bias', Catherine Lu calls the circumstances arising from colonialism *structural* injustice and argues that the rendering of justice should go 'beyond victims and perpetrators and toward the institutional, normative and material conditions in which they interact'.[75] This, of course, has not occurred, in part because, returning to Charles Mills, race has underpinned the entire liberal framework of social and political thought from the outset, and at the same time it has largely been excluded from liberal debates on rights.[76]

Differentiations in access and entitlement to human rights within Western states that have made racial civic stratification the norm can be traced to the first acts of European colonization, when tortuous debates over the rights of indigenous peoples resulted in indigenous and enslaved peoples simply becoming inferior rights-bearing subjects within the larger colonial order.[77] I will have more to say on the continuities in these particular patterns in chapter 5, but differential treatment of indigenous peoples in settler colonial states reinforces the fact that Europeans have long represented indigenous peoples as biologically, culturally and – therefore – juridically inferior.

One of the measures of this today is in Canada where huge rates of murdered and missing indigenous women and girls have sparked substantial activism. A national enquiry on the subject published in 2019, as part of which over 2,300 affected people were interviewed, concluded that this amounted to genocide in both sociological and legal terms. The report argued strenuously that these tragedies were structurally embedded in Canada's settler colonial society. 'Ultimately, and despite different circumstances and backgrounds, what connects all these deaths', the report stated, 'is colonial violence, racism and oppression'.[78] Police and medical authorities either did not respond appropriately, or in some cases were implicated in rapes and deaths. In Australia, the abduction of Aboriginal children who formed the 'stolen generations' underlies the common experience of denial of human rights to indigenous populations in settler colonial states. Scholars using Raphael Lemkin's original definition of genocide as involving the forcible transfer of children from one group to another and the elimination of culture have classified this as genocide.[79] In the liberal states of Canada and Australia, indigenous peoples are still victims of the murderous acts that prompted the formalization of human rights.

## Rightlessness

Looking within the internal European context, we could say that civic stratification was given more immediate impetus in the uprooting, removal and deportation of populations, especially across Central and Eastern Europe, in the late nineteenth and into the early twentieth centuries. This was done to create ethnically homogeneous zones under specific government authority as part of nation-building exercises. The processes by which rights were segmented, stratified and denied in Europe echoed the differentiation of rights under colonialism, and are articulated today as nation-states claim exclusive powers to define citizenship.

In the early twentieth century, men were conscripted and moved all over Europe to train in various national armies, and they were used by nations aligned against each other to protect, and sometimes enlarge, their highly stratified internal *national* orders. Although commemorated on the medal I inherited from my grandfather as 'The Great War for Civilisation', the result was 50 million dead from 1914 to 1919 in World War I. British writers who fought in that war, including Siegfried Sassoon, Robert Graves and Wilfrid Owen, often depicted it as being fought for no greater principles than the national vanities of governments and politicians. The unwilling recruits whom Sassoon wrote of in *Memoirs of an Infantry Officer* were inducted into a mechanical and inhuman undertaking. 'What in earlier days had been drafts of volunteers', he writes, 'were now droves of victims'.[80] Later in his recollections, he describes the purpose of his and other soldiers' sacrifices as being the upholding of a society of extreme class privilege. As he put it following conversations with Lady Brassey of Chapelwood Manor, Sussex (fictionalized as Lady Asterisk at Nutwood Manor), where he was convalescing: 'outwardly emotionless, she symbolized the patrician privileges for whose preservation I had chucked bombs at Germans and carelessly offered myself as a target for a sniper'.[81] These 'patrician privileges' allowed members of higher social classes simply to become officers, with access to recuperation in manor houses in England, while working-class recruits shortened their odds of survival in makeshift hospital tents at the front. Additionally, the 3 million troops from the Commonwealth, including a million from British India, were also enlisted in what was depicted as an imperial cause. They fought on the Western front and they were not given the same food, medicines or remuneration as white soldiers.[82]

The reinforcing of internal British class divisions through World War I was mirrored by Germany where, as Schmitt commented, 'to demand seriously of human beings that they kill others and be prepared to die themselves so that trade and industry may flourish for the survivors or that the purchasing power of grandchildren may grow is sinister and crazy'.[83] In the same milieu of violence and class rivalry, ethnic and national divisions were changed as the boundaries of European states were continuously redrawn to create several distinct nation-states that were previously under the dominion of various Empires. The interwar period was also a period of mass unemployment, poverty, widespread malnutrition, starvation and economic depression throughout mainland Europe. As Hannah Arendt observed in 'The Decline of the Nation-State and the End of the Rights of Man',[84] numerous peoples simply either became unwanted 'minorities' in these new states or were deprived of all rights because they did not have a nationality that coincided with the state they happened to live in. This provoked another mass exodus of such peoples to other states in which they sometimes had a nationality, but, because they were not born in the territory, they did not have citizenship rights. Only nationals could be citizens, and only citizens could have rights. Within each state, there could be people of varying juridical statuses, and scores without citizenship guarantees. As with many of those caught up in the 'migration crisis' in Europe today, there were people who had no human rights in the territories they were born in and, likewise, no rights in the places to which they fled.

For Arendt, the realignment of states following World War I catalysed the problem of human beings who may be refugees, minorities or stateless, but who to one degree or another are without the right to have rights. Those who fell into these categories were victims of the establishment of nation-states, the preconditions for which are 'homogeneity of population and rootedness in the soil'.[85] The problem was that, within the reconfigured boundaries of mid-twentieth-century Europe, the national homogeneity that was the underlying premise of citizenship and hence access to rights, did not prevail, especially in Eastern Europe. In these circumstances, the link between birth and nation could be severed, and rightlessness became public policy applied to specific ethno-national groups. Both Germany and the Soviet Union along with numerous other European countries, de-nationalized and disowned population groups. Most notoriously, German Jews lost all rights of nationality overnight under the Nuremberg Laws of 1935. This became the groundwork for the murder of 6 million Jews by the German state.

One response to this horror was the migration of European Jews to Palestine, followed by the creation of the state of Israel in 1948 out of the British Mandate colonial administration. But, as Arendt notes, this 'produced a new category of refugee, Arabs, thereby increasing the number of rightless by another 700,000 to 800,000 people'.[86] As a Jewish state, Israel established differential citizenship rights according to ethnicity and religion, as have other countries up to the present. In 2019, India's lower chamber passed a bill that would grant residency and citizenship to non-Muslim migrants only.[87] The stripping of citizenship was given great force by the Bush administration policy during the Iraq war by asserting that those they captured were 'unlawful combatants' who had no rights under the Geneva Convention. In such a scenario, all means of violent and inhumane practices could be, and were, exercised against them because they were rendered stateless, and, hence, rightless. No international enunciation of the human rights of refugees has been able to affect any of these state actions that, in effect, seal the fate of hundreds of thousands of people as being without the right to have rights.

Under the rubric of the Global War on Terror, several Western liberal states, including Britain, the USA, Australia, the Netherlands and Austria, have taken measures to compel citizens to denationalize. Although 'the force of Arendt's "right to have rights" aphorism may seem attenuated, at least with respect to liberal democratic states of the twenty first century', as Macklin points out, this depends on the 'right to enter and remain in the state'.[88] In 2017, 100 British ISIS fighters were rendered stateless by the UK government as the caliphate succumbed to military defeat.[89] Added to this number was the tragic case of the pregnant teenage ISIS bride Shamima Begum, who in 2019 attracted media attention because she was found by a BBC journalist in a refugee camp in Syria. Home Secretary Sajid Javid argued that Ms Begum would not be stateless because she was entitled to Bangladeshi nationality through her parents. Denied both British and Bangladeshi rights, she had to remain in Syria, where her infant child died, largely due to physical conditions in the refugee camp shortly after Javid's pronouncement. Actions such as these amount to an admission of varied British citizenship categories, because citizens with foreign parents can more easily be stripped of their nationality,[90] resulting in the right-lessness of the camp.

Other countries have removed citizenship from their nationals under global counter-terrorism and security legislation. While these instances had internal causes, it is not insignificant that such legislation was globalized by the US and British-led war on terrorism. Bahrain, for example, denationalized almost 1,000 people, including some minors, and part of this was done through mass trials of defendants *in absentia*. Michelle Bachelet, the Director of the UN HRC, criticized Bahrain for violating the right to a nationality under Article 15 of the UDHR.[91] India did the same on a much larger scale to residents of Assam, who had to prove that they had lived in India before the Pakistan civil war of 1971 in which many were forced to flee what is now Bangladesh. In 2019, the final National Registrar of Citizens list determined that 1.9 million people were illegal immigrants subject to detention and deportation. As of August 2019, 1,000 people failing appeals at the Foreigners' Tribunal have been placed in detention centres, and children separated from parents.[92]

Arendt speculates that the alternative to refugee status or right-lessness would be to condemn such people to the status of colonial peoples.[93] This, however, was not unthinkable, and is the subject of Mark Mazower's *Hitler's Empire*, in which the historian argues that part of Hitler's plan was to reproduce the colonial relationships Britain had created outside Europe. The Nazis saw little difference between the racial superiority the British used to justify colonialism and their own variant. 'The mighty British Empire', Mazower concludes, 'had long set the bar for German imperialists',[94] and the Führer was a great admirer of British colonialism. Once refugees were present within nation-states, there were three main options, according to Arendt. Firstly, these populations could be assimilated by re-education and citizenship classes, all of which were intended to cause the disappearance of non-national cultural uniqueness. This became necessary for the maintaining of the national cultural homogeneity, and was, incidentally, already a major policy for indigenous peoples in settler colonial states such as Canada, Australia and the USA. Secondly, they could be deported or forced to migrate, and many did go to the Americas, Australia, Palestine and South Africa; or, thirdly, they could be liquidated, which was the choice of the European fascist regimes that took power in the 1930s. By the end of World War II, as Timothy Snyder has documented,[95] German forces had killed about 10 million civilians in mass extermination actions, over half of them Jews. Another 3 million Soviet soldiers died of starvation in German prisoner-of-war camps. The Soviet government killed 15 million Soviet civilians, many of whom were national minorities such as Ukrainians, Kazakhs and Byelorussians, in the 1930s and 1940s. About half a million Germans and Hungarians starved to death while prisoners of the Soviets.

By comparison, 'civic stratification' seems tepid, but Arendt shows how ethnic, national or racial differentiations in human rights can become ratcheted up to genocide. If rights become, as they always have been, the enforceable prerogative of the nation, then the kinds of actions undertaken by Nazi Germany and other European states in the 1930s and 1940s to deprive non-nationals of the same rights as the citizen, even though they may have been born in the territory, are always possible. The Third Reich issued mandates by which Jews who left Germany under pressure from pogroms and racial laws, or were deported from it, had no rights of return. The stateless, being rightless, were, as Arendt argues, at the mercy of the police forces, who took it upon themselves to enforce whatever they chose. In fact, the very being of the stateless person was criminalized. They had no rights to work, but, if they did, they were committing a criminal offence. The irony was that only by committing a criminal act could the stateless person gain rights – as a criminal in the state criminal justice system. The paralysing effects of this are described in W. G. Sebald's *Austerlitz*, as German decrees on the Jewish Czech population meant that, among other restrictions of her rights, the protagonist's mother 'could go shopping only at certain times; she must not take a taxi, she could sit only in the last carriage of the tram, she could not visit a coffeehouse or cinema, or attend a concert or any other event'.[96]

If nothing else, Arendt's 'The Decline of the Nation-State and the End of the Rights of Man' points to the dangers of the nation-state being the guarantor of human rights, and here we realize that the abstract 'Rights of Man' was a guarantee to individuals only insofar as they were under the protection of the state. The state, as Arendt contends, under its self-asserted sovereignty, is free to act with no recourse to any concept of natural rights. Indeed, as Schmitt argues, states as political entities construct differentiations between internal friend and enemy.[97] This means that human rights do not elevate anyone from the condition of 'bare life', since rights can be removed at any time, depending on politically concocted human taxonomies. In Agamben's reading, this precarity of 'bare life' is enabled by the French Declaration of Rights itself, which asserts the rights of man and citizens, leaving open the possibility that universal rights are subsumed under citizenship rights, and the sovereign enters into 'more intimate symbiosis' with the jurist, doctor scientist, expert and priest.[98] Therefore, the sovereign power over the individual is absolute, creating 'a new living dead man',[99] signifying a major shift, at least in the European world, from earlier, more diverse sources of authority.

Shortly after World War II, under Article 14 of the UDHR, all persons were given the right to seek asylum, and *all* peoples 'are equal before the law and are entitled without any discrimination to equal protection of the law' in Article 7. Subsequent human rights instruments, such as the International Covenant on Civil and Political Rights Article 26, also granted all persons equality before the law, free from discrimination. These enunciations, however, face the contradiction that, while the state was urged to guarantee these rights, it was also the guarantor of national, class, racial and ethnic privileges and inequalities. Indeed, as Arendt recognized, the creation of the state of Israel in British Mandate Palestine in the same year as the UDHR, while providing a 'homeland' for Jews, simply created another group of peoples with lesser rights. We know that this situation has continued to the present.[100]

Rightlessness and civic stratification are both political processes within states that are regulated by laws, and sometimes even Constitutions. Many years before the European Holocaust, the US Constitution held that black people were outside its reach. African-Americans only became citizens through the 14th Amendment in 1868. This was after the infamous *Dred Scott* case in 1857, in which a slave kept in non-slave states was ruled not to be a citizen. The first impulse of the US government was to restrict citizenship to Europeans, and this was inscribed in the 1790 Naturalization Act which limited citizenship to 'white persons'.[101] As we will discuss more in chapter 5, a similar ruling in the USA, *Lone Wolf* v. *Hitchcock* in 1903, invested Congress with 'plenary powers' over Native Americans.[102] If people can be classified as not protected by the laws, subject to absolute state authority, outside of any social contract, then anything is possible. Although the victims of rightlessness and inferior rights have fought back through social movements, organized acts of resistance, oratory and art, their effects on a wide range of groups today cannot be overestimated.

## The Structural Embeddedness of Non-universal Human Rights

Both an antecedent and continuing dynamic, hierarchical comparison of cultures has underpinned hierarchies of rights. Dehumanizing images and practices, scientific racism, cultural evolutionism, intelligence tests and paternal tutelage were all widely espoused by liberals to rank human communities. Hence, human rights arrived within a liberal world that had already constructed numerous concepts of invidious human difference. Decolonization and the UDHR did not lead to reflection on how these concepts could be challenged and colonizing could be avoided, but to a kind of triumphalism that heralded a new international order based more on peace, cooperation and economic development. Buzan and Lawson maintain of the post-World War II international society that, while 'many status inequalities lingered on ... the package of colonialism, human inequality/racism, the "standard of civilization" and divided sovereignty unravelled'.[103] In its place, a 'new package' consisting of universal human rights, anti-racism and aspirations to equality was said to prevail.

While they each have different specific concerns and theses, many human rights scholars equate human rights with progress and show this with discrete indices and measures of liberal social, legal and political advances internationally. But, aware of the painful histories of colonialism and slavery, some are quick to situate all this in the post-World War II era. Jack Donnelly, a prominent human rights scholar, for example, commented that, although the West was in the past a purveyor of 'racist imperialism', the age of decolonization and more enlightened theoretical models have spelt its demise. Since World War II, 'the rise of universal human rights presents a story of moral progress'.[104] More recently, Kathryn Sikkink asserts that 'human rights, as defined in current human rights law, provides a morally defensible starting place for talking about progressive change in the world'.[105] Others, such as Kathryn McNeilly, believe that there are possibilities for re-engagement with human rights and the universality within them to realize radical and transformative potentials.[106] This all presupposes that a line can be drawn under colonialism and enslavement and that, after the 'sordid nature' of it was revealed – as liberal human rights analyst Samuel Moyn contends – it 'ultimately ended once and for all'.[107]

For Moyn, in his most recent book, the French Revolution had 'introduced human rights as a *lingua franca* of politics for modern states', as well as initiating the humanitarian concern for social welfare.[108] Although Moyn later notes 'exclusions' and is concerned more with how social welfare is abrogated through neoliberalism, the idea of progress and original European virtue implicitly remains. When he does proceed to analyse global politics of distributive justice as an aspect of human rights, Moyn begins not with colonialism but with the 'postcolonial states', as well as with the attempts of colonial powers to instil more concern with humanitarian welfare prior to decolonization.[109] In Moyn's upbeat narrative, these new states led the charge for global human rights and justice that the West had proposed through many international conventions and instruments, abetted by a host of mid-twentieth-century liberal scholars.

The inconsistencies between the espousal of this 'new package' so soon after Europe reluctantly released its grip on darker-skinned peoples did not go unnoticed among observers of decolonization. The reflections on the deep social, political, economic and psychological damage that colonialism inflicted in the eyes of anti-colonial activists and scholars contrast with human rights theorists' buoyant optimism. While universal human rights were being declared in 1948, just after Europe had been 'responsible for the highest heap of corpses in history',[10] Aime Césaire suspected that these rights were only enunciated because of the *European* tragedy of the Holocaust and World War II. Declarations of the magnitude of the UDHR had never been made in the contexts of European colonizing or enslaving. Although there were reformers and humanists among colonizers, their calls for change stopped well short of universal human rights, and when non-European peoples asserted claims to human rights by resisting colonialism and slavery, their aspirations were often violently denied. Even the founding meeting of the UN in San Francisco in 1945 explicitly rejected representations for decolonization or any specific enunciations of the rights of colonized peoples. While establishing universal human rights, the Preamble to the UN Charter authored by apartheid leader Jan Smuts did not disavow apartheid or Empire.[111]

Given the colossal human rights deficit accumulated by the colonial powers and settler colonial states, can the slate be wiped clean by enunciations, aspirations and examples of progress? Can the undoubted success of some social movements to deploy human rights to reverse numerous adversities be seen as having great potential for social change, or is there something more structurally embedded within the European colonizing experience that makes the link between colonialism and the denial of human rights persist? Can we speak of a colonialism *of* human rights? Equally important is how states built on colonization and slavery can extend meaningfully enforced human rights to those who were categorically excluded from such rights, and upon whose exclusions settler states were shaped. 'An absolute and immense democracy is not all we find in America', Alexis de Tocqueville tells readers at the outset of the final 'Three Races' chapter of *Democracy in America*.[112] As a consequence of Africans and Native Americans being situated outside democracy, he thought that conflict would persist in the USA because democratic rights only applied to the European population. It might not be much of a stretch to consider that similar provisos need to be made about 'universal' human rights.

# 2

# The Uneasy Present of Colonialism

You must not wonder where your lavatory went when you flushed it …
Oh it might all end up in the water you are thinking of taking a swim
in; the contents of your lavatory might, just might, graze gently against
your ankle as you wade carefree in the water, for you see, in Antigua,
there is no sewage disposal system. But the Caribbean Sea is very big
and the Atlantic Ocean is even bigger; it would amaze you the number
of black slaves this ocean has swallowed up.[1]

Jamaica Kincaid

## Uneasy Memories

Today, a realization that so many of our human and ecological losses are
attributable in some way to colonialism is becoming more tangible and
is a large part of the current moment. There seems to be some echo that
calls us to recognize that the inhumanities that induced loss continue.
Something profound lurks in the fact that those who bore the brunt of
colonization are not doing well, making the present poverty, racism,
displacement, corruption and inequalities stand out against other futures
that colonialism denied. In 2018, Jamaica Kincaid's *A Small Place*
was turned into an experimental play at the Gate Theatre in London.
The source work is an essay that illustrates the profound uneasiness
that followed British withdrawal from Kincaid's native Antigua and
the ensuing arrival of white tourists where once-manacled people had
toiled. The black inhabitants of the island, often ignored backdrops for

the tourists, are traces of the expendable humans that the British sent to their Caribbean plantations, while the sea is the forgotten grave of the many Africans who died, or were murdered and tossed overboard by slave-ship crews, en route to the Americas. The effluent in the otherwise clear waters is an unsettling reminder that an idyllic holiday spot is not a modern paradise. There is no closure. Slavery is a 'wrong that can never be righted' Kincaid tells us later in the essay, a wrong that cannot be addressed by an apology, money or the 'death of the criminal'.[2]

Recognition of the historical roots of criminality and human rights violations inform current preoccupations with the significance of colonialism and slavery. One indication of this is the attention surrounding public commemorations of prominent figures who feature in state narratives, portraying the nation as inheriting unqualified achievements through exploration, discovery, inventions, humanitarian social policies, intrinsic cultural virtues and economic wellbeing. The fact that 'achievements' were often accompanied by, and relied upon, acts that killed, maimed, violated and deprived non-Europeans of their livelihoods and lands, however, is increasingly subject to vigorous exposure.

The ubiquitous public monuments to prominent sponsors or agents, who may well have pioneered, explored and discovered, but also plundered and committed atrocity, are an affront to those who believe that injustices and inequalities have followed from a mindset associated with these actions. While monuments and street names honouring European monarchs, soldiers and imperialists were commonly removed immediately after decolonization across African and Indian cities, a movement to question public commemorations of people and events related to colonialism has been renewed. In 2018, Berlin renamed some of the streets which were named after the figures associated with its 1884 to 1914 occupation of South West Africa.[3] Under Kaiser Wilhelm II, the German military killed between 60,000 and 100,000 Herero at the beginning of the twentieth century through a mixture of shootings, induced starvation, and drought caused by the sealing of wells and poisoning of water.[4] Although street names and other memorials to those carrying out Germany's lethal occupation of parts of Africa remain, the first stirrings of conscience have appeared with the opening of an exhibition at the German Historical Museum in Berlin to explore the genocide and discussions of reparations.[5] Despite the material evidence of beheaded Herero skulls housed in German museums, these commemorations, ambivalent and belated as they are, could not have occurred without the Herero and Nama activists and their supporters in Germany pushing national memory to extend beyond World War II.[6] In a formal handing-over ceremony in 2018, the German government returned human skulls and bones derived from the genocide and used for eugenics research, but it has delayed an official apology and has therefore avoided compensation claims.[7]

After some street and other names that honoured colonial and apartheid figures were removed in South Africa in the early 1990s,[8] the Rhodes Must Fall movement has campaigned to remove the statue of the racist magnate Sir Cecil Rhodes at the University of Cape Town, located in a city containing some of the countries remaining colonial-era commemorations. The Rhodes Must Fall movement, as Achille Mbembe has suggested, represents a questioning of how Rhodes acquired the land he 'donated' and upon which the university is built.[9] Likewise, as part of a general movement of universities in the UK and the USA to recognize the substantial benefits they continue to accrue from slavery and colonialism, students at Oriel College Oxford demanded the removal of the Rhodes statue on the front of a college building (see figure 2.1). This was criticized by celebrity historian Mary Beard and others on the grounds that one cannot judge past figures such as Rhodes by contemporary standards. But, as Gopal points out with a string of literary examples, there was significant dissent towards the inhumanity and racism of Britain's colonial enterprises.[10] To date, college authorities have refused to remove the Rhodes statue, and in a public opinion poll 59 per cent of the Britons surveyed thought it should not come down. Only 11 per cent thought that the statue should be removed.[11]

The well-publicized furore over Rhodes and his legacy adds to a general re-evaluation of other figures in Britain's imperial past, including Sir Winston Churchill for his racist views and his role in the Bengal famine in 1943, when Churchill's war cabinet ordered the confiscation of grain and the destruction of boats and cars in Bengal. This is the subject of *Bengal Shadows*, a documentary film made by Joy Bannerjee and Patho Battacharya in 2017. Referencing Satayajit Ray's moving portrait of victims of the famine in his 1973 film *Distant Thunder*, through survivors' memories and expert commentaries, the film shows that prioritizing the war effort over Bengali lives led to suffering and death on a vast scale. Although Churchill's colonial policies and dehumanization of Indians have led to some reassessments of his heroic status, no public monuments of Churchill have been removed in Britain. This is not the case, however, with more distant and lesser-known figures. In the former slave port of Bristol, where, as the rows of grand Georgian houses testify, a prosperous mercantile city was built on proceeds from the slave trade, a social movement has arisen dedicated to the removal of a monument to 'father of the city' Edward Colston in the city centre. A generous benefactor to Bristol, Colston was a high official in the Royal Africa Company, and over his tenure almost 85,000 Africans were forced onto company ships to be transported to Britain's plantation colonies in the

**Figure 2.1** *Statue of Cecil Rhodes, High Street frontage of Oriel College, Oxford. Source: Christopher Hilton, 2017.*

Caribbean.[12] Bristol authorities have resolved to rename the Colston concert hall and some schools bearing his name, but the monument has remained, with a plaque providing information on Colston's associations with slavery. Colston, however, is just one of many publicly celebrated Bristolians who were intimately connected to and profited from the enslavement of black people going back to the sixteenth century. The conflict in Bristol is about public history and relating past crimes to current discrimination and disadvantage.[13]

Likewise, in the USA, public symbols associated with racism, such as those connected with the Confederacy of Southern states, arguably a political union dedicated to the permanent enslavement of African peoples, have also been at the centre of vigorous debate and violent conflict. This includes the reinvigoration of white supremacism manifest in numerous rallies in support of Confederate monuments, including one in Charlottesville, Virginia, in 2017, which ended with the murder of 32-year-old white anti-racist protester Heather Heyer. The incident is now iconic for President Trump's remark that there were 'some very fine people' on both sides. This was taken as sympathy for whites claiming preferential citizenship, and the controversy deepened in 2019 when Trump reiterated this view, stating that the enslaver Robert E. Lee was 'a very great general'.[14] While vocally opposed by Trump and many Republican politicians, as of 2017 monuments to racists and enslavers have been removed from about two dozen US cities, and many other removals are planned across the country.[15] Beyond this, as Stephen Small observes,[16] the more significant sites of contestation are the numerous plantation houses that provide guided tours, and in so doing provide platforms to obliterate the realities of slavery, glorify enslavers and distort facts. As Small shows, these have been challenged by black social movements, NGOs concerned with public history and tourism, and by sites that are owned or managed by African-Americans and offer counter-narratives. In related developments, memorials to the role of slavery in many cities, and to incidents of racial injustice such as the numerous nineteenth- and twentieth-century lynchings of African-Americans – and, more recently, Latina/os – have sprung up across the country.

The memorialization of Canada's first Prime Minister has been attacked by indigenous rights movement Idle No More and other coalitions of activists and academics. They have demanded the removal of statues of Sir John A. MacDonald, one of the architects of Canada's notorious Indian boarding-school system, and a person widely regarded as a racist. In 2017, schools in Ontario removed MacDonald's name from nine schools in the Province,[17] and in 2018, the municipal government of Victoria, British Columbia, decided to remove a statue of MacDonald from the front entrance of the City Hall.[18] As part of the same general movement, a French immersion school in Vancouver has covered up a plaque honouring Cecil Rhodes, after whom the school was originally named.[19]

While in Europe there are museums and galleries in which special exhibitions detail commentary on past colonialism with clear implications for the present, many tend to be tepid affairs that underestimate or ignore the criminal dimensions and human rights implications of colonialism. This might have gone relatively unnoticed a few decades ago, but it is being highlighted now. For example, reviewing the 2015–16 'Artist and Empire' exhibition at London's Tate Britain museum, Nicola Gray maintains that 'despite some of its declared aims, it is almost a celebration of empire, glossing over and obscuring the damage, destruction and profound changes that British imperialism wreaked on "other" cultures and lives'.[20] This is perhaps even more remarkable given that, as she points out, the museum was funded by Henry Tate who made his fortune through sugar procured from plantation slavery, and the site itself was formerly Milbank penitentiary from where Britain dispatched its unwanted petty criminals to Australia. Similarly, Small discusses many museums and country houses across Europe that 'symbolically annihilate' slavery and colonialism, in part by denying that they owe their collections and wealth to colonies and slaves.[21] Some, however, still practise 'bold national self-praise for colonialism'.[22]

In Belgium, monuments to the genocidal King Leopold II still decorate town and city spaces, and voices seeking to comment on the effects of the state's actions in Congo, Rwanda and Burundi have been marginalized.[23] The memory of the estimated 10 million murders and countless mutilations and rapes by Belgians in the Congo, however, have surfaced only occasionally in art exhibitions, and Belgium's new building dedicated to colonialism at the Royal Museum of Central Africa features little about them.[24] Over two decades earlier, Adam Hochschild came to the same conclusion about the museum. 'But of any of the larger injustices in the Congo, there is no sign whatever', he observed; 'in none of the museum's twenty large exhibition galleries is there the slightest hint that millions of Congolese met unnatural deaths'.[25]

While some public memorials to colonizers have fallen, memorials and museums to educate people about colonialism and slavery have gone up. In one of France's remaining colonies, Guadeloupe, a museum of slavery called ACTe was opened in 2015 in a nineteenth-century sugar factory in Pointe-à-Pitre,[26] but there is debate on the island as to how much this museum links past enslavement to present human rights. This is also the case with the National Museum of African American History and Culture which opened in Washington, DC, in 2016. The museum takes the visitor from the capturing of people in Africa to plantations, the Civil War, Emancipation, and struggles in the twentieth century, including lynching, but after 1970, the objects and text are replaced with videos, music and entertainment. It starts with the Walmart Welcome Center, and is festooned with corporate sponsorship. One reviewer indicates that it culminates with 'feel good creativity' as 'the tragic story of Black America is folded into a happy coda'.[27] Perhaps more directly evocative of the realities of enslavement and its aftermath is the National Memorial for Peace and Justice which opened in 2018 in Montgomery, Alabama (see figure 2.2). A product of the Equal Justice Initiative, it presents various displays to remember the history of white supremacy in the USA, to commemorate its victims and to place it as much in the present as the past.

> At the center is a grim cloister, a walkway with 800 weathered steel columns, all hanging from a roof. Etched on each column is the name of an American county and the people who were lynched there, most listed by name, many simply as 'unknown'. The columns meet you first at eye level, like the headstones that lynching victims were rarely given. But as you walk, the floor steadily descends; by the end, the columns are all dangling above, leaving you in the position of the callous spectators in old photographs of public lynchings.[28]

Furthermore, memorials to massacres, relocations and removals of American Indians have appeared in the USA, and many of these, such as the Sand Creek Massacre trail that traverses Colorado and Wyoming, or the many memorials in the South to the Trail of Tears of the 1830s, 'invite discussion of the power of race and colonialism in the present'.[29]

Portugal, the country that was responsible for sending by far the largest number of slaves to the Americas,[30] has been reluctant to memorialize those that it sent to forced servitude and death. Although Portuguese citizens voted to erect a monument to the 4 million Africans their nation shipped to the Americas, progress on it has been slow, no design has been developed, and the project is marked by internal indecision within the government and populace. The party Unidos Podemos in Spain has also proposed a plan of public education to teach the population about Spain's role in slavery and colonization, and to promote recognition of Afro-Spaniards. A memorial to slavery is also part of their twelve-point plan of action.[31]

The actions to memorialize colonialism and slavery, and to contest the public honouring of perpetrators of colonial violence and injustice, are not just about past events, as some of these initiatives show. If they were, wrongdoing could easily be admitted, since the evidence for the

**Figure 2.2** Nkyinkim *by Kwame Akoto-Bamfo at the National Memorial to Peace and Justice, Montgomery, Alabama. Source: Ron Cogswell, 2019.*

incredible inhumanities perpetrated by European and North American states are abundant. The individual culprits may be dead, but the structures that supported them are alive, and inequalities, discrimination and victimization cannot be separated from them. Aborigines and their allies in Australia reminded the world of this when they protested outside the opening ceremony of the Commonwealth Games on the Gold Coast of Australia in 2018. Widely disseminated in the media, the protesters depicted the sporting events as 'Stolenwealth Games'. One protester was quoted as saying, 'And we don't want nothing of the Commonwealth here. They've stolen the land, built this country on stolen wages, built this country on the blood and bones of our people.'[32]

Anti-colonial movements are sometimes triggered by a sudden realization that authors of atrocities have been continually aggrandized, or, as in the 'Stolenwealth Games', they emerge at moments celebrating something linked to exploitation of peoples and lands. These movements are remarkable because the memories of the crimes are articulated by peoples who have endured continuous violence, assimilation campaigns, state schooling and modernization projects that denied them choice over their futures. Nonetheless, the memorials may just be the tip of this iceberg. A whole raft of visual culture, fine art, journalism, activism and academic scholarship encourages the perception of the past within the present.

## Obliterating Colonial History

The linking of past colonialism and current human rights issues, however, faces obstacles. It depends on the availability of official historical records, as well as on the depiction of the histories of colonial states in museums, textbooks, mass media and cultural expression. While many former colonial powers and settler states generally have free and accessible schooling, thriving visual arts communities, huge numbers of museums, well-ordered historical archives and freedom of expression, these can all be fashioned to deflect, hide or obliterate evidence of the most exploitative aspects of colonialism and obscure its connection to current lived realities.

One area that is particularly crucial is the ability to research the activities occurring under colonial authority. Information about these is available, but most of the materials are produced by and from the point of view of the colonizing powers, who in turn administer access to them. The views and experiences of those under colonial dominion were less scrupulously recorded, although, as we shall see, recent scholarship has started to reveal some of them. Correspondingly, the actions of colonial governments and views of officials that could offend national self-image as represented by states have been suppressed. For example, despite the excellent archival facilities, some scholars who want to research the actions of the British government in its colonial possessions have found myriad roadblocks and deliberate fabrication of the records.

One of the most startling examples is that uncovered by American historian Caroline Elkins. When Elkins went to find records of Britain's dealing with the Mau Mau rebellion, which was in part directed against the handing over of indigenous lands to British settlers at the close of Empire in Kenya, she discovered that 'countless documents pertaining to the detention camps either were missing from Britain's Public Record Office and the Kenya National Archives or were still classified as confidential some fifty years after the event'.[33] The disappearance of these records was not an accident. The human rights abuses, including torture, rape and castration of Mau Mau rebels, perpetrated by the British authorities in the 1950s[34] violated numerous parts of the Geneva Convention – including those on the execution of prisoners – that Britain had so recently and reluctantly endorsed.[35] Records taking up 200 feet of shelving were removed for thirty years to a storage depot in Hayes, Middlesex, and then to a secret site at Hanslope Park. 'The rumours in Nairobi had been correct', Ian Cobain relates, 'the packing crates loaded aboard a British United Airways flight to Gatwick on the eve of independence had contained the 1,500 files ... Inside the crates were some – but not all – of the British colonial authority's most sensitive documentary archives.'[36]

Much of this was revealed during the lawsuit against the British government launched by Mau Mau survivors of torture and abuse. At that time, it was disclosed that the British government possessed secret files outside the public records system. In 2013, in what Foreign Secretary William Hague emphasized to be 'full and final settlement', the UK government paid out almost £20 million in total damages to 5,528 Kenyan survivors who were imprisoned and tortured in detention camps.[37] The original number of Kenyans detained under the 1952 emergency laws and 'Operation Anvil', in what Elkins calls a 'pornography of terror ... public brutality, rape and starvation'[38] reaching to scores of villages, was about 320,000.[39] While concealing official records is a violation of liberal democratic codes of accountability, it also prevents any kind of thorough reckoning with or learning from the past. As part of an out-of-court settlement to the claims brought by the survivors a monument was erected in Nairobi's Uhuru Park in 2015 (see figure 2.3).

The return of archives to independent African states is therefore as pressing as, and complementary to, the return of plundered human

**Figure 2.3** *A memorial in honour of victims of torture in Kenya, including Esau Khamati Oriedo, during the British colonial era.*
*Source: Wikimedia Commons, 2016.*

remains and cultural artefacts. However, this task is particularly difficult when it comes to Britain. Official suppressing of the colonial records for Kenya is just one instance of a wider policy known as 'Operation Legacy', in which vast numbers of documents were not only secreted away but incinerated and destroyed in what Cobain calls 'the bonfires that accompanied the end of Empire'.[40] Sato, who has analysed some of the 20,000 files that were only declassified in 2017, from thirty-seven colonies, additionally notes the attention British officials paid to selecting out which documents could be given to the independent state government, and, in East Africa, they maintained a racial policy whereby only persons of European descent could handle the documents.[41] Numerous other public records potentially embarrassing to the state, including those relating to Mandatory rule of Palestine and the military occupation of Northern Ireland in the 1970s, have also disappeared from the National Archives.[42] While Britain has made no moves to cease concealing such documents, in 2018 France announced that its archives from the end of its violent rule of Algeria would be opened.[43]

Other colonial powers blocked access to records, or destroyed the evidence of their atrocities. Belgian King Leopold II was so desperate to suppress any knowledge of his personal fiefdom, the Congo Free State, that it took eight days to burn all the records in furnaces near his palace, 'turning most of the Congo state records to ash and smoke in the sky over Brussels'.[44] Colonial powers were also reluctant to divulge damaging information about the atrocities of other colonial powers. For example, Britain compiled detailed Parliamentary records of the genocide of the Herero and Nama in German South West Africa to support its case for reparations against Germany at the end of World War I. But, when the German colony had been handed over to the British Dominion of South Africa after World War I, these records, known as the Blue Book, were destroyed 'as part of a postwar reconciliation effort to better integrate the German-speaking white settler population of the territory within the new South African mandatory colonial project'.[45]

The current criticisms of museums in Britain extend even further, however, to the actual collections themselves, which represent a continuing violation of the human right to culture. The world's oldest national museum, the British Museum, has long been accused of benefitting from the display of many important, valuable and sacred objects that were removed during Britain's imperial adventures. Its collections are protected by the British Museum Act of 1963, which stipulates that the Museum can only sell, give away or dispose of an object 'vested in them' dating before 1850 if it is either a duplicate or useless. So keen is it to counter accusations of theft and present the case for its ownership of these objects that, in 2018, the British Museum begun a series of 'Collected Histories' talks to change widespread perceptions that much of what it houses was looted.[46] Museum directors defend their acquisitions in terms of showcasing them to a wide international public, and on the basis that there are no facilities to preserve and show them in the places where they came from. However, many of these countries now do have such facilities, and items could easily be repatriated.[47]

In the context of pressure from activists in movements giving informal 'Stolen Goods' tours and challenging corporate fossil-fuel sponsorship,[48] the British Museum and others, such as the Victoria and Albert and Pitt Rivers museums, have begun to investigate more systematically the provenance of many of their objects.[49] Many collections of plant and animal specimens that were donated or sold to the Natural History Museum and the British Museum were collected under slavery.[50] Even with some acknowledgement of this, the fact that Britain possesses so much of the world's tangible cultural heritage denies many people the opportunity to know and learn about their own histories and world-views, to honour and recognize ancestors, and to assess the impacts of colonialism. The scale of purloined human remains alone is vast: 'in Britain alone, there are at least 61,000 remains [of indigenous peoples] in around 132 different collections'.[51]

Britain's diplomats and politicians have also been attentive to redirecting memories in formerly colonized countries. In 2007, Chancellor of the Exchequer Gordon Brown asserted on a tour of East Africa that Britain had nothing to apologize for. He urged Africans to 'move forward', and focus on the British values of tolerance, liberty and civic duty.[52] The Prime Minister Brown served, Tony Blair, echoed these sentiments, arguing that Empire required neither bad conscience nor apology, and David Cameron invoked Britannia ruling the waves to urge on his Conservative supporters.[53] A few years later, the British ambassador to Nigeria was insistent that Nigeria *not* look to colonialism to explain its lack of industrial development, but to its own internal politics. Showing that the infantilization of Africans survives, the ambassador noted that Britain would 'no longer be a parent'.[54] Instead, he, like Prime Minister Theresa May in her visit to the country in 2018, was looking for Nigeria to see itself as a beneficiary of new trade deals that Britain would need after Brexit in the short-lived promotion of a 'Global Britain' brand. The attitude of French governments to the linking of colonial history to perceived problems in their former African colonial possessions differs only in details from that of the British, as we will see in chapter 4.

The extrication of colonialism from any culpability for the thorny humanitarian problems of the present is also a feature of the secondary-school curriculum in Britain and France. While the history of Empire was taught in Britain, it was largely done from a vantage point that celebrated Britain's achievements. The treatment of this history became more critical in the 1970s and 1980s, but with the introduction of a national curriculum in 1991, pedagogy on Empire became less prominent. Politicians in Margaret Thatcher's cabinets, and more recently Tony Blair, Gordon Brown and the former Conservative Education Minister Michael Gove, have all variously called for emphasis on the positive aspects of 'Britishness'.[55] Of recent political leaders, only Labour's Jeremy Corbyn has suggested that British students should learn more about colonialism and slavery and incorporated this into his party's 2019 election manifesto.[56] In 2016, historians in Britain called for a more balanced view in the history taught to British youth.[57] University lecturers routinely find 'students who are educated through a school history curriculum that focuses almost entirely on English political and religious history – with bits of 20th-century European history thrown in. [Students] therefore know practically nothing about empire and its legacies – including in Britain.'[58] In France, a law in 2005 required school curricula and scholarly research to recognize 'the positive role of the French presence overseas, notably in north Africa'.[59] This followed about forty years in which French colonialism was culled from the curriculum, and the Algerian war was heavily edited.[60] The law, however, lasted only one year due to outrage by historians over the article directing how knowledge of history was to be presented. Government control of how history is taught, and thus how succeeding generations think about the nation-state itself, is of course a breach of the human right to education, since education presupposes knowledge independent from the state.

Settler colonial states have also established practices for concealing elements of their histories that reflect their treatment of indigenous and minority populations. For example, a Canadian history textbook published in 2017 insinuated that the dispossession of Aboriginal peoples was voluntary.[61] This builds on a longstanding Canadian narrative, flagged by the 2015 Truth and Reconciliation report, that many church and governmental residential school policies amounted to 'good intentions' gone awry.[62] This narrative was present when I visited the Canadian Museum of Civilization in Ottawa in 2005. Under a tableau on residential schools, the text read, 'some graduates of residential schools recall good teachers and warm relationships. But for other graduates, the pain of sexual abuse and cultural loss has overshadowed good intentions and practices.' In at least one part of the USA, the history of indigenous dispossession and colonization is not even sugar-coated in this way. In Arizona in 2010, the HB2281 statute outlawed the teaching of courses in secondary schools deemed inflammatory to the United States. It cites specifically Mexican American Studies programmes that include coverage of Spanish, Mexican and Native American histories and Anglo-European colonization.[63]

While universities do not explicitly omit instruction on colonialism and slavery, the narrowing of academic disciplines to circumscribed theoretical, practical and historical themes promotes Eurocentrism, to which many in the contemporary generation of scholars and activists are objecting. In Britain, the narrowing of knowledge is furthered by bureaucratic control via 'benchmarking', whereby curricula are standardized by professional associations. In philosophy, for example, one of the disciplines in which more truly universal knowledge would be important to impart to students, European and North American figures predominate. To its disciplinary guardians, Western philosophy is singularly universal because it is rigorous and rational,[64] but, of course, it is only so – as Godwin Sogolo has observed – because certain ideas are deemed to be non-universal.[65] In the view of many Western philosophers, African and other worldviews do not conform to the paradigmatic rules of formal logic. The policing of knowledge in this way led to reactions from students and scholars calling for decolonization of the curriculum across the Western world. Summarizing this critique of Western universities, Small maintains: 'The problem with the academy is that it claims to operate through principles of objectivity, impartiality and scientific inquiry that is open to all perspectives. But when it comes to the study of racism and the experiences of Black people most European universities are limited in scope, narrow in methodologies and restricted in access.'[66]

Within the wider public, however, some linkages between current human rights abuses and colonialism cannot be suppressed because they became widely known through media coverage. In 2018, activists, journalists and private individuals exposed the British Home Office hounding of people who, as children, had arrived legitimately from the Caribbean Commonwealth countries in the 1950s and 1960s. Accused of being illegal immigrants because they could not produce paperwork detailing when they entered the country, these individuals had accompanied their parents who were recruited to work in public services after the ravages of World War II. In what is known as the Windrush scandal, many of these now elderly people were, after successive immigration acts in 2014 and 2016, denied employment rights after paying taxes during decades of service to the UK.

As part of an official Conservative Party policy initiated in 2012 to create a 'hostile environment' for illegal immigrants and to accelerate deportations, then-Home Secretary Theresa May remarked in Parliament in 2013 that her government would 'deport first and hear appeals later'. To maintain their livelihoods in Britain, many of these migrants had to provide copious documentation, including receipts going back five decades. Key evidence of their legitimate status, such as the original landing slips, were destroyed while May was Home Office Minister. In a glaring example of racialized civic stratification, some Windrush migrants were denied health treatment in the NHS or presented with huge bills for treatment of serious illnesses. Others have been deported.[67] A 42-year-old woman who had been in Britain since she was 1, committed suicide after being incarcerated in the notorious Yarl's Wood detention centre.[68] As redress for the victims of her policy, Prime Minister May established a grant for activities to celebrate Caribbean migrants and a complex compensation application containing forty-five pages of Guidance Notes for those who lost their jobs because of the policy. Nonetheless, many victims did not receive the promised government apologies, and several have died since the announcement. Relatives have suggested that sudden deaths of victims since 2018 related to the stress of loss of income, denial of health benefits, and inability to travel abroad to see family and loved ones.[69] The Home Office offered to pay for the funeral of one Windrush victim in 2019.[70]

The denial of human and citizenship rights to legal Caribbean migrants is closely linked to government policies from 1948 onwards to restrict 'coloured' migration as Britain formally withdrew from its colonies.[71] While media and activists have revealed the human sides of the story, many of the records of these discussions and the ways in which British government officials regarded 'coloured' migrants are shielded from public scrutiny, with 'closed extracts' prominent in the Commonwealth Immigration files in the National Archives.[72] Ironically, simultaneous with the revealing of the hostile treatment of Windrush citizens, some of whom were originally recruited to help build the NHS, was a new scheme to recruit Jamaican nurses on short-term contracts to fill vacancies caused by under-investment in nurse education in Britain. Significantly, the cost of training these nurses will have been borne by the Jamaican government, and, under the scheme, the nurses will have to leave Britain after three years.[73]

## Colonial Laws Today

Within former colonial territories, however, knowledge of colonialism is more immediate and difficult to suppress, in part because it is woven into the legal system. Laws discriminating against groups and activities were introduced by colonial powers and many are still on statute books, to the great convenience of autocrats. For example, the realization that vast numbers of British Commonwealth countries retained British colonial-era anti-sodomy laws that criminalize LGBTQ people – and this includes severe penalties for people found to be in same-sex relationships – forced Prime Minister May into an apology. Such laws, in formerly colonized countries in Africa, Asia, the Caribbean and Indian Ocean territories such as Mauritius, are known to encourage violence against people who do not identify as heterosexuals.[74] Other colonial-era laws, and the homophobic norms on which they were based, are still on the books to suppress gender-based human rights in other ex-colonial territories. Often these are in societies where diverse forms of sexuality were accepted prior to colonialism with no attempt to persecute or ban. Additionally, the British also introduced laws to suppress non-European religious practices and spiritual beliefs in the Caribbean. These were only recently repealed,[75] and Rwanda, where over 1,000 laws originally benefitting colonial regimes operate, has started annulling such legislation.[76]

Further instances in which colonial legal systems have served, directly or indirectly, as conduits for racially segmented rights have been unearthed by socio-legal and historical scholarship. While both the French and British permitted some customary laws within their overarching colonial authority, in West Africa native laws could not conflict with 'French civilization', according to a 1903 decree. Any relations between Natives and the state in French African colonies were governed by the *Indigénat* which specified severe punishments, forced labour and land expropriation for transgressors.[77] Even though many colonial laws have been removed from penal codes in independent states, they remain as precedents for the politicians, judiciaries and police, since colonial legal systems such as the *Indigénat* so frequently permitted massive discretionary authority. In Sudan and other Muslim-majority territories, the British imposed legal plurality by folding Shari'a law into an English common law-based colonial legal system. According to Massoud, the incorporation of Shari'a into the colonial legal system led to the suppression of more open and liberal interpretations of Shari'a after independence.[78] This was because the elites that formed the independent governments adopted the colonial legal system and alienated large numbers of the populace that wanted Shari'a. The survival of the colonial legal system pushed them towards advocating more stringent versions of Islamic law.

Colonial laws used to suppress dissent are also in operation in several countries. For example, a British Assembly law that prohibits various unlawful assemblies of more than five people, which was passed in 1914 but repealed in 1928, has been injected with new vigour by various Egyptian regimes. The Cairo Institute for Human Rights reported that 'from 2014–2017, the Assembly Law was used to sentence at least 474 Egyptians to death in 11 cases. In 2017 alone, it was cited to imprison more than 120 people for sentences ranging from 2–25 years.'[79] The colonial law has been used with great gusto by President Abdel Fatah al-Sisi, who has effectively banned both peaceful protest and the largest opposition group, the Muslim Brotherhood. In 2018, a further 700 people were arrested for a sit-in protest over the *coup d'état* in which Sisi came to power, and 75 people were sentenced to death for the protest, provoking the incoming HRC President Michelle Bachelet to urge Egypt to relent on these sentences.[80]

Across West Africa, the new decolonized states inherited criminal justice systems that were in part designed to quash local rebellion against European power. This included militarized criminal justice systems and the death penalty, and represented a divergence from traditional African restitutive methods of conflict resolution which gave prominent roles to women.[81] Since 2016, journalists in several sub-Saharan African countries have been targeted by colonial-era legislation designed to suppress dissent and manipulate public opinion. This includes prosecuting a newspaper editor in the Democratic Republic of Congo under a defamation law created by Belgium, five Zambian journalists under a British law for calling a member of the ruling party a 'useless person', and a newspaper editor in Botswana under British anti-sedition laws, as well as attacks on the media in South Africa using apartheid-era laws.[82] Many former colonies have also used British-designed anti-sedition laws to suppress rights to political and cultural activities.[83]

In South East Asia, colonial powers implemented strictures against local protest and opposition to state authority, and some of these continued after independence. For example, according to Benedict Anderson, 'Malaysia inherited (and later improved on) the colonial regime's draconian anti-subversion laws and steely bureaucracy'. Anderson continued, 'the country has had a permanent authoritarian government throughout its existence, but the basis of its permanence has ... everything to do with a collective determination on the part of the Malay ethnic group (52 per cent) to monopolise real political power'.[84] In Guyana, another former British colony, current anti-sedition laws have also been linked to earlier colonial laws relating to British attempts to suppress Marcus Garvey's Universal Negro Improvement Association.[85] As Cheeseman and Fisher argue in relation to Africa,[86] the ease with which autocrats use repressive colonial laws was facilitated by the forced transformation of African societies under centralized authority structures, and through corrupt collaborations between colonial administrators and local leaders. This also extended to vote rigging, the first instances of which in Africa were organized by Britain and France.

## From Decolonization to Neocolonialism

Another powerful indication of the uneasy present of colonialism is that, centuries after the first acts of European intrusion, few of those living in territories that experienced colonialism are thriving, either economically, politically or in terms of justice. This also holds for indigenous peoples and descendants of formerly enslaved people in settler colonial states. Fieldhouse's observation that the 'optimistic' expectations around 1960, among European policymakers and economists, that political independence in African countries 'would lead to rapid and sustained economic and social growth and development',[87] is a salient reminder of the gross exaggeration of the beneficence of colonialism. Although there are many competing explanations for the failure of the forecasters, and there have been some cases of limited economic success, decolonization has been followed by generalized poverty and instability. The societies that were hastily configured at the close of the colonial era are known variously for their poverty, human rights problems and social injustice.

One reason for this is that newly independent states needed to rely on income from raw materials and monocrop farming, which they traded for manufactured goods and cash for infrastructure. The inbuilt inequalities in these exchanges, flagged by political theorists such as Samir Amin and Andre Gunder Frank in the 1970s, meant that decolonized states frequently had to negotiate loans to balance their economies, leading to spiralling debt, capital flight and dependency, causing some to see colonization and neoliberal globalization as continuous.[88] Newly independent countries inherited an economic system that delivered vast rewards for the owners of capital and the politicians that facilitate their profits, while impoverishing most of the citizenry. With debts, inefficient tax-collecting systems and corporate avoidance of taxes, the new states largely omitted to incorporate social welfare provisions. Indeed, the same kinds of prejudicial differentiations of rights that colonial powers used were taken forward by some states after independence.[89]

There were, of course, warnings from African leaders and intellectuals at decolonization. The Congolese Patrice Lumumba – who was assassinated with the assistance of Belgian colonial agents and US funds and logistics – and Ghanaian Kwame Nkrumah both foresaw a rapid transition from colonialism to neocolonialism. In the Congo and Ghana, as well as elsewhere in Africa, the state quickly became authoritarian with several factions vying for power, which often translated into personal command over national treasuries. While there are those who contend that the neocolonial argument had adverse effects on African populations because it justified authoritarian rule,[90] the suggestion that the peoples of the decolonized states would remain dominated by the former imperial powers through new means, especially economic, appears correct.

Some lives in former colonial territories may have improved over the last decades, but any measure is relative to a very low base. A major analysis of the UN's Millennium Development Goals by the Brookings Institute showed that infectious diseases have diminished, more children have formal education, and income has increased in targeted parts of Africa and Asia.[91] Yet fewer people have good access to water, and more suffer from undernourishment. A study of malnutrition in *Nature* found that 'at these rates, much, if not all of the [African] continent will fail to meet the Sustainable Development Goal target – to end malnutrition by 2030'. It further stated that 'no country in Africa is likely to achieve all the WHO GNT [Global Nutrition Targets] in all of its territory if current trends continue'.[92] The authors were concerned at the scale of stunting and wasting among children and the vast disparities in the prevalence of child growth failure within African countries, as well as persistent lack of improvement across the Sahel. Around 60 per cent of the population of sub-Saharan Africa has seen declining calorie intakes.[93] An important indicator of the status of formerly colonized populations in the Global South is life expectancy. Many countries have a life expectancy of just 50 compared to an EU life expectancy of 80.6 years. In India, the life expectancy is 67, and, as Lessenich points out, 'when at the age of 60, we [Europeans] look forward to a new chapter in life, one in two people in India have already died'.[94]

Despite widespread perceptions of India as an emerging global power, rural populations have suffered greatly from poverty, malnutrition and hunger. Using official statistics and sources, economist Utsa Patnaik argued in her essay 'The Republic of Hunger' that increasing numbers of Indians suffered from hunger into the 2000s, and that this was due to globally oriented neoliberal economic policies which lowered prices for the products of rural areas and rewarded urban economic activity.[95] Because of these adversities, the state of Andhra Pradesh 'has seen more than three thousand farmer suicides in the last five years [of the early 2000s] as well as suicides of entire families of weavers ... in 2002 alone ... as many as 2,580 deeply indebted farmers killed themselves mainly by ingesting pesticides in three districts alone'.[96] In India, recent official records showed that around 18,000 farmers were taking their lives every year, and epidemiological studies have shown that these suicides were principally a result of crushing debt.[97]

Similarly, contemporary indigenous peoples and descendants of enslaved Africans in the Americas are hugely disadvantaged according to the indicators of wellbeing established by Western countries and international organizations. There are approximately 370 million indigenous peoples around the world and, although they represent 5 per cent of the world population, they constitute 15 per cent of the world's poor.[98] A major epidemiological study of 28 indigenous groups in 23 countries found 'poorer outcomes' for indigenous peoples over non-indigenous populations within these countries. This included evidence of lower life expectancies, and correspondingly higher infant mortality, maternal mortality and both child malnutrition and child obesity, as well as adult obesity among indigenous groups. Added to this was lower educational attainment and economic status for indigenous populations.

Regarding Afro-descended people, a recent UN report linked colonialism and slavery directly to the poverty-stricken lives many black people live, both within countries that were colonized by Europe and in those that have developed from the foundation of enslavement:

For centuries, people of African descent living in the African Diaspora, were marginalized as part of the legacy of slavery and colonialism.

> There is a growing consensus that racism and racial discrimination have caused people of African descent to be relegated in many aspects of public life, they have suffered exclusion and poverty and are often 'invisible' in official statistics. There has been progress but the situation persists, to varying degrees, in many parts of the world.[99]

The Afro-descended peoples of the Americas have also not done so well. Recent studies have found that the median white family income in the USA is thirteen times greater than that for the median black family, and that this exists for every education level. A third of black families have no assets at all. The differences in wealth between black and white Americans are accelerating.[100] As Baradaran remarks, 'injustices sown in the past grow imperceptibly in the present'.[101] Similarly, communities of indigenous peoples have been killed in vast numbers, moved to relatively small plots of land, and largely marginalized. Their lands now fall within states that deny them autonomy, while also exploiting them – as we shall see in chapter 5 – for what remains of their resources.

By focusing on statistical indices of incomes, such as national per capita GDP figures, capitalist economists and institutions such as the World Bank continue to argue for global economic 'convergence',[102] and to encourage the same patterns of global economic activity that place the socially and environmentally high-cost extractive and other industries in the Global South, and the consumption of the products in the wealthier, often former colonial, states. The Africa Rising narrative is another manifestation of this,[103] as is Tony Blair's Africa Initiative, which under the strapline 'making globalization work for the many' is now called the Tony Blair Institute for Global Change. Both present a narrative of future incremental improvements through continued neoliberal economic development and good governance.

The singular path to wellbeing echoed by the supporters of bootstrap capitalism has turned out to be a cul-de-sac for many of the formerly colonized territories, as well as people on reserves, reservations and other indigenous territories. With, according to one recent estimate, 1 per cent of the world's population owning 82 per cent of the wealth,[104] the prospects for democracy and human rights cannot obviously be based on universal access to material wellbeing. In 2015, the International Labour Organization (ILO) warned that some 75 per cent of the world's workers are now employed in temporary, contingent jobs or in unpaid family jobs.[105] Despite being inducted into a 'development'-oriented blueprint for capitalist decolonization, and it being tied to US foreign policy towards Latin America in the 1960s,[106] few states labelled as 'developing' have come anywhere close to the overall standards of living and institutional stability of Europe and North America. While the development agenda may have been concerned with amelioration of the effects of prior colonial intrusion, the conditions for continued wealth accumulation in the 'third world' by today's multinational corporations are less attentive to local betterment, since this is considered the province of the independent states. The structural economic realities make it unlikely that these states will realize either material prosperity in their populations or a high regard for human rights. Instead, states that did not follow the neoliberal developmental prescription, such as China and other autocratically directed economies with poor human rights records – including Russia, Singapore and the Gulf states – have been successful.

Significantly, in both African and East Asian countries, democracy is extremely weak and could never be tied to economic success. Furthermore, what economic gains have been made were often achieved through clientelism and crony capitalism. This is being reinforced by what some see as a new version of colonialism through Chinese economic investments in Africa, creating debt and dependency. President Xi Jinping has pledged $60 billion in investment to Africa as part of the Belt and Road initiative. It is also tied to a proviso that African countries will send exports to China, and move away from their ties to Taiwan.[107] Like its liberal counterpart,[108] this more ruthless state-directed economic liberalism continually undermines Native ways of life because economic growth requires that their lands and labour be diverted from customary uses for the huge infrastructure projects envisioned by Chinese investments.

## Undemocratic Democracies

Liberal human rights are associated with representative democracy. States that are not regarded as democracies are not expected to be advocates of the human rights of their citizens or those of other nations. This may be a problem, however, since the democracy that many states assert to embody and promote was never a part of the colonialism they practised – or, in the case of settler colonial states, still operate. As Ibhawoh points out, colonialism 'was premised on the notion of basic native exceptionality. The civilizing and modernizing agenda of Empire was everywhere mediated by assumption about the essential difference of the colonized other. Colonial law, even in the aspiration towards universalist British justice, departed from the common law in its ascription of privileges, immunities, and distinctions between civilized and uncivilized.'[109]

Thus, the enunciation of respect for justice, and by extension human rights, was selective. Although laws and rights in the Western tradition are regarded as absolutes and universals, colonized populations were differentiated internally, as well as from the colonial state's citizens and settlers. While law requires equality in its applicability to serve as the regulatory framework for democracy, colonial laws varied in to whom they applied. It is then hardly surprising that the post-independence states assumed this model of the nation-state, since that was the model deposited by colonial powers. In her short essay 'Nation-State and Democracy', Hannah Arendt emphasized the residual inheritance of the undemocratic and racist imperialist state. 'The fact that the peoples of Africa and Asia', she writes, 'can only imagine political freedom in the mold of the already failed nation-state is only the most minor of the dangers that the legacy of the imperialist age has left to us'. The biggest danger is that racial thinking 'has taken hold of such large strata of recognizably different peoples everywhere'.[110]

Legitimacy in a democracy also depends on state authority being transparent and representative. While this was never the case in any European colony, or regarding the treatment of indigenous or enslaved populations under settler colonialism, it also appears not to obtain in democracies themselves. The franchise, for example, is a basic human right, with a lineage that can be related to the Enlightenment idea of the social contract. Admittedly, the franchise has been extended in Western countries beyond propertied white males since human rights principles were first articulated. While women, ethnic minorities and indigenous peoples can formally vote, in many democracies elections are today tainted by large corporate donations and gifts from wealthy citizens. Candidates almost exclusively originate from the very richest segments of the society. Massive propaganda and, more recently, online manipulation of voters have taken place. Questions are now arising about what democracy may mean in liberal Western states.

If the vote is a vital element of democracy – a literal indication of the social contract – then the denying of the franchise because of sex, race, immigration status or lack of property means that the most fundamental formal human right is lacking in many liberal states, and perhaps none more so than the USA. Most Native Americans, for example, only became citizens through the Indian Citizenship Act in 1924, and their rights to vote were often not respected until many years later following the passage of the 1965 Voting Rights Act. Their basic democratic rights to participate in the selection of officials were abridged even after that by 'employing a host of election rules that made it difficult, if not impossible, for Indians to vote and elect their candidates of choice'.[111]

Karen Hansen's closely observed study of the contrasting fates of Dakota Sioux and Scandinavian immigrants on the Great Plains at the turn of the twentieth century shows precisely how citizenship was racialized. Even though Dakota were granted some citizenship rights as wards of the state – itself a subaltern status – under the Dawes or Allotment Act of 1887, their rights to vote were continually blocked by North Dakota state officials on several grounds, including that they were not civilized.[112] By contrast, the path to citizenship and the exercise of citizenship rights for foreign-born Norwegians was relatively easy. Only after tireless efforts, the hiring of lawyers and court appearances were most of the Dakota able to vote. Voter suppression was bizarrely replayed in a recent Supreme Court decision in *Brakebill* v. *Jaeger*, in which the Court upheld a new North Dakota law which potentially minimizes the indigenous vote because it requires voter identification to have a street address and many reservation dwellers have only Post Office boxes. Only through huge efforts by the tribal governments in North and South Dakota to get identification cards issued was the legislation neutralized, but this was not the only problem. Some voting stations near reservations were closed, and others were relatively long distances from reservations.[113]

Likewise, African-Americans have long been disenfranchised as a result of deliberate Federal, local and party policy. Poll taxes, literacy tests, income tests, property tests and complex ballots that confused illiterate ex-slaves in the Southern states prevented black people from voting,[114] contrary to the 15th amendment of the Constitution. In the 1960s, organized voter intimidation in districts with large ethnic-minority populations occurred, with William Rehnquist, later a Chief Justice of the Supreme Court, being one of the participants in these activities.[115] As will be discussed more in chapter 3, in what is now a new era of voter suppression, the Republican Party has devised policies – including gerrymandering, restrictive voter identification laws and the reduction in the number of polling places – to discourage and suppress African-American voting.[116] The idea that the universal franchise defines democracy, and therefore is integral to a social contract, in which 'the people' are sovereign rights-bearers, clearly does not apply.

Besides the non-universal characteristics of the franchise, Western democracy also suffers from a kind of hollowing out of its institutions. Stuart Hall has observed that democracies have increasingly centralized power within the executive, marginalized local sources of political power, and outsourced and privatized government functions with no clear public accountability.[117] In part, this is facilitated by the similarly undemocratic means by which people come to serve in government. Documented for the USA in C. Wright Mills' *The Power Elite* almost seventy years ago, elected officials of state are overwhelmingly drawn from the rich, representatives of corporate interests and institutions such as the military that have important power bases within the state. Mills argued that the entire democratic process, from the selection of candidates to governmental decision-making and the mass media, operated to maintain elite control over the state.[118] This view was echoed by Mills' friend Ralph Miliband in *The State in Capitalist Society*, in which he emphasized the influential role of businesses in the USA and Britain in government policies, including the pervasive practice of distributing government funds to commercial enterprises.[119]

These links between wealth and political power seem only to have intensified. Ten of the thirteen British Prime Ministers since 1945 studied at Oxford, and successive government cabinets have contained vast representation from those who benefitted from Britain's two-tier educational system. For example, 'privately-educated politicians make up more of Prime Minister Theresa May's new [2018] Cabinet than her last one and ministers are now five times more likely to have gone to a fee-paying school than the general population'.[120] Furthermore, over a third of MPs returned at the 2015 election attended private fee-paying schools, compared to 7 per cent of the population, and the number of MPs from manual working backgrounds declined from 16 per cent in 1979 to 3 per cent in 2015.[121] The broader trend in Britain – of which the massive governmental over-representation of those with inherited privileges is just one illustration – is an 'old boys' network' that extends across all major sectors of British economic and cultural life.[122] Within the British government itself, access to the Prime Minister is regularly purchased. In 2017–18, donors and benefactors paid almost £7.5 million to have dinners with Theresa May,[123] and other moneyed donors paid up to £50,000 to dine with her predecessor, David Cameron.[124]

Similarly, American legislators operate on short election cycles, and because of the high costs of campaigning must either be independently wealthy or receive financial backing, the most lucrative of which is from corporations seeking to influence policy. This effectively means that legislators' tenure as representatives of the people is dependent on them voting for policies and laws that benefit the corporations that sponsor them. The median worth of members of Congress in 2013 was over $1 million, some 18 times larger than the median income of US households at $56,335. Around 3 per cent of state legislators are blue-collar workers, and only 9 per cent of city council workers.[125] One does not have to dig too deep to discover that corporations and the very rich bankrolled the election of candidates for public office, and therefore ensured the passing of economically favourable legislation to privatize public services, lower taxes on the rich, enable tax avoidance and weaken civic organizations and labour unions that defend the rights of less wealthy citizens.[126]

In 2016, the first billionaire President was elected. He joins a long list of extremely wealthy occupants of the White House. Donald Trump became the second President in the twenty-first century to have been elected by fewer voters than their opponent. It is worth recounting that only about 25 per cent of voters selected Trump. Hillary Clinton received almost 3 million more votes, and 6 million disproportionately African-American voters were disenfranchised because of felony convictions.[127] Trump's Presidency is notable in its open attacks on democracy. From his perch in the Oval Office or his Florida resort, Trump frequently calls for the imprisonment of private citizens and rival politicians. During his 2016 campaign, he urged his followers to attack protesters and opponents physically. Like many political leaders, Trump uses public office for even greater personal enrichment, with evidence that he has made foreign policy based on states' patronage of his businesses,[128] and, as we know from the 2019 impeachment enquiry, on a willingness to investigate his political opponents. Former FBI Director James Comey's memoir warned that 'we are experiencing a dangerous time in our country … with a political environment where basic facts are disputed, fundamental truth is questioned, lying is normalized and unethical behavior is ignored, excused or rewarded'.[129] Comey was the first of many commentators working inside the Trump administration to observe how government business was being conducted through dishonesty and manipulation.

Equally significant for any democracy is a free press. As documented in David Frum's *Trumpocracy*, the press is the institution that Trump has attacked and undermined more than any other.[130] In his first six months in office, Trump's tweets against the press were the largest single category of his numerous online opinions.[131] He has also incited violence towards the press, which continued at rallies into his Presidency; redefined well-researched investigative reporting as 'fake news'; drastically reduced journalists' access to the workings of the White House; and joined forces with other world leaders, such as Sisi in Egypt, who have attempted to disempower the mainstream press, which he has repeatedly characterized as an 'enemy of the people'. In 2018, the UN Special Rapporteur on the Freedom of Expression and the Special Rapporteur for the Inter-American Commission on Human Rights issued a joint statement urging Trump to cease his attacks on the media because it jeopardized fundamental democratic rights.[132] This, however, may be redundant since heads of states and politicians increasingly sidestep public scrutiny through refusing media interviews and communicating via social media, where they can set the agenda rather than be questioned and challenged.

These patterns of deeply antidemocratic behaviour, of which the attacks on journalists are only one instance, put Trump in the same frame as similar authoritarians, demagogues and fascists in history, and those who emulate them today, such as Recep Tayyip Erdogan, Viktor Orban, Rodrigo Duterte and Vladimir Putin.[133] Britain's Prime Minister Boris Johnson, with his repeated threats to circumvent established law and democratic protocol and his unlawful suspension of Parliament, could be added to the list. Anti-democratic executive actions within the USA and other Western countries find counterparts in the condoning – and, in Trump's case, expressed admiration – of similar actions elsewhere. Trump has venerated Putin, who orders the jailing and assassination of political opponents, rigs elections, controls the media and likewise operates a kleptocracy. The President's support for the Saudi monarchy in the face of institutionalized human rights abuses, state-ordered murders of political opponents and silencing of journalists has been linked to his family's financial ties in that country.[134] The ability of Trump to act undemocratically, however, is facilitated by the Constitution, 'which is virtually silent on the president's authority to act unilaterally'.[135]

Western countries have persistently failed to adhere to the democratic prerequisites for human rights. Besides the fact that numerically losing candidates won two recent US elections, the momentous 2016 Brexit vote to leave the European Union in Britain was assisted by breaking electoral rules on campaign contributions, illegal data-harvesting by British company Cambridge Analytica and Facebook, and donations above the legal limit to the Canadian digital company AggregateIQ. There have also been allegations that the financial backers of the Leave campaign financed their contributions from Russian business deals,[136] and a report on this by the Parliamentary Intelligence Committee was withheld from public scrutiny by Boris Johnson ahead of the 2019 election.[137] Britain's own Electoral Commission confirmed much of the fraud perpetrated in the Referendum. Other elections were also influenced by interference by social media and foreign governments, as was claimed by executives of Cambridge Analytica, in the USA, Britain, Kenya, India, Brazil, Mexico, and Trinidad and Tobago.[138]

Over 130 million Americans were exposed to advertisements bought by Russian state parties to influence the 2016 election in favour of Trump, whose campaign included a public appeal by Trump for Russian operatives to hack into his rival's emails, something that occurred hours after the invitation.[139] This is in addition to numerous false news stories planted by Russian state operatives in US social and other media ahead of the election.[140] As the bipartisan Senate Intelligence Committee determined in 2018, this included the special targetting of African-Americans through Instagram and Facebook accounts to influence them to favour Trump.[141]

While there is legitimate outrage in the US Congress about Russian electoral interference, it is important to recall that the US government has engaged in similar activities, systematically intervening in Latin America to bring about undemocratic political outcomes. This includes installing and supporting dictators in virtually every country south of Mexico, and mounting military invasions of Cuba, the Dominican Republic and Guatemala. The Nixon administration spent millions of dollars to destabilize the economy of Chile and subsequently depose and murder elected Socialist President Salvador Allende. This led to the seventeen-year genocidal dictatorship of Augusto Pinochet, representing perhaps only one of the most gruesome of scores of American interventions to subvert democracy.[142] The USA has also financed and supplied military and logistical support to remove democratically elected leaders in the Middle East, Africa and Asia.

## Muscular Lockjaw

From the point of view of those who were or are colonized, the visible shunning of democracy and universal human rights inside Western countries is layered onto knowledge of the West's violent colonial past, long-term occupation of others' lands, dispossession of countless numbers of peoples, trading and ownership of slaves, as well as numerous one-sided wars. That the inheritors and emissaries of the rational humanitarianism of the Enlightenment might themselves be operating from a highly compromised, even irrational, position is underlined by the lack of much serious political discussion of links between colonialism and human rights.

Many of the mass media, politicians and national institutions of European states that colonized, and settler colonial states, are partial to accounts of both colonialism and decolonization that place no direct blame on European rule for current adversities, especially regarding human rights, in these territories. In fact, the emphasis of Western politicians is often not on blame for past wrongdoing, but on praise for the humanitarianism of the colonial project itself, and a redirection of scrutiny towards indigenous leaders, or indeed the retarded character of the formerly colonized society itself. British and French leaders have directly or indirectly argued that colonialism uplifted non-European peoples by exposing them to literacy, science, government, technology, industry and organized religion.

Indeed, the sentiment that colonialism demonstrates the veracity of the idea of progress that was held by many European imperialists and thinkers of the nineteenth century is echoed today. Much of the British public believes in the beneficence of the British Empire and colonialism. A 2014 YouGov poll found 59 per cent of Britons were proud of the Empire, while 49 per cent thought it had made the colonies 'better off'.[143] Academic debate has also returned to questions regarding how colonialism should be interpreted today. Although not without opponents who have shown the reverse to be the case,[144] prominent scholars have forwarded forthright arguments about the virtuous nature of the British Empire, and these have been expressed in print and in television documentaries. Contributions to 'global welfare' cited by celebrity historian Niall Ferguson, for example, include the building of physical infrastructure, free trade, law and governance.[145] A controversy related to this narrative of colonialism was ignited in 2017 when Bruce Gilley, an American political scientist, published 'The Case for Colonialism' in *Third World Quarterly*, precipitating mass resignations from the board of the journal. One of the most prominent defenders of Gilley was Nigel Biggar, a Professor of Moral and Pastoral Philosophy at Oxford, who argued that there was too much guilt being expressed over Empire,[146] and who established a course in 2017 entitled 'Empire and Ethics' on the positive and negative aspects of colonialism.

Perhaps emboldened by public backing, and exuding a sense of confidence in British rectitude, in 2017 then Foreign Secretary Boris Johnson began reciting 'Mandalay', a colonial poem by Rudyard Kipling while at a holy site in Myanmar. He only ceased when discreetly stopped by the British ambassador to the country.[147] Although this poetic evocation of the charity of British military rule was potentially insulting to his hosts, it was widely reported as a 'gaffe', as were Johnson's other expressions of casual racism.[148] The trivializing of racism underscores an assumption of much of the praise for colonialism: that those subject to it were, and are, backward peoples to whose aid the British had come. However, when people are assumed to be inferior, it can be a short step to violence. Indeed, the Brexit referendum in 2016 was characterized by unrepentant xenophobic and extreme nationalistic campaign platforms. It led to the murder of pro-Remain Labour MP Jo Cox and was associated with violence against many perceived 'foreigners' afterwards. Brexit also invoked among the public and in the popular press images of a proud, independent, powerful Britain, renewing a type of national pride associated with Empire, as several commentators have observed.[149] Beyond Brexit, there are more general indications of renewed reliance on the history of Empire to defend national pride in Britain and France.

To find perhaps the most trenchant observations about the effects of trumpeting imperial virtues, we need to rewind to the age of decolonization. Writing of the constant reminders of 'the wealth of Western values' in colonized societies, Frantz Fanon stated: 'every time Western values are mentioned they produce in the native a sort of stiffening or muscular lockjaw'.[150] To avoid lockjaw today, as then, humanitarian crises, mass killings, atrocities of war and forced removals of peoples must be depoliticized and pinpointed to specific and contemporary local settings. While Fanon referred to the context of French colonialism in the Caribbean and north Africa at the close of the formal colonial period, the treatment of indigenous peoples and the descendants of those who were formerly colonized within Western states contains the same dynamics: the professing of allegiance to human rights values, but the refusal to acknowledge state violations of them.

Hence, events such as the Grenfell Tower fire disaster in the summer of 2017 in London involving residents – many of whom were recent migrants – and others whose ancestry can be traced to former colonies, was framed, and then only superficially, by the government as a matter of public policy and local government accountability and not international human rights. The incineration of seventy-two people in a tower block clad with cheap combustible materials in the most unequal borough in the UK was not depicted – even by human rights lawyers, as Andrew Fagan notes[151] – as a matter of international human rights. Only in March 2019, almost three years after the tragedy, did Britain's Equality and Human Rights Commission report that human rights laws – protecting life and providing safe housing – were breached.[152] Despite this, Kensington and Chelsea Borough Council officials awarded themselves over £90,000 in bonuses the year after the fire.[153]

Fagan interprets this as illustrative of the liberal human rights community refusing to consider the adverse effects of political economy – specifically neoliberalism, a model embraced by the British state. He sees human rights becoming 'gentrified', and hence mirroring the process by which wealthier people displace poorer residents from their homes in fashionable districts of London. Only after a considerable amount of time had elapsed was the combustible cladding and other unsafe building features at Grenfell raised as a human rights issue.[154] While this is important, when the Grenfell inferno was investigated through a public inquiry, it ignored questions of human rights, and the Equality and Human Rights Commission and the United Nations Special Rapporteur on the right to adequate housing were denied admission to the inquiry.[155]

## Moral Equivalences

Western politicians and liberal scholars make claims to the broad values of freedom, democracy and justice that can be construed as the embrace of a political mythology of human rights.[156] This mythology is, of course, dependent upon removing colonialism and slavery from any assessment of blame for either internal scandals in Western countries – such as those surrounding cruelties towards minority and indigenous populations – or, more particularly, human rights problems within former colonized territories.

In examining the 'precarious boundaries of the classical distinctions from the colonial era to Mobutuism', V. Y. Mubinde observes[157] that the Congolese dictator and overseer of numerous atrocities, Sese Seko Mobutu, obtained some degree of legitimacy by contrasting mythic memories against each other. Many of the narratives of these derive from the representations about Native societies made in the colonial period. Aiding the emergence of figures like Mobutu is the fact that, while colonizers faced a multitude of overlapping and sometimes conflicting cultural traditions among the colonized, they presented indigenous societies as imparting one unified and coherent system of thought. Mubinde further posits that the myriad African traditions transformed through colonialism were eventually merged into new unified social orders such as those fashioned by whatever leaders gained power.[158] If there is a single Native society over which colonizers preside, those who succeed them can easily build images that solidify autocracies such as that of Mobutu, based on appealing to that constructed unified identity.

A more extreme example is the suggestion by Mahmood Mamdani that the genocide of up to a million mostly Huutu in Rwanda was intimately linked with the violent history of European colonial occupation. Mamdani argues that colonial violence was the precondition for 'genocidal impulses'.[159] Despite the genocide occurring some thirty years after independence, it cannot be disentangled from the racializing of different populations – and particularly the inculcation of the notion that Tuutsi were superior – by the Belgians, Germans and British. Pioneered by explorers John Hanning Speke in 1861, and Henry Morton Stanley in 1876, this 'Hamitic hypothesis' held that, wherever there was evidence of what they deemed to be organized societies – and specifically in the Great Lakes regions – the populations must have come from elsewhere, and therefore they more closely approximated Europeans.[160] Belgian law and administration built divisions between the Huutu as 'ordinary negroes' and a ruling class of Tuutsi.[161] Similarly, the tragedies of the Darfur region which led to the indictment of Omar Hasan Ahmad al-Bashir, the President of Sudan, in the ICC in 2008 had their roots in British colonial policies. As Mamdani observed,[162] the British reidentified, marginalized, and provided complex differences in land and other rights to different 'tribal' groups that were configured for purposes of colonial administration.

Colonial precedents, as well as Western support for dictators, supply vital contexts elsewhere in Africa for human rights. Helen Epstein's account of state corruption, brutality and murder in several parts of central Africa links the many atrocities, and even the Rwandan genocide, to US and British backing of dictators and military aid.[163] As far back as the Reagan era, the US government befriended Ugandan President Yoweri Museveni, whose leadership relies on several sham elections. Epstein argues that, for strategic reasons connected with anti-terrorism, the USA and UN suppressed investigations into the role of Paul Kagame's Rwandan Patriotic Front in the genocide of Huutus in Rwanda and the Congo. In fact, US actions directly abetted parts of the Rwandan genocide: '[Susan] Rice, Clinton's special assistant on Africa, supported the brutal Zaire invasion and has long been a stalwart friend of Museveni and Kagame. As Obama's national security adviser, she even attempted to block a UN report linking them to Congolese warlords responsible for atrocities.'[164]

US and British generosity to autocracy includes support for the Ugandan military, and aid funds that were earmarked for health, transport and education and diverted to the regime. Epstein also contends that the current humanitarian crises in Uganda can be related to British rule. She cites a particularly vivid example: 'in Acholiland, Acting Commissioner J. R. P. Postlethwaite, nicknamed "chicken thief" by the Acholi, publicly strung up a rebellious chief and lowered him headfirst into a pit latrine until he died'.[165] Furthermore, the British, like European colonists elsewhere, cultivated certain tribal groups as favoured subjects, and these divisions can often be mapped onto contemporary human rights conflicts in Africa more generally.

Other atrocities carried out by colonizers cannot entirely be disentangled from current human rights concerns. The massacres of Muslim Rohingyas in their villages in Rakhine state in Burma/Myanmar have been among the very worst human rights crises of the twenty-first century. About 1.2 million Rohingya have been forced out of their homes and across the border into Bangladesh through Buddhist Burmese troops incinerating houses with families inside, hacking and beating survivors to death, and raping women. The gruesome murders of civilians by the Burmese state, presided over by Nobel Peace laureate Aung Sun Suu Kyi, and supplied with arms by Britain, have been documented by many news agencies, and NGOs such as Human Rights Watch.[166] The refugee encampments around Cox's Bazaar in Bangladesh were in 2018 the largest such temporary settlements on the planet. The attacks that precipitated the mass exodus were in some instances reprisals, albeit astronomically disproportionate, for Rohingya attacks on the Burmese military.

Yet the murders and forced relocations occupy a context that began with Britain granting Burma independence in 1947. This was within a British-demarcated territorial boundary after a promise to grant the Rohingya a state. This guarantee was subsequently rescinded, as was a petition by the Rohingya to be part of the new state of East Pakistan in 1971. Azeem Ibrahim, in his much-praised account of the Rohingyas, identifies the British decision to incorporate Arakan (now Rakhine state) into its Burma colony as 'a purely administrative decision [which] led to the situation we are in today'.[167] After Burmese independence, the Rohingya minority were persecuted through several laws, including a 1982 Citizenship Act which effectively denationalized Rohingya and justified continued persecution.[168] It created a different category of humanity, ending in statelessness and brutal removals. A few years after the Citizenship Act, 'In 1989, colour-coded Citizens Scrutiny Cards (CRCs) were introduced: pink cards for full citizens, blue for associate citizens and green for naturalised citizens. The Rohingya were not issued with any cards.'[169] Six UN Special Rapporteurs urged the Burmese government to repeal and amend the Citizenship Act in 2007, but this had no effect.

These cases illustrate that current atrocities need to be situated in colonial as well as contemporary contexts, but they also indicate that human rights concerns require broader understanding that highlights the selectivity used in raising a human rights concern and identifying perpetrators and victims. In 2018, a statement for general debate in the HRC submitted by the UK government illustrated the strategic nature of invoking human rights. It warmly endorsed the remit of the UN Office of the High Commissioner for Human Rights (OHCHR), then proceeded to express concern about restrictions of freedom of expression in Bangladesh, the erosion of democracy in the Maldives, unfair elections in Cambodia, the imprisonment of bloggers in Vietnam, state-authorized killings in the Philippines, political prisoners and humanitarian aid in Venezuela, and the burning of villages and schools in Cameroon.[170] A month later, the Foreign Office Minister Lord Ahmad of Wimbledon addressed the HRC, flagging up human rights violations in Burma, Syria, the Maldives, Sri Lanka and, interestingly, Yemen.[171] These ahistorical snapshots were also notable in ignoring human rights violations in Western liberal states – for example, the US President has encouraged criminal violence against journalists, ordered the incarceration of child migrants and separated them from their parents, and the 2016 Presidential election is widely suspected of having been fraudulent.

Significantly, states with equally severe human rights problems, such as Saudi Arabia and Egypt, whose autocratic regimes are also supported by the UK, were ignored. Britain and the USA sell arms to Saudi Arabia. BAE Systems alone took orders for fighter planes and military hardware in 2018 for £3.2 billion, and American munitions sales to Saudi Arabia were estimated to be £5 billion between 2015 and 2017.[172] These have been used in military operations in Yemen[173] that the UN Secretary-General called 'the world's worst humanitarian crisis'.[174] The USA and UK are muted on human rights in the Kingdom, including the credible reports of torture, arbitrary detention, sexual harassment, assault of Saudi women human rights activists, and unfair trials of female critics and journalists.[175]

The execution by dismemberment of *Washington Post* journalist and critic of the Saudi autocracy Jamal Khashoggi, in the Saudi Arabian consulate in Istanbul in October 2018, brought these hypocrisies to the fore. Motivated by a desire by the Saudi government to eliminate a source of dissent, the murder was met only with tepid condemnation by the British government, and Canada's Liberal Prime Minister Justin Trudeau even claimed that the cost of complaining would be 'in the billions of dollars'.[176] Canada subsequently banned seventeen named individuals thought to be connected with the murder from entering the country. Britain took no action. Although US legislators withdrew US military assistance to Saudi Arabia and condemned Prince Mohammed bin Salman for his role in directing the murder, President Trump reinforced the primacy of trade over human rights, telling NBC's *Meet the Press* interviewer Chuck Todd in 2019, 'I only say they spend $400 to $450 billion over a period of time, all money, all jobs, buying equipment ... I'm not like a fool that says, "We don't want to do business with them."'[177] This followed an HRC Report concluding that the extra-judicial killing was directed by the Saudi government, which had lied and concealed evidence, most spectacularly by dressing up a lookalike who walked out of the embassy in Khashoggi's clothes and by forensically cleaning the embassy before Turkish investigators were allowed to enter it. Special Rapporteur Agnes Callamard additionally found Saudi Arabia violated the Vienna Convention on Consular Relations, along with the peacetime prohibition against the extra-territorial use of force, and the convention against torture and enforced disappearance.[178]

Western silence and rationalization of atrocities within powerful nations extends to China, where a one-party state continues to use extreme repression against large sectors of the population, surveils its citizens, and imprisons large numbers of dissidents. In 2005 alone, China executed somewhere between 5,000 and 12,000 people,[179] but remains relatively immune from human rights accountability. The violations include, most recently, mass re-education internment camps for Uyghurs and other Muslim peoples, where up to 1 million people were detained in October 2018, and children separated from their families.[180] Detention in the camps has lasted many years and people have been subjected to continual brainwashing and Chinese cultural immersion.

It is equally important to the strategic ideological management of human rights problems to ignore, downplay or censor links between past state actions, present injustice and both enslavement and the settlement of indigenous lands. If settler colonial histories – and they are multiple and manifold – were better known, the same American government which selectively comments on restrictions of freedom, unfair trade and 'dictatorship' around the world would have to face sterner tests of its sincerity. The massacres of Native Americans – many of which, such as those in California, have only recently been fully documented[181] – forced removals, duplicitous and broken treaty agreements, removal of indigenous children from their families to be transported – some as prisoners of war[182] – to boarding schools, are not readily consistent with exhortations to abide by the 'rule of law' elsewhere in the world. Like the USA, Canada implemented a duplicitous treaty system, but more recently implemented a land claims process that requires indigenous peoples to forfeit ownership over their lands. It presides over horrifying statistics on Aboriginal health, suicide and alcohol abuse.[183] Nevertheless, Canada freely criticizes other states – most recently, Burma for the genocide of Rohingya,[184] and Saudi Arabia for women's rights and arrests of activists, despite also selling $15 billion of arms to the Kingdom, widely believed to be a cause of civilian deaths and starvation in Yemen.[185]

What might be at issue is moral equivalence, the situating of human rights concerns in different places and times on the same plane. If human rights are universal, then the universality extends across time and space. Events cannot logically be extricated from history and geography, set apart and judged independently, either of each other or of the state parties. A final example to illustrate this is that massive stain on Western liberalism of the Holocaust and the carnage of two World Wars. The singular culpability for the Holocaust, with its gruesome, calculated and unprecedented mass killings of 6 million Jews and others, was pinned on Germany, even though British and American officials were aware of the Holocaust as early as 1942, but did nothing to stop it.[186] It is also despite parallel (although numerically much smaller) slaughters committed by the Allied forces, such as the killing of an estimated 25,000 people by the British RAF and the USAF in the fire-bombing of Dresden, immortalized in Kurt Vonnegut's *Slaughterhouse Five*, and the American nuclear bombing of Nagasaki and Hiroshima, carried out with the agreement of the British, which killed 129,000 civilians. Similarly, the 1940 Red

Army summary execution of about 22,000 prisoners of war, including Polish officers, in Katyn forest was known to the British and American governments, but they did not raise a murmur towards Joseph Stalin, the architect of the massacre. Instead, they condoned Russian occupation and the imposition of Soviet communism in Poland.[187] Neither Russians, British nor Americans were prosecuted for these acts, and they were not classified as war crimes or acts of genocide.

Marcel Ophuls' recently restored film *Memory of Justice* speaks to the problem of moral equivalences. It is a powerful indictment of Nazism, interspersing interviews from the late 1960s with former Nazis, including Albert Speer, with footage from the Nuremberg war crimes trials. The film shows many sides of the Nazi story – remorse, convictions of righteousness and, perhaps most of all, evasion of responsibility. However, at the beginning, and increasingly towards the end of the film, Ophuls questions US and British prosecutors Telford Taylor and Sir Hartley Shawcross, who are asked about the conduct of the Vietnam War. With the aid of additional interviews with journalist Daniel Ellsberg and former US soldiers, viewers begin to see affinities between what was condemned at Nuremberg and the massacres, bombings and chemical attacks that largely escaped legal judgment in Vietnam. Interviews with former French soldiers billeted to Algeria who witnessed torture and summary executions of Arabs complete the picture. Using the technique of dialectical montage employed in his other films,[188] Ophuls leaves viewers with questions about whether those who judge others are themselves free from the same – or similar – condemnation.

In the 4½-hour documentary, the moral equivalence is not, of course, about the scale or the explicit intention to kill people, but about justice and guilt being placed within the same frame of reference. Ophuls' questions about how supposedly ordinary people could commit horrendously sadistic acts recall Hannah Arendt's *Eichmann in Jerusalem*. Almost forgotten though it has been, *Memory of Justice* punctures any national claims to unique moral authority. Far worse to the contemporary viewer, perhaps, are suggestions that the German state designation of inferior peoples as non-nationals and, hence, rightless peoples might have some similarities with the treatment of refugees and asylum seekers in liberal Western countries today. 'The refugees I work with', says Natasha Walter, who runs a charity in Britain, 'don't have the right to work, they are exploited, they live in limbo, they wait years for citizenship, they are detained, and they deal with all of that while they are on the move from the trauma they are fleeing'.[189] That there might be, as Agamben has suggested, an 'inner solidarity between democracy and totalitarianism'[190] in the treatment of those who have become subjects with different and inferior rights is obvious.

# 3

# Slavery and Its Afterlives

The African slave trade is the most dramatic chapter in the story of human existence.

Zora Neale Hurston[1]

## Introduction

Against all the odds, Barack Obama was elected the first black American President in 2008. He was re-elected in a close-run contest in 2012. Although Obama's ancestors on his father's side were not slaves, they were colonized by the British in what is now Kenya. Obama as a black person from a background of colonialism was also identified with peoples brought to the Americas by Europeans as slaves. The fact that such an articulate and worldly man was elected to succeed one of the least fluent and cosmopolitan Presidents could have been an indication of some sort of new order in which the assignment of people into races graded according to worth was diminishing. This would be a significant sign that, contrary to Alexis de Tocqueville's bleak prediction that 'although the law may abolish slavery, only God can obliterate its traces',[2] the traces are getting dimmer.

But perhaps it takes more than a Presidential election to alter the effects of the 'most dramatic chapter in the story of human existence'. Over a decade before Obama's election, Paul Gilroy began *The Black Atlantic* with the concept of the memory of slavery.[3] This memory is something that binds white and black people together. For Gilroy, the same Enlightenment culture that is credited with creating democracy, Parliamentary systems and human rights valued slave trading and commercial enslavement, and was infused with racial ideologies.

The Black Atlantic relationship originates from purchasing, shackling and transporting Africans to the Western Hemisphere on British, French, Dutch, Danish, Spanish, Portuguese and American ships financed by governments, banks and insurance companies. Packed into compartments often only as high as 3 feet, incidences of death, sickness, rape and beatings of slaves en route to the New World were common. With 'bargains sharp and sinful on both sides', Hurston tells us, in her delayed memoir of 'the last slave', Kossula, of 'their journey from humanity to cattle; with storing and feeding and starvation and suffocation and pestilence and death; with slave ship stenches and mutinies of crew and cargo; and the jettying of cargoes before the guns of British cruisers; with auction blocks and sales and profits and losses'.[4]

Kossula was taken as one of 116 captives on an American slaver, the *Clotilda* out of Mobile, Alabama, in one of the last acts of the US slave trade. Beginning over 250 years earlier, the scale of the North American trade in slaves was phenomenal:

> The European international slave trade to what became the US lasted for almost 200 years, and after it was legally abolished in 1808, the domestic trade in enslaved people (the so-called 'interstate trade') within the US continued for more than 55 years. During the international trade at least 800,000 Africans were kidnapped, transported, or landed in the US. From the 1770s to the 1860s, the 'interstate trade' involved the sale of more than 650,000 enslaved African Americans from the Upper South to the Lower South. Another 1.3 million were sold locally in the South.[5]

This trade had provided wealth for British shipping companies transporting a yearly average of 74,000 people[6] to their colonies in the Caribbean and the Americas, and during part of this time Britain monopolized the slave trade to Spanish colonies. Between 1751 and 1850 alone, Britain sent over 2.8 million African captives to the Americas.[7] Altogether about 12.5 million Africans were seized and transported to the Americas, mostly from the seventeenth to the nineteenth centuries. Captives were obtained by European and American trading companies through various methods – directly kidnapping them, encouraging existing conflicts among Africans, and by exchanging goods with African rulers and merchants who had already captured prisoners. One estimate claims that the slave trade may have cost Africa as many as 50 million people.[8] We can see why Hurston describes the slave trade as she does in the quote which opens this chapter. Of the 12.5 million transported captives, about 10 million did not survive to the European and American plantations[9] because they were too sick, old, young or rebellious, and were thrown overboard and entombed by the Atlantic Ocean in the infamous Middle Passage. One of the most notorious incidences of maritime murder was the massacre on the British ship *Zong* in 1781, in which 130 captives were thrown overboard by crew because the ship's doctors considered them to be commercially useless.[10]

In 1619, the first Africans arrived in what is now the United States, probably on a Dutch warship, and became indentured servants. After that, the slave trade lasted officially until 1808, although it persisted illicitly, as was the case with the *Clotilda*, up to the time of the Emancipation Proclamation in 1863. Despite the banning of the slave trade, traffickers were rarely punished. In fact, Presidents Jefferson, Madison, Monroe, John Quincy Adams and Jackson all issued Presidential pardons to owners of slave ships that were apprehended in violation of the ban on slave trading, and Thomas Jefferson even pardoned the same owner twice for violating the law. W. E. B. Du Bois concludes that 'execution of these laws was criminally lax'.[11]

There were many types of slavery practised in the USA. In the nineteenth century, most slaveholders held only a few, with less than ten captives, enslaving Africans on farms, but some were also taken to cities. Big plantations growing tobacco, sugar and cotton were more common in the Deep South. Here, commercial breeding and rearing of slaves was common, according to some historians,[12] and separation of families was the rule. Plantations were, of course, schizophrenic institutions run by people for whom morality and coherent human values could not survive. Slave owners would often give concessions to slaves for days off and weekend passes but also severely punish them for minor transgressions of rules, mainly through whipping and flogging. Despite these regimes of terror, there were frequent and numerous rebellions, an organized anti-slavery movement, and when it came to fighting to end slavery many black soldiers served in the Union Army.

American law selected Africans for unique treatment through State and Federal Slave codes. These covered every aspect of an enslaved person's life: they would have no standing in the courts; could not offer testimony except against another slave; their oaths were never binding; ownership of property was forbidden; a slave could not strike a white person even in self-defence, and could not leave plantations without permission. In Mississippi, a special law prohibited slaves from blowing horns or beating drums. Most petty digressions from these laws were punishable by whipping, while branding, imprisonment and death penalized what the enslavers considered more serious infractions.

## The Uneasy Present of Slavery

Memories of uprooting, transportation, exploitation and murder are *contemporary* experiences that connect the histories of the Americas and Europe. There are also widespread memories of resistance, resilience and rebellion.[13] Other cultural forms may have emerged – literatures, music, theatre and philosophy among them, but relationships of servility and dominance loom large in the shared memories of white and black peoples. Indeed, the delayed publication of Zora Neale Hurston's *Barracoon* is part of this movement.

Slavery is often a starting point, or at least a reference, for scholarly works on race in Europe and North America. Likewise, black activist groups such as the Black Panthers of the 1960s, the Rastafarian movement in Britain in the 1970s and 1980s, and more recently Black Lives Matter in the USA, often refer to current conditions as not dissimilar to slavery. The 2016 documentary film *The 13th* by Ava DuVernay, about the ironies of the 13th Amendment's inability to prevent the reproduction of captivity conditions for African-Americans in the USA into the twenty-first century, is in many ways an extension of these movements.

Numerous contemporary visual artists are also preoccupied with the present significance of slavery. To cite just one, Kara Walker has become internationally recognized for her moving, eerie, ironic, sometimes humorous pen-and-ink silhouettes and drawings depicting the many brutalities of slavery, often by using stereotypes of black physicality. Her sculpture/installation of a sphinx-like sugar-coated black woman – the full title of which is *A Subtlety: Or … the Marvelous Sugar Baby an Homage to the unpaid and overworked Artisans who have refined our Sweet tastes from the cane fields to the Kitchens of the New World on the Occasion of the demolition of the Domino Sugar Refining Plant* – shown originally at the Domino Sugar refinery in Brooklyn in 2014, speaks powerfully to the endurance of slavery. The enslaved woman, part mammy, part sex object, is outrageously over-sized as per many white stereotypes, and around her are small blackamoor children hoisting heavy baskets of the products of the sugar. In 2019, Walker's *Fons Americanus* installation in the Tate Modern Turbine Hall recreates the Victoria Monument outside Buckingham Palace as a memorial to slavery, with the Winged Victory goddess replaced by an African woman whose clothes have been ripped off and throat slit; her breasts spurt the water cascading down to pools where sharks rise up amidst thrashing black bodies. Around the central plinth there is a noose dangling from a truncated tree. A poster on the wall in the style of slave auction announcements credits 'that celebrated Negress of the New World,

Madame Kara E. Walker, NTY'. One reviewer calls the layered cake effect of the installation a kind of 'rot after the celebration'.[14]

Slavery has, of course, been part of literary culture for a long time. One need only think of Toni Morrison's *Beloved* which won the Pulitzer Prize in 1983, but there are also the writings of Americans Alice Walker, James Baldwin, Octavia Butler and Charles Johnson, Britons such as Andrea Levy, Edwidge Danticat from Haiti, Derek Walcott of St Lucia, and Fred D'Aguiar of Guyana. Slavery has also been a prominent theme of film, with British artist Steve McQueen's 2013 adaptation of Solomon Northrup's 1853 narrative *Twelve Years a Slave* winning three Academy Awards.

Theatre and performance art are capable of drawing audiences back into the memory of slavery in all its immediacy. This is the case with Robbie McCauley's 1998 performance art *Sally's Rape*. In what the artist calls a 'social experiment', this theatrical piece makes viewers directly visualize, feel and think about what slavery means. The performance, consisting in large part of a dialogue between the black character of Robbie McCauley and Jeannie Hutchins, who is white, and in shifting narrations of the rape of McCauley's great-great grandmother (Sally) by her white slave master, underlines the importance of the social relationships between whites and blacks that have so deeply shaped US society. The crime of being 'bound down on the ground', as McCauley says, deepens the multi-generational violation that slavery represents. The performance shows slavery as deeply traumatic social engineering, transforming the way people see and think about themselves for generations.

*Sally's Rape* oscillates between everyday friendly chatting of the two women and the memory of slavery, which McCauley evokes from her own lineage through the rape of Sally. Her origin is in 'being done it to'. McCauley makes the past contemporary in melancholic reflections on rape, and by her acting out the part of a person being sold at auction, in which the audience are encouraged to participate by bidding on her disrobed body. In this way, McCauley lured audiences into an uncomfortable relationship in which they are directly confronted with the living consequences of the actions of past generations of whites. Hutchins listens to the narrative of rape patiently, half-smiling and fidgeting, and at one point mentions a friend who was raped and went to a rape crisis centre. McCauley retorts that there were no such centres on the plantation. The performance shows how a social institution that ended some 160 years ago may continue to affect how people feel and act towards one another. Inter-generational female suffering and sexual violence is one of the main vehicles for this.

As is now well known, the persistent lasciviousness of white men on plantations in the South and in the British plantation colonies of the

Caribbean often knew few limits. Like Kurtz, Joseph Conrad's ivory trader in the Congo who 'lacked restraint in the gratification of his lusts'[15] in *Heart of Darkness*, enslaved women were infinitely violable for sudden pleasures, quick gains, and in the attainment of power by these rudderless masters of black people. Polite society in the South sometimes ostracized such men, but often the local white communities and the wives of the masters ignored their crimes. The pain and anguish caused to black women and the enslaved communities by rape, commented on movingly in Harriet Jacobs' 1861 narrative, *Incidents in the Life of a Slave Girl*, went unhealed, and perpetrators were unpunished. As Jacobs described it, 'my master met me at every turn, reminded me that I belonged to him, and swearing by heaven and earth that he would compel me to submit to him'.[16] These sexual advances began when she was 15 and he was 50. The master enslaver threatened to kill Harriet if she told anyone of his actions. He was, she tells us, already the father of eleven slaves,[17] who were his property.

American and European societies are shaped by this lucrative exercise in dehumanization. The slave economy, with its vast output of cotton, sugar, rice, tobacco and other products, propelled industrialization. Human beings were defined as commodities and, as such, were simply mediums of production. Their dehumanized blackness, underpinned by racist ideologies shared in the European Enlightenment, singularly consigned them to servitude. Slavery, therefore, is a vast system for the enunciation of the rightlessness of black people. This was admitted in the three-fifths compromise in the 1787 Constitution, which made enslaved people count as three-fifths of a person for the purposes of taxation and the calculation of the number of state representatives in Congress. Other passages in the Constitution underpinned the legitimacy of slavery. Most prominently, these were: the fugitive slave provision which mandated the return of 'runaway slaves' to their owners; the prohibition of a tax on slaves; and a clause preventing Congress from ending the slave trade within twenty years.[18] Built into the Constitution was the idea that there exists a taxonomy of humanity, arrayed along a continuum of human rights.

Notions of the Constitutional inferiority of Africans persisted, and in the 1850s when Congress debated a return to the legal slave trade, President James Buchanan sided with enslavers who were fearful that new African slaves would depreciate the value of their own captives. In a message to Congress in 1859, he asserted that, 'of the evils to the master, the one most dreaded would be the introduction of wild, heathen, and ignorant barbarians among the sober, orderly quiet slaves, whose ancestors have been on the soil for several generations. This might tend to barbarize, demoralize and exasperate the whole mass, and produce the most deplorable conditions.'[19] Abraham Lincoln, the sponsor of the Emancipation Proclamation and Buchanan's successor, had in the previous year displayed similar beliefs when, in debate with Stephen Douglas, he argued:

> I am not, nor ever have been, in favor of bringing about in any way the social and political equality of the white and black races (applause) that I am not nor ever have been in favor of making voters or jurors of negroes, nor of qualifying them to hold office, nor to intermarry with white people; and I will say in addition to this that there is a physical difference between the white and black races which *I believe will forever forbid the two races living together on terms of social and political equality.* And in as much as they cannot so live, while they do remain together there must be the position of superior and inferior, and I as much as any other man am in favor of having the superior position assigned to the white race [my emphasis].[20]

Outside of the discussions among Abolitionists, the deliberations over secession among white people in the South showed few significant differences of opinion. As the statement of secession from Georgia put it, 'the subordination and the political and social inequality of the African race was fully conceded by all'.[21] The secession statement from Texas made it abundantly clear that racially coded rights were natural, grounded in the founding of the United States, and decreed by the Christian God:

> We hold as undeniable truths that the governments of the various States, and of the confederacy itself, were established exclusively by the white race, for themselves and their posterity; that the African race had no agency in their establishment; that they were rightfully held and regarded as an inferior and dependent race, and in that condition only could their existence in this country be rendered beneficial or tolerable.
>
> That in this free government all white men are and of right ought to be entitled to equal civil and political rights; that the servitude of the African race, as existing in these States, is mutually beneficial to both bond and free, and is abundantly authorized and justified by the experience of mankind, and the revealed will of the Almighty Creator, as recognized by all Christian nations.[22]

The conviction of black inferiority, and its corollary attachment of inferior rights, continued after slavery was officially abolished in 1863. In fact, racism could flourish in all realms of public and private life, untainted by its associations with a system that came to be identified as at least compromising the very democratic and rights-based principles of the Declaration of Independence, Constitution and national narrative.

But abolishing slavery in the USA and its counterparts elsewhere need not presage emancipation, which implies a whole different set of socio-cultural and economic associations.[23] In fact, the legal ending of slavery produced a new class of victims: white people, whose centuries-long rights to enslave were curtailed. This precipitated extreme ambivalence within US institutions regarding the role black people should assume in society and what rights they should be entitled to in comparison to whites. This can be seen in the stuttering and moralistic ideas and actions of the author of the Declaration of Independence.

## Jefferson, Human Rights and Slavery

The third American President, Thomas Jefferson, is known for his contri-butions to the understanding of democracy and human rights. He is also known for his ownership of African slaves. Enslaved Africans built and maintained his fabulous estate at Monticello. One of his human properties, a mixed-race woman named Sally Hemings, who was his wife Martha's half-sister and herself the child of an enslaved woman and a white enslaver, was his secret mistress. Sally Hemings, referenced also in Robbie McCauley's performance, gave birth to six children fathered by Jefferson. When he got married, Jefferson's wife's sizeable dowry included 132 slaves. As one author put it, 'Jefferson was intimately associated with slavery from cradle to grave. His first memory was of being carried on a pillow by a slave; and a slave carpenter made the coffin in which he was buried at Monticello.'[24] The newly independent American state's emphasis on liberty and rights while also operating an extensive system of human slavery was incarnated in the figure of Thomas Jefferson.

Jefferson is considered an Enlightenment thinker because of his broad intellectual horizons and his drafting of the Declaration of Independence. His contributions to formulating the nature of rights are a main tenet of liberal thought. It is due in large part to Jefferson that the USA is so often depicted as the pre-eminent liberal democracy, and even the 'Applied Enlightenment'. In the words of the prolific historian Henry Steele Commager,Jefferson heroically 'combined the sturdy provincialism of the frontiersman with the cosmopolitanism of the philosophe'.[25] Along with other men of letters, science and politics such as Thomas Paine, James Madison, Benjamin Franklin and Benjamin Rush, he embodied what Commager and many others, including Alexis de Tocqueville much earlier, saw as the new nation's aspirations to reason, logic, science and political freedom, as well as the unity of humankind. Due to these and other Founding Fathers' wishes for the new nation to embody progress, the liberal values of freedom of expression, tolerance and democracy were inscribed in the US Constitution before they were recognized by any European power.

Jefferson is known as a champion of the rights of a people to self-government and self-determination. Even before the American Revolution, he was continually exposing the tyrannies of the British monarchy towards the colonists, and advocating greater autonomy for the latter. In the 1774 pamphlet *Summary View of the Rights of British America*, Jefferson articulates what would become a distinctly American concept of rights. Much like John Locke in *Two Treatises on Government*, he situates the English monarch as nothing other than 'the chief officer of the people',[26] circumscribed by the laws, and charged with running the government. The monarch is thus dependent on the institutions of the country and the will of the people. Following Locke again, Jefferson rejected the Divine Right of Kings, preferring a 'social contract' between the state and the public. In his pamphlet, Jefferson railed against the injustice of Britain maintaining authority over the colonists and treating the colonists as unequal citizens.[27] Significantly, Jefferson believed that American settlers possessed a 'natural right' to govern themselves. This was the main thrust of the Declaration of Independence of 1776, which has been interpreted as perhaps the first enunciation of human rights, self-government and democracy of the Enlightenment age. The most famous phrase in the *Declaration* that Jefferson largely drafted is:

> We hold these truths to be self evident: that all men are created equal; that they are endowed by their Creator with inherent and inalienable rights; that among these are life, liberty and the pursuit of happiness; that to secure these rights, governments are instituted among men deriving their just powers from the consent of the governed; that whenever any form of government becomes destructive of these ends, it is the right of the people to alter or abolish it, and to institute new government.

This was a truly revolutionary idea at a time when England was a feudal society mired in class, rank, status, inherited privileges, aristocratic birthrights, titles and a monarchy. The assertion that all men are created equal was not only a guide for the independent American society, but a forceful rebuttal of the main organizing principle of the British state. In enunciating this, the USA was the first nation to make equality part of its official ideology.[28] The 'inalienable rights' to 'life, liberty and the pursuit of happiness' could only be possible in a new form of society: a democracy. A final blast at feudal England was the idea that state authority must be based on the consent of the governed. Although John

Locke had, a century earlier, developed the architecture of the social contract, and his ideas became an important foundation for the concept of liberal democracy, he still assumed that the English monarch ruled by consent. Jefferson clearly believed otherwise. Much of the rest of the *Declaration* is a denunciation of British rule over the American colonies, referring to it as 'absolute tyranny'.[29] Against this, Jefferson proposed that the government is a creation of the people. It is held in place by the people, and composed of the people. If it was not accountable, the people have a right to abolish it, as the American colonists did in winning the War of Independence in 1776.

While the *Declaration* was a challenge to European feudalism, its extension of rights and the franchise excluded women, completely ignored enslaved Africans and only briefly and disparagingly mentioned American Indians. When Jefferson drafted the Virginia Constitution, he also excluded from voting those who did not own property, which of course included the enslaved Africans who were considered property. The original draft of the *Declaration* criticized the slave trade, but all references to it were taken out by the Continental Congress, one-third of whom were owners of enslaved Africans. Jefferson owned over 175 enslaved people when he wrote his treatise of democracy and human rights.[30] He supported the ending of the slave trade by the USA in 1807, but not slavery itself.

From other documents, we know that Jefferson regarded slavery as 'a blot in our country', a 'great political and moral evil', but he stopped short of abolishing the institution, saying only that 'the minds of our citizens may be ripening for a complete emancipation of human nature'.[31] In his thoughts and actions, however, Jefferson expressed great ambivalence, summarized in his reference to white Americans having the 'wolf by the ears': 'Justice was on the one scale and self-preservation on the other.'[32] He initially argued angrily that Britain's avaricious trade in African slaves was to blame for slavery, but later focused more on the USA, believing that slavery had caused deep animosities that would have long-lasting effects. When he did suggest that slavery could eventually be abolished, Jefferson felt that this would have to be balanced by mass European immigration. One of the ever-present problems of slavery was the fear of black insurrections against numerically inferior white enslavers and white people in general. Jefferson swiftly sold any of his slaves involved in sedition to distant plantations, sometimes those known for extremely harsh conditions.[33] Some slaves interpreted efforts to free themselves from tyranny as exercising a type of legitimate self-determination, seen in many slave narratives and orations such as Frederick Douglass' 1852 speech 'What to the Slave is the Fourth of July?' But Jefferson saw no parallel with the War of Independence, preferring a racial basis for the conceptualization of human rights, something Douglass well recognized: 'This Fourth [of] July is *yours*, not *mine*. *You* may rejoice, *I* must mourn. To drag a man in fetters into the grand illuminated temple of liberty, and call upon him to join you in joyous anthems, was inhuman mockery and sacrilegious irony.'[34]

Fears of enslaved Africans exercising the same 'self-determination' as the white colonists, under the same vaunted liberal principles – along with the precedent of the successful Haitian Revolution – spurred the passing of many laws to embed the rightlessness of black people in American society. Hence, in Jefferson's Virginia:

> Other than deportation of insurgent slaves, the provisions of these laws included the creation of a public guard to protect public property in Richmond; the arming of town militias in time of emergency, the prohibition of slaves' hiring themselves out; the requirement that free blacks register with the local court clerks in resident localities; and the authorization of slave testimony against free blacks [but not whites] in criminal trials.[35]

Two years before his death, Jefferson hatched a plan to nationalize and deport slaves, by the government purchasing them for $900 million and sending them to West Africa.[36] This was part of the 'colonization' project which involved the transporting of black people to new colonies in West Africa, in Sierra Leone and Liberia. Dierksheide remarks on the morality of this plan.

> Jefferson's colonization plan allotted compensation for slave owners, the slow disappearance of older slaves from the continent, and the colonization of younger slaves outside boundaries of the United States. Though Jefferson conceded that 'this subject involves some constitutional scruples' and that the 'separation of infants from their mothers ... would produce some scruples of humanity', he insisted that gradual colonization of black slaves was the only way to remove their presence from the union.[37]

The forcible separation of families was something that surely tested Jefferson's 'scruples', as indeed did his long-term relationship with his enslaved mistress, but it indicated that in his mind a white racial state could be the only means to achieve universal human rights in the USA. Neither Jefferson, the American Colonization Society whose president was his friend and former President James Madison, or the government which sponsored the movement were particularly concerned about the effects of a new colonization on West Africans, who sometimes became subjects of often brutal imperialistic control funded by the USA.[38] Their main concern was to preserve a white American settler state. Jefferson knew that slavery was a 'blot' on the vaunted civilization of the USA, but instead of aspiring to make rights universal, he advocated physical removal of black people, to whom he did not want to apply universal human rights.

Like many Enlightenment and later liberal thinkers, Jefferson believed that Africans were inferior, and this was 'fixed in nature'.[39] Their supposed inferiority, he believed, was not merely an effect of slavery, because intermarriage produced 'an improvement of blacks in body and mind'.[40] Africans, in his mind, were physically less attractive, had shallow emotions, reacted intuitively and possessed no depths of judgement. Even their music (along with that of the American Indians) was less sophisticated than European music.[41] In the end, Jefferson's racial convictions made him conclude that 'the unfortunate difference of color, and perhaps of faculty, is a powerful obstacle to the emancipation of these people'.[42]

At the end of his life, Jefferson professed the necessity of emancipation, but resigned himself simply to making slavery more tolerable through white benevolence,[43] as he estimated himself to be doing at Monticello. Overall, Jefferson was paralysed by conflicting sentiments about slavery, and he never freed any of his human property, many of whom he simply treated as business assets. A bad bookkeeper, Jefferson constantly ran up debts and used his enslaved people as capital to clear these, often selling members of families and breaking deep bonds between spouses, and parents and children, without any apparent concern for the trauma this might have caused.[44] Among the list of his possessions when Jefferson died was 'Sally – an old woman worth $50'.[45]

## Segregation

Looked at in retrospect, slavery was the crucial precursor to the institutionalization of rightlessness and inferior rights for black people in the USA. W. E. B. Du Bois had seen this clearly. Perhaps the most famous passage of *The Souls of Black Folks*, published in 1903, was 'the problem of the twentieth century is the problem of the color line – the relation of the darker to the lighter races of men in Asia and Africa, in America and the islands of the sea'.[46] In his mind, the colour line was reinforced by attitudes of whites, out of guilt from slavery, but also from convictions about their cultural superiority that made them unable to listen to or understand black people. Du Bois saw this as connected to the forced subjugation of huge swathes of the globe to European colonialism. This problem was not American in origin, but slavery, segregation and racism in the USA were all outcomes of European colonialism. The colour line, and thus the selectivity of rights, was built into the institutional structure of European settler societies such as the USA.

Many of the most stringent laws ordering the *separate* treatment of African-Americans were established during a period of white backlash to equal rights, immediately after official abolition. Just two years after enslaved Africans were freed, President Andrew Johnson instated Black Codes. These established a system of semi-servitude through tenant farming and apprenticeships, and forbade blacks from travel in the same railroad cars as whites. Segregation of schools took place promptly.[47] Vagrancy and curfew laws were put into operation and convict labour punishments such as 'chain gangs', used during slavery, were reinstituted. Under the Black Codes, a black person could be arrested simply for being unemployed.[48]

There were, of course, responses from freed people, including many uprisings against these laws, leading in 1867 to their abandonment in many Southern cities. In 1866–7, Federal civil rights legislation followed suit, invalidating or relaxing the enforcement of the Black Codes. The Reconstruction period from 1868 to 1877 coincided with formal equality and gains for African-Americans while there was a military occupation of the South by Union forces. C. Van Woodward, in his landmark study of racial laws known as Jim Crow, cites the writings of many black travellers in the South who reported no difficulties on railroads and public accommodations.[49] Yet, despite some changes to reduce racial inequality in law, segregation immediately took shape. Outside of the South, the farther West a black person travelled, the harsher the conditions, on account both of white hostility and of white fears of the devaluation of their labour. Several Western states restricted the number of African-Americans that could enter their territories – Indiana, Illinois and Oregon, most prominently.[50]

A series of Civil Rights Acts were passed in the 1860s and 1870s granting African-Americans political rights which had long been denied, in the North as well as the South. In 1867, more blacks than whites voted in the South. State assemblies often contained numerous black representatives. Southern states elected ten black men to the US House of Representatives in the Reconstruction era. Up to 1901, almost every Congress had Southern black elected officials.[51] The apex of this rights-conferring was the 1875 Civil Rights Act which enshrined formal equality in law. It stated:

> That all persons within the jurisdiction of the United States shall be entitled to the full and equal enjoyment of the accommodations,

advantages, facilities, and privileges of inns, public conveyances on land or water, theaters, and other places of public amusement; subject only to the conditions and limitations established by law, and applicable alike to citizens of every race and color, regardless of any previous condition of servitude.[52]

This legislation followed the 13th Amendment to the Constitution, which abolished slavery and involuntary servitude (1865); the 14th Amendment, which prohibited states from denying any citizens the privileges and immunities of all US citizens, due process of law, and equal protection of the laws (1868); and the 15th Amendment, which protected the right to vote of all male citizens of the USA, regardless of colour (1870). These were all correctives to the Constitution that made it operationally legitimate to own and enslave human beings, and as such to deny the enslaved normal rights of citizenship.

Reminding us that the gradual expansion of civil and political rights is not – as per the narrative of liberal progress – inevitable, the conferring of these rights was rapidly nullified by other political and judicial developments that either ignored them, or found loopholes to enable inferior rights to continue to be applied to African-Americans. Within the post-slavery society, racism did not disappear, and white supremacist sentiment gained traction as Southern whites felt that their sacrifices in the Civil War should be rewarded with the preservation of racial hierarchies in the reunified American state. To keep the fragile peace, the rights of freed slaves were not rigorously enforced, voting rights were quickly rescinded, and segregation quickly became normalized under what was in effect white supremacist rule.

After Reconstruction, white fears that black people would take control of American institutions were openly and widely expressed. The nightmarish scenario envisioned by Jefferson's 'wolf by the ears' came to be expressed in D. W. Griffith's 1915 film *The Birth of a Nation*, depicting the Ku Klux Klan (KKK) as heroic defenders of the sanctity of racial hierarchies and a white American state. The film, adapted from Thomas Dixon's 1905 novel *The Clansman*, shows mixed-race men as menacing, lascivious, corrupt and braced to take control of towns and cities. Through the heroics of the Klan, including the lynching of a black villain, the white order of American society is preserved. The fears expressed in Griffith's film are linked with the character of Silas Lynch, the 'mulatto' Lieutenant Governor, black magistrates becoming a 'new aristocracy', and blacks rigging the ballots, while whites anticipate disenfranchisement. Equally grave from this perspective was possible legislation allowing racial inter-marriage. In the film, the KKK appears in defence of the pure Aryan birthright and the stabilization of a racial social order of absolute white dominance.

As faithfully represented in *The Birth of a Nation*, the fear that racial equality would lead to intolerable participation – and, by extension, human rights – for black people was the impetus for the KKK and other white supremacist groups across the country. Founded after the Civil War, the Klan became an organizational foundation for the assertion of white privilege, and hence its counterpart, the social, political, economic and legal ostracism of people who differed from them. The KKK was well organized with numerous projects (including anti-immigration and anti-Jewish campaigns, and those to affirm the Nordic 'indigenous' culture of the USA) and platforms (supporting creationism, for example). Much of the ideology of the KKK during its periods of resurgence, the 1920s and 1960s, was to promote the idea that Protestant white men were losing position and status to blacks, Jews, Catholics and foreigners. The uniforms, parades and often violent shows of strength spoke to a palpable sense of white emasculation. When they violently attacked people they believed represented a threat to them or US society, they often did so as representatives of the criminal justice system, since police and judges were also in the Klan.[53]

White supremacist violence was deemed necessary by the Klan despite the vigorous enforcement of Jim Crow laws that promoted the civic isolation of black people. Many Southern states prioritized these laws over the Constitutional amendments guaranteeing universal rights. The right of African-Americans to vote, for example, was withdrawn by Southern states through poll tax requirements, complex written ballots and literacy tests. Black voter turnout in South Carolina went from 96 per cent in 1876 to 11 per cent in 1898.[54] Whites also used unchecked violence, terror and economic reprisals to keep black people from voting well into the 1950s.

While the Southern states descended into authoritarian single-party government, the Northern states and the liberals within them either condoned Southern violations of African-American rights or were silent on them.[55] Northern liberals, like many white people of the time, were against slavery, but they were not necessarily for racial equality. Showing how moves towards the recognition of supposedly equal rights can quickly be annulled, Reconstruction measures were reversed in a series of judgments in 1883, and the Supreme Court invalidated the 1875 Civil Rights Act, which, in specifying that 'all persons ... shall be entitled to the equal enjoyment of the [public and private services]', was aimed especially at hotels and restaurants. With this, the prohibition of the practice of refusing service or accommodation to black people was lifted – indeed, it was held as unconstitutional. After the rapid reversal of this position, there would be no further civil rights legislation by the US Congress until 1957.[56]

This abrupt backtracking on universality was a stark reminder of the racial contract. 'When a man has emerged from slavery, and by the aid of beneficent legislation has shaken off the inseparable concomitants of that state', stated Justice Bradley in delivering the Supreme Court majority opinion voiding the 1875 Civil Rights Act, 'there must be some stage in the progress of his elevation when he takes the rank of a mere citizen, and ceases to be the special favorite of the laws, and when his rights as a citizen, or a man, are to be protected in the ordinary modes by which other men's rights are protected'.[57] As he went on, Bradley considered being a 'mere citizen' as living within a society in which racial discrimination by private establishments is normal. The elimination of the freedom to discriminate, Bradley concluded, was not covered by the Constitutional Amendments, and such discrimination when it did occur could not be construed as following from past conditions of servitude.

The sanctification of segregation, and with it the differential treatment of African-Americans, through the 1883 Supreme Court decision was, as Rothstein reminds us,[58] a means of preventing Congress from enforcing the 13th Amendment by prohibiting practices perpetrating the characteristics of slavery. It was therefore, according to Rothstein, an erroneous decision by the US Supreme Court that led to violations of the Constitution by making African-Americans second-class citizens. This was further embedded through a Supreme Court test case of Jim Crow laws in 1896, *Plessy* v. *Ferguson*, which introduced the 'separate but equal' doctrine. Passed by a 7–1 majority, the plaintive Plessy was a passenger, who, because he was one-eighth black, was required to travel in the coloured person's carriage. He was arrested for refusing to vacate the white person's carriage when instructed by a conductor, thus breaking an 1890 Louisiana state law requiring separate but equal accommodations for blacks and whites on railroad cars. The ruling upheld the Louisiana law, and was adjudged not to violate any of the Constitutional Amendments because, the majority argued, the Constitution merely upheld equality. As Bradley had stated just over a decade earlier, it could not invalidate social and legal distinctions between blacks and whites. The Court concluded that 'legislation is powerless to eradicate racial instincts', continuing: 'if one race be inferior to the other socially, the Constitution cannot put them on the same plane'.[59]

Beliefs such as that which held that black and white people are by nature unequal underpinned the selectivity in access to citizenship rights. Across the USA, daily life in business establishments, entertainment, the military, employment, housing and the criminal justice system were characterized by the provision of inferior access rights to black people.

States and municipalities enacted laws, particularly in the South, to enforce segregation further. For example, in 1905, Georgia passed the Separate Park Law to push African-Americans out of public parks. A Louisiana law mandated racially separate ticket windows, entrances and exits, and that blacks were to be kept 25 feet from whites at sporting events, circuses and tent shows.[60]

Much African-American resistance in the twentieth century was concerned with the fight for equal facilities within this framework of segregation. This struggle was waged in part against 'racially explicit laws, regulations, and government practices [which] ... combined to create a nationwide system of urban ghettoes surrounded by white suburbs'.[61] It culminated in the civil rights and Black Power movements of the 1950s and 1960s. Activists directly challenged and critiqued the Federal government because it legitimated racialized human rights. The state had, for most of the twentieth century, used its power to impose segregated race relations among its employees and through its programmes.[62] The pattern adopted largely in the South was nationalized by the government, which rigorously enforced segregation and thereby institutionalized white attitudes that blacks were inferior to them.

The embedding of racism came straight from the top. President Woodrow Wilson, a main force behind the League of Nations, shows the affinity between liberalism and racism exemplified also in Thomas Jefferson. A strong advocate of racial segregation, Wilson believed that racial separation encouraged both social harmony and the elevation of African-Americans.[63] He even screened *The Birth of a Nation* in the White House in 1915.[64] Two years earlier, Wilson ensured that, in government offices, curtains were installed to separate black and white clerical workers, separate cafeterias were created, separate basement toilets were built for African-Americans, and black supervisors were downgraded to prevent any black person having authority over any white person.[65] These policies continued through the Great Depression and the New Deal as Congress used various stipulations on funding to prevent extensive black participation in government social programmes. By 1938, blacks comprised only 8.4 per cent of all government employees in Washington, and 90 per cent of these were employed as janitors or cleaners.[66]

While racial segregation had been associated with the South, with its plantations and small towns divided by railroad tracks, Northern cities were always bastions of racial segregation. This was prominently identified in Du Bois' 1899 study *The Philadelphia Negro*.[67] Attempting to understand racialized patterns of poverty, Du Bois looked at the social conditions in which many black people found themselves. He discovered widespread experiences of denial of employment, education and criminal justice rights. A high proportion of the Philadelphia black population was

Southern migrants, and hence, he argued, their problems stemmed largely from their past condition of servitude as they tried to negotiate a position in a highly competitive industrial setting. Many black families that Du Bois surveyed lived in only one room with little ventilation. Few dwellings had sanitation or water, and there were extreme health hazards. All this gave rise to profound demoralization expressed in family break-ups, alcoholism, gambling, crime and violence. There were only limited areas of the city where black people could rent accommodation. According to Du Bois, this stemmed from the undeniable fact that most whites preferred not to live in the same areas as blacks. This aversion was enforced by real estate agents and by landlords raising rents to make occupancy of certain districts beyond the meagre budgets of most black families, whose sources of income were not largely from unionized industrial labour, which heavily favoured whites. Rather, black employment was concentrated in service jobs ministering to wealthy whites near the centre of the city.

This pattern of segregation and urban poverty continued well into the twentieth century. In a very detailed study of the 'Black Belt' in Chicago at the end of the Great Depression, sociologists St Clair Drake and Horace Cayton's *Black Metropolis*[68] uses similar techniques to Du Bois to address the relationship of the black population to the white, to the economy and to the wider politics of the city. It combines social surveys, statistics and maps with social-anthropological style interviews with whites and blacks by a team of interviewers. Like Du Bois' study of Philadelphia, it attempts to explain why it is that an urban black population is rooted in poverty, have much worse health problems than other groups and experience little residential mobility. The explanation for residential segregation was simple: it was a policy actively pursued by the American government to deny black people equal entitlement to housing. It was abetted both by 'white flight' out of the inner cities and the corresponding creation of all-black ghettos. In turn, these ghettos produced vastly reduced life circumstances for all their inhabitants.

The 1939 Housing Act cemented these differential rights in law. For the social stability of neighbourhoods, it permitted white homeowners, landlords and real estate agencies to discriminate to maintain occupation of housing districts by the same social and *racial* classes. Thus, it was difficult for blacks to secure loans to buy houses anywhere other than predominantly black neighbourhoods. Restrictive covenants that excluded black people from renting or owning homes in specified places were used well before the Housing Act. They were drawn up by organizations of real estate agents, homeowner associations and community builders, as Gotham shows, for many cities and towns across the USA in the first half of the twentieth century, to protect property values from members of racial or national groups that were thought to lower them.[69]

Although the Supreme Court declared such covenants unenforceable, they were widely used until the end of the 1960s. As Drake and Cayton illustrate,[70] restrictive covenants could also be used by realtors and landlords to charge higher premiums to black people, a pattern Du Bois discerned in Philadelphia several decades earlier, and connected to the familiar patterns of residential racial homogeneity still seen in American communities today.

Continuing in the same vein as Du Bois, and Drake and Cayton, Kenneth Clark's *Dark Ghetto*, a study of Harlem in the 1960s, starts from the inescapable fact that Harlem is a ghetto, a racially segregated district of New York City. In 1960, one-third of black people lived in districts that were more than 90% black. But within the ghettos, the concentrations of black people were particularly high. Harlem in 1960 was 98% black, the Brooklyn ghetto was 96% black, and the Queens ghetto, 94% black.[71] Clark highlights Harlem's ugliness – its dirt, filth and neglect. There was no museum, art gallery, art school or theatre, and only five small libraries, but Harlem contained hundreds of bars, churches, and scores of fortune tellers. 'Everywhere there are signs of fantasy, decay, abandonment and defeat', he tells readers.[72]

Clark noted that the rents and profits from housing in Harlem, as in other black ghettos, were high, and that largely white landlords deliberately crowded as many people as possible into housing units to increase profits.[73] The effects of overcrowding – inadequate ventilation increased risks of airborne transmitted diseases, respiratory conditions and gastro-enteric conditions, as well as accidents and fires – were also common. The infant mortality rate for Harlem was double that for New York City. There is little to choose between Clark's descriptions of black Harlem in the 1960s and Du Bois' black Philadelphia some sixty years earlier. With only one in seven adults employed in Harlem, the unemployment rate was double that for the city. Those who did have jobs were relegated to the lowest-status and most menial jobs.[74] Clark found that the experience of being denied jobs because of skin colour, despite it being illegal, was very common and extended to employment agencies. Harlem residents reported to Clark the regular experience of having their applications discarded, and being made to wait for hours in employment offices. All of this took a huge toll on family life, with massive numbers of family break-ups occurring, and ensuing impacts on adolescent crime, delinquency and drug use.

The studies mentioned are part of a long line of scholarship on the phenomenon of the black ghetto, and these emphasize that the Federal government instigated the segregated residential patterns. In turn, these served as the basis for reducing the life chances and rights of African-Americans. Across the USA, city governments and private real estate and housing associations went to great lengths to ensure that African-Americans were effectively quarantined in separate residential districts, and that white people would be as insulated – preferably, in some cities, by actual physical barriers – from interacting with black people.[75] The historical differentiation and outright denial of rights to black people is the backdrop for similar exercises of hierarchically structured human rights in the United States. One illustration of this is seen in the policing of black people.

## African-Americans and Criminal Justice

Whereas arbitrary justice, including summary executions, was practised on slave plantations, it was permissible because plantations could operate subject principally to codes formulated by master enslavers. Importantly, such gross injustice could stand because the guarantees of the 5th and 6th Amendments to the Constitution for due process of law, speedy, public trials and impartial juries of peers did not apply to enslaved people as they were property rather than citizens. Even the 14th Amendment introduced after abolition never applied to African-Americans equally. The racial codes of justice initiated by enslavement carried forward in the implementation and enforcement of rights into the present. In *The Collapse of American Criminal Justice*, William Stuntz called attention to the persistently biased implementation of criminal justice by police and judges. All implementation of law and the recognition of rights require discretion, and, as Stuntz notes, 'discretionary justice too often amounts to discriminatory justice'.[76] Consequently, in major cities in recent times, about 80 per cent of young African-American males have criminal records; 1 in every 15 black males aged 18 or older is incarcerated (as against 1 in 36 Hispanics, and 1 in 106 whites).[77] African-Americans are incarcerated at almost six times the white rate according to Sentencing Project.[78]

Black incarceration is in part due to zealous enforcement through the 'War on Drugs' which began in the 1980s and carries with it the enforcement of mandatory jail sentences, directives to imprison offenders for 85 per cent of their sentences, and the 'three strikes' laws which impose lengthy prison sentences for cases where the offender has two previous felonies. Black Americans comprise 28 per cent of those with two felonies.[79] Over the course of a lifetime, 1 in 3 black men will be imprisoned, compared to 1 in 17 white men; 1 in 18 black women will be incarcerated, compared to 1 in 111 white women.[80] Most disturbing is the racial imbalance in the death penalty, which represents a continuity from the eighteenth century in which black people were more likely to receive capital punishment and to be sentenced to more severe forms of it and for more categories of crimes than whites.[81] Evidence also shows that the highest likelihood of receiving the death penalty is in situations where the victim of a capital crime is white and the perpetrator African-American.[82] Indicating how sensitive this evidence is to some US authorities, the North Carolina legislature, which in 2009 became the only state to have enacted legislation to allow appeals against the death penalty (but not the conviction) based on racial-disparity evidence and jury selection, repealed its Racial Justice Act after less than four years.[83] Reviewing the extensive evidence of persistent, and often widening, racial disparities in criminal justice, Flynn and her colleagues remark: 'at every stage of the criminal justice system, the rules are stacked against black Americans, making it more likely they will come in contact with law enforcement in the first place and essentially guaranteeing that when they do, they will be treated more harshly than whites'.[84]

While there have been many instances in which police used excessive force resulting in killing people, the fatal shooting of Michael Brown, an unarmed black teenager in 2014 in Ferguson, Missouri, resulted in renewed public and media outcry about police behaviour itself. Zimring argues that this was because of its typicality, and that it raised the issue from being purely about police conduct to civil rights.[85] Because of the unreliability of official statistics, this coincided with attempts to document independently both the extent of the police killings and their racial character. Both the *Guardian* and the *Washington Post* did this through several online techniques, such as searches of local newspapers and news sources. The *Guardian* found that 26.1% of the fatalities from police patrol and service calls in the first six months of 2015 were African-American, and that they accounted for 48.4% and 45%, respectively, of the Taser deaths and deaths in police custody.[86] African-Americans comprised 12.2% of the US population in 2015, so their over-representation among those to have been killed by police is two to three times higher than their proportions of the population.

Since the death of Michael Brown, many others have followed. Eric Garner, a 43-year-old African-American father of six in New York City, was killed by a police officer while being placed in a chokehold, in the course of being arrested for selling single cigarettes on which no duty had been paid. His last words, 'I can't breathe', repeated eleven times, were filmed by bystanders. When an officer at the scene dispatched the news that Garner would probably be dead on arrival to the police commander at Staten Island, the lieutenant answered, 'Not a big deal', adding that it was lawful because it was in the course of the arrest. Trump administration Attorney General William Barr ordered the dropping of a civil rights charge against the officer whose chokehold killed Garner.[87]

In North Charleston, South Carolina, on 4 April 2015:

> A video shows an apparently unarmed 50-year-old black man, Walter
> L. Scott, running away from an officer after an incident during a traffic
> stop in North Charleston, S.C.
>     The officer, Michael T. Slager, fires his weapon eight times, striking
> Scott in the back, upper buttocks and ear.[88]

The officer has since been indicted for murder. A week later in Baltimore, the National Guard were called to quell civil disturbances, as had also been the case in Ferguson. Protests were mounted to contest the killing of 25-year-old Freddie Gray, who 'was chased and restrained by police officers, and suffered a spine injury, which later killed him, in their custody. The police say they have no evidence that their officers used force. A lawyer for Mr. Gray's family accuses the department of a cover-up, and on Tuesday the Justice Department opened a civil rights inquiry into his death.'[89] The police officers involved were exonerated in 2017.

Since these police killings, many more have followed and the circumstances include '"a senseless, asinine shooting" of an unarmed man during a minor traffic stop',[90] and the execution-style shooting of 32-year-old Philando Castile in his car. Castile's girlfriend Diamond Reynolds filmed the aftermath on Facebook live with her 4-year-old daughter in the backseat.[91] The officer was charged with manslaughter, but not convicted. Testimony to the suffering and injustice of this police killing, as well as the inability of black people to be heard within systems of rights and criminal justice, was rendered by artist Luke Willis Thompson, who won the 2018 Deutsche Börse photography prize for four short films of Diamond speaking to herself. The audience can see Diamond's anguish and her lips move, but there is no sound except the whirring of a film reel. Thompson was also nominated for the 2018 Turner Prize for this work.

The killing of 12-year-old Tamir Rice, who was playing with a pellet gun in a Cleveland park, predated the killing of Michael Brown. The trial of the police officer resulted in another exoneration. The *New York Times* reported it as follows:

> A grand jury declined on Monday to charge a Cleveland patrolman
> who fatally shot a 12-year-old boy holding a pellet gun, capping more
> than a year of investigation into a case that added to national outrage
> over white officers killing African-Americans. In announcing the
> decision, Timothy J. McGinty, the Cuyahoga County prosecutor, said
> he had recommended that the grand jurors not bring charges in the
> killing of the boy, Tamir Rice, who was playing with the gun outside
> a recreation center in November 2014.[92]

In early 2019, two other white police officers were cleared of charges of murdering black men. Officer Betty Shelby shot and killed Terrence Crutcher in Tulsa, Oklahoma, in 2016. A video recording of the shooting showed Crutcher with both hands in the air when he was shot.[93] Two officers who shot and killed 22-year-old Stephon Clark in his grand-mother's backyard in Sacramento were relieved of charges. The shooting of Clark continued after the victim had fallen to the ground from the earlier bullets.[94]

In 2015, the *New York Times* reported that Michael Brown's hometown of Ferguson was almost exclusively reserved for black people, who, because of their poverty, were restricted to government-subsidized Section 8 housing, and effectively locked out of more diverse and prosperous areas of St Louis:

> Such is the case in Ferguson. The part where Mr. Brown died is a predominantly black east side neighborhood where residents have complained of police harassment and high crime in a cluster of apart-ments that stretches into the census tract with the most Section 8 renters in Missouri. Life is much different just two miles away in the city's amenity-filled central business district, surrounded by pockets of predominantly white, affluent neighborhoods with sturdy brick and clapboard homes.[95]

Barabaran points out that not only is Ferguson one of the most segregated cities in the USA, but more than 20 per cent of the population live under the poverty line, the schools are almost entirely segregated, and 26 per cent of the black population is unemployed. She argues that the inter-generational lack of wealth or assets is the context for segregation and crime.[96] Similarly, North Charleston, where Walter Scott was shot and killed, is 'South Carolina's third-largest city, with a population of about 100,000. African-Americans make up about 47 percent of residents, and whites account for about 37 percent. The Police Department is about 80 percent white.'[97]

Police targeting of black people is bound up with historical adversities that put African-Americans in places in which crime is likely to occur, and indeed where crime is a viable option of survival. The fact that police treat black people differently follows both from perpetual lack of access to human rights, including rights to life, in these rough urban locations, and from stereotypes of black people linking them to criminality. At the end of Attica Locke's recent novel *Bluebird, Bluebird*, about a somewhat troubled black police detective investigating a double murder in a small town in east Texas, the protagonist unveils a web of racial violence and stigmatized inter-racial love. So conflicted was the detective about his role as a law enforcer that 'he got confused sometimes, on which side of the law he belonged, couldn't always remember when it was safe for a black man to follow the rules'.[98] Obeying the law in some instances can simply lead to suspicion, racial profiling, punishment and sometimes death for uncommitted crimes, as in the case of the 4,700 people murdered by lynch mobs, where 99 per cent of the perpetrators went unpunished,[99] or even the victims of police pistols over the last five years or so. Similarly, 'for black folks, injustice came from both sides of the law, a double-edged sword of heartache and pain', as the narrator of *Bluebird, Bluebird* tells readers: 'for every story about a black mother, sister, wife, husband, father or brother crying over a man who was locked up for something he didn't do, there was a black mother, sister, wife, husband, father or brother crying over the murder of a loved one for which *no one* has been locked up.'[100] In December 2018, the Senate passed a bill to make lynching a crime for the first time in US history. This comes a little less than a century after the highpoint in lynchings of African-Americans.

The experiences so vividly narrated by Attica Locke and numerous other writers, journalists, artists and social scientists illustrate the structural nature of the denial of human rights to black people. In 2016, when the UN Special Rapporteur on the rights to freedom of peaceful assembly visited the USA, he discovered that, although his mission was not focused on race, he could not ignore it as a huge factor in violations of the enjoyment of the rights to freedom of peaceful assembly and of association. The vast numbers of African-Americans in prison and denied the vote, and for whom peaceful assembly and protest are heavily compromised, are indicative of the histories that I have briefly traced back to slavery. As the Special Rapporteur put it:

> An aggressive emphasis on street-level 'law and order' (or 'broken windows' approach) policing combined with wide police discretion means that African-Americans are subjected to systematic police harassment – and sometimes much worse – often for doing nothing more than walking down the street or gathering in a group. Convictions and incarcerations dramatically increased once the 'War on Drugs' was set in motion, without a corresponding increase in drug use.[101]

## Voter Suppression

If African-Americans feel that their human rights have been violated, the ballot box has not been there to change much. The democratic legitimacy of the American state and the human right to participate in open elections as enshrined in the UDHR were not meaningfully addressed until 1965 when the Voting Rights Act was passed. Despite a brief period after the Civil War in which black people had few obstacles to political participation, the post-slavery era up to today has been characterized by suppression of black people's rights to participate in electing the leaders under whom democracy supposedly functions. As is well known, poll tax requirements and literacy tests implemented in many states prevented all poor and illiterate people from voting, but disproportionate among these were African-Americans, who had been banned from reading under slavery, and had started their economic lives after slavery with virtually nothing. Criminal disenfranchisement also disproportionately affected black people, and this continues today, with more than half of those disenfranchised through incarceration being African-American.[102]

The 1965 Voting Rights Act was designed to eliminate the structural barriers to black people exercising the franchise that so many state legislatures had put into effect. One vital element of it was Section 5, requiring that states with a history of discrimination had to submit any changes to election procedures, and hence voting rights, to the Justice Department. Even after the Act, some Southern states were notorious for suppressing the black vote and submitted numerous discriminatory changes. Nevertheless, it has been estimated that the Act prevented over a thousand attempts to change local laws that would have discriminated against black people.[103] This notwithstanding, in 2013 the Supreme Court decided, in *Shelby County* v. *Holder*, to eliminate the Voting Rights Act's 'preclearance' process from Section 5 of the 1965 Act. This opened the door for procedures such as identification laws and disenfranchisement through incarceration, which are more likely to stop poor people and African-Americans from registering to vote. Writing for the Court's 5–4 majority, Chief Justice John Roberts said, 'Things have changed in the South.'[104] This has opened the door for a new era of voter suppression.

The Brennan Center for Justice identified fifteen states that developed new voting restrictions for the 2016 election.[105] President Trump's former Attorney General, Alabama Senator Jeff Sessions, was one of the main architects of voter suppression in his state and an enthusiastic supporter of *Shelby*.[106] He defended voter ID laws that have been shown to discriminate against black voters, and prosecuted black community leaders for voter registration drives on the basis that they were advising people on how to vote. ID laws are more likely to disenfranchise poor people, and African-Americans are a high proportion of poor people who may not have the right kind of ID. Flynn et al. cite evidence showing that ID laws substantially increase the gap in voter turnout between white and black people.[107] According to the Sentencing Project, 6.1 million Americans were denied the vote in the 2016 election because they had committed a felony, and more than 1 in 5 African-Americans were disenfranchised in four Southern states.[108]

Another tactic to reduce the impact of the black vote has been through Republican state legislatures gerrymandering districts to ensure that Democratic votes – again, those disproportionately cast by African-Americans – are neutralized by complex geographical districting. Partisan political gerrymandering was defended and upheld as beyond judicial comment in the consolidated Supreme Court cases of *Rucho* v. *Common Cause*, and *Lamone* v. *Benisek*, in 2019. In North Carolina, where Federal judges ruled that the state's electoral districts were gerrymandered in favour of Republicans and had to be altered, ten of the thirteen districts had Republican victories for House of Representative seats despite the state being evenly divided between registered voters in the two major parties.[109] As reported in *Nature*, mathematicians using algorithms to generate possible district maps have demonstrated that only a tiny fraction of the thousand possibilities would have generated the Republican majorities that the Republican-drawn boundaries delivered in the 2016 North Carolina state assembly elections.[110] This means that all black people, not simply those incarcerated in the racialized prison system, are affected by rules and manipulations of the electoral system designed to disenfranchise them.

## Racial Rules and Demography

Writing shortly after the 2016 US election, Toni Morrison portrayed Obama's successor's supporters as being motivated not only by feelings of white emasculation, but by perceptions of being eclipsed by people of colour. Before running for office, Donald Trump had publicly challenged Obama's legitimacy as an American, and presented himself as aggressively preventing any further erosion of white privilege, through both his hostility to civil rights and racial abuse of Mexicans. 'Under slave laws, the necessity for color rankings was obvious', Morrison writes: 'but in America today, post-civil-rights legislation, white people's conviction of their natural superiority is being lost. There are "people of color" everywhere, threatening to erase this long-understood definition of America. And what then? Another black President? A predominantly black Senate? Three black Supreme Court Justices? The threat is frightening.'[111] Despite the persistence of ethnic differences in access to and recognition of rights, Morrison senses that the fears evoked in *The Birth of a Nation* a century earlier have energetically resurfaced.

While African-Americans do not account for a growing proportion of the US population, the white population is diminishing in several ways, in what is a rapidly expanding and more complex ethnic matrix. Whites comprise about two-thirds of the US population today, but this will dip to below 47 per cent by 2050.[112] Another change is that far fewer people are identifying themselves with any one ethnic or racial group. One in seven new marriages is between people of different ethnic/racial groups.[113] This is a genuinely new trend and could signal the weakening of race as a concrete concept and organizing principle through which US institutions have allocated differential rights.

This means that the massive differences in the experiences of black and white people created by racialized rights and laws may be in jeopardy, but the accumulated effects of denial of rights cannot be erased by demographic changes. As Flynn and her colleagues show, racial rules have characterized US history, and the result is a chasm in life chances, with black women being particularly disadvantaged, in wealth, income, education, criminal justice, health and democratic participation. Disparities in wealth, for example, are getting wider. The net worth of a black household in 2011 was lower than it was in 1984, but the net worth of white households was 11 per cent higher over that time.[114] After reviewing the most recent literature on racial wealth gaps, they link this situation to slavery, arguing that 'the legacy of this expropriation of wages, which would have served as an asset-building platform that would have compounded over time, certainly explains some percentage of the racial wealth gap'.[115] By the same token, whites have been massively advantaged by slavery, and this provided a platform for subsequent wealth accumulation. Financial houses in New York, Paris and London, including names such as Baring, Brown and Rothschild, owe their transition to modern investment capitalist operations to their interests in goods produced from American slave labour, such as cotton and tobacco.[116] Indeed, the wealth of numerous finance capitalists, including Lehmann Brothers, Aetna, JP MorganChase and Wachovia, originates from slave labour.[117]

As Trump's aggressively white nationalist ascension symbolizes, with shifting demographics, the continuation of white privilege may no longer be assured. In the past, even poor white Americans could benefit from the racial contract, but it is less clear that this can continue into a more ethnically complex era. But, in some places, such as east Texas – the setting for Attica Locke's *Bluebird, Bluebird* – racial rules may still apply to permissible conduct, but white folks' 'oppressive and intrusive gaze into every aspect of black life' may continue within this maelstrom of racial order. Trump's 2016 victory and his public outcries over all adversities that befall him may be like Locke's whites who have 'a preoccupation that weakened a man looking anywhere but at himself'.[118] Indeed, this is the inheritance of colonialism and slavery, systems that made those who dominate so self-assured that they looked everywhere but at themselves. They started off creating a vast empire from the control and labour of black people, and ended up shooting, imprisoning and disenfranchising their descendants. All along, the US authorities exclaimed commitment to equality, democracy and human rights. The constant denial of the human rights of black people in the USA, from slavery to the contemporary era of mass incarceration and voter suppression, signals the durable qualities of differential human rights.

# 4

# The Less Than Human

'Are there any witnesses?'
'Yes five, two men and three Arabs.'
Or again,
'It was an Arab but dressed like a person.'

Pierre Nora[1]

## People But Not People

Arabs were not people. Using observations made by fellow historian
Pierre Nora, Alastair Horne illustrates responses to a judge's request for
evidence in court in twentieth-century French Algeria. Horne summarizes the French settler or *pied noir* view as one of indifference borne of
deep convictions of cultural and racial superiority. Indifference is echoed
in Kamel Daoud's *The Meursault Investigation*, a retelling of Albert
Camus' *The Stranger* from the point of view of Harun, Daoud's fictional
brother of 'the Arab' whom Camus' protagonist murders on the beach
midway through *The Stranger*. Enmeshed in the torpor and despair that
followed colonialism, Harun constantly dialogues with Camus, berating
the famous writer for making his brother anonymous. The replicability
of 'the Arab' is part of the cascade of anonymity that marked colonial
subjects as simply part of France's real estate inheritance.[2] Harun thinks
that the writer 'could have called him "2 p.m." like that other writer
who called his black man "Friday"'.[3] According to the narrator, the
word 'Arab' appears twenty-five times in *The Stranger*, but there is not

a single named person attached to that epithet.[4] Throughout, Harun remarks on Camus' obsession with the internal vanities of Meursault and the 'legendary indifference … and chilliness in a country flooded with sunlight and covered with fig trees'.[5] Camus mirrors the colonist, 'giving names to whatever he appropriates and taking them away from whatever makes him feel uncomfortable'.[6] Indeed, the very anonymity of 'the Arab' is a metaphor for a colonial process that makes subjects and their ways of life uniform, and therefore insignificant.

Camus, hailing from a working-class *pied noir* home headed by his deaf and illiterate mother, was of course sensitive to the cruelties of colonial Algeria, but stopped short of supporting the decolonization movement. Part of this had to do with the use of terror by the National Liberation Front (FLN), the main anti-colonial political movement. But the anonymity of Camus' 'Arab' betrays a parallel indifference that Ann Laura Stoler calls colonial aphasia,[7] common to prominent French intellectuals, writers, film makers and anthropologists who were born in Algeria or spent significant amounts of time there. These individuals, and by implication the wider French public, became unable to connect words with events, so that forms of commentary and analysis of colonialism in France may have admitted some specific French faults, but failed to situate these within the larger colonial enterprise embarked upon by the nation itself. For example, regarding anthropologists, Stoler comments: 'These scholars and others were outspoken in denouncing the value of race as a scientific category, but the colonial institutions and practices that eviscerated the social lives and economic prospects of French colonial subjects were rarely registered as core features of their analysis.'[8] The colonization of Algeria shows dehumanization of subject peoples could be propelled by the very forces of self-belief that derive from Enlightenment and Republican ideas stressing human rights.

One of the first commentaries on how best to colonize Algeria was by Alexis de Tocqueville. He believed that 'modernization' was inevitable and that, over time, societies would change from being hierarchical and tradition-bound to being open and democratic. The democratic society Tocqueville had perceived in the USA provided a model that he thought would be followed by Europe. His *Democracy in America*, and his comments on the colonization of Algeria, were the products of travel and direct sociological observation some ten years apart. While his remarks on the USA were more conceptual and contained a certain personal distance, those on Algeria were closer to works of nationalist advocacy. Tocqueville had earlier contemplated settling in Algeria, and obviously wished that this colony would be a place where a refined but effective French model of settler colonialism could be built, thereby avoiding the brutalizing aspects of American democracy, tied up as it was with enslavement and dispossession. In the early period of French colonization, he made two journeys to Algeria, in 1841 and 1846. The frontier spirit, which he had already seen in the USA, had made Muslim society far more 'disorganized, ignorant and barbarous than ever it was before it knew us'.[9]

But Tocqueville was more critical of methods of colonization than of colonization itself, which he believed was a step towards modernization of the peoples of North Africa. The task was to colonize as humanely as possible. In the reports on Algeria, Tocqueville attempts to reconcile what he depicts as the democratizing ideals of French occupation with the differing interests of the settler and indigenous Muslim populations. He made several suggestions as to how colonization could be most effective, stipulating that the use of force should always be preserved. At times, Tocqueville's prescriptions border on the Machiavellian, treating Natives as characterless objects of rule and transformation. The extension of rights, albeit differential ones, is implemented through the initial use of violence, a fact that Tocqueville readily acknowledged. Following this, Tocqueville maintains, in his 'Second Letter on Algeria' in 1837, three principles. The first was that his government should not have destroyed the existing institutions of state, bureaucracy and social organization of the occupied population. Rather than lighting their pipes with administrative records left by the vanquished Ottomans,[10] these should have been carefully studied, analysed and commandeered. In Tocqueville's calculations, it was important 'for a time' even to have 'bent to their ways',[11] and it was vital to avoid creating what did not exist in the local cultures, but to use their norms for French purposes. 'We must give up that taste for uniformity that torments us', he tells his French readers.[12] This benign version of colonialism was also shared by Albert Camus who, a century later, in his documentation of the famine in the Kabylia mountainous area east of Algiers, would advocate French assistance in helping preserve distinctive cultures. Instead of incorporating the local within their authority, he believed, the French had become 'anxious conquerors'.[13]

The maintaining of some indigenous cultural distinctiveness under colonial control anticipates 'indirect rule'. This was a technique used by the British in Africa to enable natives of occupied territories to govern through political institutions and forms of authority that might be indigenous to some extent, but which were under the ultimate authority of the colonizers. If local institutions were all destroyed, as Tocqueville feared they might be in Algeria, only total anarchy would result. Various tribal groups would begin to fight each other, brigandage and crime would explode, and confusion reign. A 'general law of humanity' is that 'people sometimes submit to humiliation, to tyranny, to conquest, but they never endure anarchy for long'.[14] Although Tocqueville was an advocate of the idea of progress, he believed that it was not always wise to implement policies to expedite the modernization of non-European peoples. This was the problem Tocqueville observed with the westward expansion of the Europeans in North America. Federal US policies had been too blunt and had resulted in carnage of American Indians, and their declines into alcoholism and community destabilization had sullied the name of progress.

Secondly, while warfare and violent conquest are to Tocqueville often necessary, these are not sufficient. Conquering a nation is not the same as governing one. Force is needed, but it should be moderate. There was always, however, a problem with controlling nomadic or migratory populations in unfamiliar territories. Instead of force, which would be difficult to unleash upon people who move around a lot and, like the Berbers (known as Kabyles in colonial society and, to a large portion of them, by their indigenous name, Amazigh), live in the mountain regions, Tocqueville's answer was to unify and centralize them in towns, but not in sufficient numbers for them to take up arms against the French. Urbanization, which would have been a vast feat of social engineering, however, was never realized in practice. Nevertheless, in the countryside, the introduction of French farming techniques, the building of roads and city infrastructure and ports, and the provision of French education were all part of efforts to instill in the indigenous populations the notion of the superiority of the colonizers.

The use of technologies as techniques of persuasion over occupied peoples has always been vital to colonialism, as Aimé Césaire and Frantz Fanon reaffirmed in the twentieth century. Visible domination of nature was the French response to the topographical challenges. But the most difficult practical problem was the Sahara. How does one colonize vast numbers of people in an area larger than Europe that contains desert, dunes a few precipitous mountain ranges, sizzling hot daytime temperatures and below-freezing nights? Nineteenth-century French plans for a Trans-Saharan railway – which was of great symbolic value as a feat of nation-building – and an inland sea created from canals dug from the Mediterranean were attempted but failed. The French never defeated the Tuareg nomads of the Sahara, numerous lives were lost, missionaries made no headway in converting Muslims, and vast numbers of camels and soldiers died in massively foolish expeditions across the Sahara.[15]

Thirdly, Tocqueville advocated the use of commerce, trade and goods to exert leverage over the Native population. By exploiting the needs and wants of those whose lands they occupied, the French could make local populations dependent and bring them under French control. As well as commerce, Tocqueville advocated the use of knowledge to induce curiosity in Algerians regarding the culture brought by the French. This would help to 'force these people to incorporate themselves with us,'[16] as well as cultivating desires for liberty, the rights of the individual and respect for private property.[17] In turn, these would help dissolve traditional cultural habits, and project Algerians along the same modernizing paths as the French. This summary cannot do justice to Tocqueville's manifold observations on the colonization of Algeria, but rather it underlines some of the ways in which an influential liberal advocate of the colonization of Algeria conceived of how a subject population could become objects of administration, and how their rights to their lands, culture and religion could necessarily be substituted for rights under colonial dominion in a process of inevitable modernization.

As an alternative to brute force, a subtler violence that serves to legitimate itself and to undermine indigenous culture was basically what Tocqueville advocated. Actions to effect this were put forward at the outset of France's 130-year occupancy of Algeria. Expensive schools were built, French was imposed as the first language, and the mother tongue of nine-tenths of the population became an alien language. Many history books began, 'Our ancestors the Gauls ...'.[18] Schools were prerequisites not only for assimilation, but for externally defined progress. Many in the French authorities saw Islam as a retardant, and consequently there were many attempts to de-Islamicize the population, showing that achieving 'civilization' and, by extension, human rights required thorough cultural transformation. Yet, even here the French only succeeded in formally educating about 15 per cent of Algerian children during their occupation. This was as a result of gross underestimates of the demographics, but also due to massively favouring *pied noir* children in the school system.[19]

The attempted replacement of local culture was fortified by French contributions to theories of race, including those of Tocqueville's young assistant, Arthur de Gobineau. Throughout the nineteenth century, the position that France had a duty to educate, develop and uplift colonized people was expressed through the *mission civilisatrice*, a narrative often drawing on comparisons with Pax Romana. To facilitate the inculcation of civilization, as indeed Tocqueville and some colonial administrators had argued, openness to intermarriage in the early years of colonization was believed to be helpful.[20] At the turn of the twentieth century, intermarriage as a goal was dropped as a growing corps of scientists and doctors were theorizing an unbridgeable biological gulf between Europeans and Africans. The *mission* then toughened into scientific racism, which held that assimilation had to yield to mere association.

By the 1950s, this had morphed again, this time into a doctrine of integration, articulated by many in the French government, including the last Governor General of Algeria, the anthropologist Jacques Soustelle. Integration assumed French cultural superiority and retained the anthropological doctrine of cultural evolutionism which placed Muslims as progressing at a slower rate than Europeans.[21] But, instead of translating this into a justification for the exploitation of the inferior, Soustelle maintained, in what Le Sueur calls a 'separate but equal' doctrine,[22] that all ethnicities in Algeria were equal, but *only* as French citizens. Predictably in colonial circumstances, this approach was haphazard in its implementation, as Lorcin observes.[23] The French decision to accompany integration with dispossessing the Amazigh of their land stoked resistance, and this has affected later ethnic conflict and associated violence in Algeria.

The simple assertion of equality inherent in the integration approach is tacitly conditional on a racial contract. The rights of the occupied population are those that can be recognized only insofar as they recognize themselves as French and bound by the French state. The colonized peoples in Algeria, however, were not solely 'Arab', but from ethnic and national groups such as Imazighen (the plural of 'Amazigh'), Tuareg, Jews, Turks and others that all became folded into one colonial polity, despite the fact that there were contrasting and overlapping colonial narratives about different groups. Highly significant in all this was the 'Kabyle Myth' expertly dissected by Patricia Lorcin. This refers to French social representations that evaluated Imazighen positively, and Arabs negatively. Because of perceptions of their adherence to private property, less pious version of Islam, and dynamic governing institutions, the Imazighen were thought to be closer to 'civilization', and hence more amenable to assimilation and integration. Indeed, Tocqueville had made this observation during his trips to Algeria at the outset of colonization. Arabs, by contrast, were represented as almost synonymous with Islam, and by nature impetuous and undemocratic. The Kabyle Myth and associated racial metaphors were ideologically instrumental to colonialism and arose 'out of the need to maintain dominance without perpetual recourse to force'.[24] Excessive violence was indeed a concern, since some military officers were openly advocating extermination of Arabs, or at least their removal to the Sahara.[25]

## Resistance

France invaded the territories now within the borders of Algeria in 1830, allegedly on the pretext that the Dey, or Governor of Algeria, had hit the French Consul-General with a fly swatter. After a period of military offensives, involving 108,000 men at its peak, effective French control was realized by 1847.[26] The Arab city of Algiers was bombarded, and French marines occupied its port and other coastal towns. At the time, it was part of the Ottoman Empire, but Arab, Amazigh and Tuareg independence had not been significantly challenged by the Ottomans, in part because of strong communal ties and cultural continuity. Imazighen occupancy of North Africa can be traced back before 4000 BCE.[27] Before the French, what is now Algeria was subject to Roman, Vandal and Byzantine periods, with the introduction of Christianity, and an Arab invasion followed by the Ottoman Turks.

One of France's first acts was to transform the Ketchwa Mosque in Algiers into a church. Muslim feast days were no longer recognized as legal holidays, and farmland was confiscated and handed over to French colonists.[28] French names were given to features of the landscape and villages. Many streets in Algiers were destroyed and replaced by French-style boulevards. The *pieds noirs* did not confine themselves to the coastal cities, but fanned out across Algeria to farm the most fertile lands. They were not shy of employing violence to take possession of indigenous lands, and this eventually led to reprisals and the need for military protection. In a revolt against French forces in 1847, about 800 Algerians were killed, summary executions were held in public squares, decapitated heads were mounted on spikes in the town of Biskra, and skulls were sent to France. In 2011, thirty-seven of these skulls were discovered by an Algerian archaeologist, and are now subject to repatriation.[29] Out of a population of some 3 million, between 500,000 and 1 million Algerians died in the first three decades of French occupation, in various wars against local populations.[30]

In line with the vision of French Minister of War General Étienne Gérard that conquest should provide 'a spacious realm for our surplus population',[31] from the 1840s onwards, France encouraged rapid settlement of Algeria by its citizens. Municipal authorities across France sponsored the policy of 'assisted emigration' of beggars, criminals, the unemployed and the poor.[32] They came in steady streams so that, by the mid twentieth century, there were a million *pieds noirs*. Settlers were drawn from those needing employment and land in France, and government officials believed that they would contribute towards the production of valuable resources.[33] Laws were put into effect to permit land confiscation and the disbanding of the tribal affiliations.[34] As in other colonial territories in the nineteenth century, some of the infrastructure for colonization was provided through penal colonies containing political dissidents.[35] Just as Tocqueville suggested, the French attempted to amalgamate their own political instruments of power with traditional village organizations that had been emptied of power.[36] But trying to make Algerians culturally like the French did not work, primarily because so many Algerians rejected it, and, significantly, because Islam was such a strong barrier to assimilation. Algerians advocated equality, but not the homogeneity of the various citizenship initiatives imposed upon them.[37] That the methods of defining subject populations to themselves failed was not for want of trying.

Assimilation and integration may have had better success if economic prosperity comparable to that of the colonists and *pieds noirs* had accompanied colonization, but this was not the case. At the end of the 1930s, Albert Camus began writing about Kabylia, drawing attention to the suffering and famine in that area. In 1939, he estimated that '50 per cent of the population live on herbs and roots in between government handouts of grain'.[38] This was supplemented by the stems of thistles. Women, he reported, walked 40 to 50 kilometres to receive relief supplies of poor-quality grain, and many desperate people were denied such support because they had voted for the pro-independence Algerian People's Party. The famine of these years was an example of French mismanagement, which, Camus believed, would only embitter Algerians. Hunger was produced by the transfer of the most productive lands from Imazighen – and, elsewhere, Arabs – to French settlers. Consequently, resistance began to grow quickly from this time onwards, across the colony.

Resistance in Algeria highlighted the differential and inferior rights accorded to Algerians within the French order. Nationalist armed struggle against French colonialism came at the end of World War II. It coincided with a high point of humiliation of the Algerian people. Although many French people inside and outside the Vichy regime had collaborated in Nazi atrocities, North African soldiers had assisted the Allied cause to liberate France in the fight against fascism. Previously, hundreds of thousands had fought in the Franco-Prussian war, World War I and numerous other military campaigns going back to 1859.[39] The reward for those who had sacrificed at the end of World War II was for Algiers to be decorated with the tricolour flag.[40]

In 1945, demonstrations sparked off across the country, beginning in the town of Sétif. After police fired on protesters, they and settlers were attacked and about 100 killed. The response, known as the Sétif massacre, resulted in a conservative estimate of 6,000 Muslims killed.[41] By the time order was restored, 10,000 Algerians were dead, thousands through summary executions.[42] Lenze estimated that violence at Sétif and Guelma, where no settlers had been killed,[43] resulted in as many as 15,000 Muslims being killed.[44] The French brought in 10,000 troops to assist the police in operations to suppress protest and civil disorder. Torture and institutionalized sexual violence were used to deal with resistance to colonial rule. The killing of Algerians under interrogation was acknowledged by French military personnel such as Paul Aussaresses,[45] who was later recruited as a training officer by the US military. The police, army, judiciary and even the Catholic church collaborated in torture.[46] French authorities pursued a policy of collective responsibility by indiscriminately arresting anyone suspected of being associated with plotting against the colonists. There were several collective reprisals by Algerians, including the massacre of thirty-eight French civilians at Philippeville in 1956, when 'attackers went from house to house, mercilessly slaughtering all the occupants regardless of sex or age'. The reaction to this, according to a French soldier, was that 'our company commanders gave us the order to shoot every Arab we met'.[47] Much of this came to public attention in France through court cases such as those of young FLN activists Djamila Boupacha and Djamila Bouhired, which exposed torture and rape as methods of interrogation.[48]

By this time there were almost 2 million French settlers in Algeria and the colonial state had a huge stake in protecting them. Settlers had French citizenship, as did Algerian Jews, who after some debate came to be categorized as 'European' and treated similarly to settlers.[49] Muslims were considered a 'nationality' and initially banned from going to France, even though France had operated Algeria as a department of the state. One problem, however, was that many Muslims had fought for the French in the two World Wars and were part of the French security forces during the most intense periods of armed conflict leading up to independence. Reluctantly, these soldiers were allowed to travel to France, not as repatriates, but as male refugees, despite the fact that almost all had families.[50] *Pieds noirs*, on the other hand, were never prevented from settling in France and came as repatriated French families, even though many belonged to the far-right terrorist group, the Organisation Armée Secrète (OAS). Algerian Jews were also allowed to travel to France as if they were *pieds noirs*. Hence, France continued its policy of differential citizenship rights, even though these Algerians had made huge sacrifices to maintain the Algerian colony itself.

Before this, governance of Algeria overall was not through any democratic process recognizing human rights, but via imperial decree, although it later shifted to elected assemblies with differential representation and voting rights for settler and Muslim populations.[51] Under the Third Republic, the *Indigénat* code 'enabled the local administrator – acting as prosecutor and judge – to condemn subjects for a wide range of offenses' and 'left Muslim Algerians with few means to resist land-grabbing by European settlers or demands for forced labor'.[52] Although Algerians and French settlers were both considered citizens, the latter had rights that the former were denied.

Under continual international and domestic pressure over the carnage in Algeria in the late 1950s, France tried to grant Algeria limited independence. Importantly, this was to be a discrete self-governing entity separate from the Sahara, where natural resources such as oil, natural gas and minerals were located. The idea was to 'decolonize' the Sahara by separating it from Algeria and making it officially a separate department of France. The government also protected the colonial economic enterprises, such as rich farming settlements, vineyards (that offended the Muslim population) and manufacturing centres in the cities. But the uprisings continued as resistance turned to nationalism in the Algerian War of Independence from 1954 to 1962. Attempts by the UN to intervene failed. When UN Resolution 1514 (XV), following from the 1960 UN *Declaration on the Granting of Independence to Colonial Countries and Peoples*, came into effect, France argued that the UN standards did not apply because Algeria was simply a department of France. Thus, the French rejection of the standard that 'all peoples have the rights to self-determination'[53] amounts to an admission of a racial contract, since Algerians gave no consent to being absorbed by France.

The War of Independence began with the establishment of nationalist independence groups in 1954, with the FLN leading the way. Historians depict this as a genuine collectivist movement, but Muslim critics of the FLN were often dealt with brutally. Groups, families and suspected opponents, or collaborators with the French, were assassinated. At Mélouza, about 300 people were executed in 1957.[54] In this atmosphere of extreme violence, France sent hundreds of thousands of troops to respond to the uprisings and protect settlers (rather than the Muslim victims of the FLN), and it issued a state of emergency, suspending human rights and imposing exceptional measures.[55] Klose calls this a 'war without rules',[56] as the French joined the British in arguing for exceptions to the Geneva Convention in order to use poisonous gas, rubber bullets and other weapons to quell colonial unrest. In fact, the French here, and the British a few years earlier in Kenya, had already violated numerous parts of the 1949 Geneva Convention they had just endorsed, including the murder of prisoners.[57] In Paris, peaceful protests against the war in Algeria in 1961 lead to 200–300 deaths from police beatings, and the corpses of Algerian protesters were thrown into the River Seine by police and the secret anti-independence movement.[58] Like the details of British suppression of anti-colonial movements, this tragic story of state murder was also concealed.

Algeria finally gained independence in 1962. Estimates of the Muslim Algerian casualties of the War of Independence vary from 300,000 to 1.5 million, with many other people also disappeared. These fatalities were at the hands of both the French and the FLN, who may have killed as many as 140,000 Algerians. The French lost somewhere between 17,000 and 25,000, mostly soldiers, and 55,000 settlers died in this anti-colonial war of liberation.[59] Eventually, Algerians were granted a referendum, and they almost unanimously opted for independence. President General de Gaulle pronounced Algeria independent two days later, upon which almost all *pieds noirs* migrated to France. This had stark economic consequences for Algerians and led to 800,000 largely landless peasants migrating to Algerian cities, with some also finding ways to leave for France.[60]

The violence of the independence struggle continued, as many Algerians were killed after the French departed. This was in part because France would only accept as immigrants a fraction of those who had served in their forces and institutions. Consequently, Algerians who had worked in one way or another for the French colonial authorities were left defenceless. About 15,000 Algerians were rounded up and murdered in the most gruesome circumstances by the new Algerian police and militias soon after the French left.[61] The French enabled this by disarming Muslim policemen on departure.

## Objecthood

Gillo Pontecorvo's 1966 film *The Battle of Algiers* is a realist dramatization of the last days of the Algerian War of Independence, from the high point of violence in 1957 onwards. The film starts with a scene in which French soldiers torture a Muslim captive. He reveals the information needed to capture Ali La Pointe and other 'terrorists' resisting French occupation, and then he is dressed by them in French clothes. A smirking French soldier gives him a military cap which is awkwardly made to fit his head (see figure 4.1). In this act, the collaborator goes from an anonymous Arab, to a valuable source. His own crazed and fearful reaction to the awareness of what it means to wear the cap, and the violence he has been made to help the French unleash, is the last scene in which he appears. While Pontecorvo humanizes his characters, the depiction of the French struggle to retain control of Algiers is of a beleaguered settler population and an overstretched security apparatus. It includes scenes of massed ranks of Arabs, to which the informant presumably returns, although, as Harries suggests, such people were often executed after they had served their purpose.[62]

The film violated the Laval Decree of 1934, a censorship measure passed in France. The Decree was intended to control the content of African films and to minimize the creative roles played by Africans in film making. It was motivated by a determination to keep cinema from playing a meaningful role in inciting and spreading anti-colonial

**Figure 4.1** *Opening scene of* The Battle of Algiers *in which an Algerian prisoner who has divulged useful information after being tortured is fitted with a French military cap.*
*Source: Gillo Pontecorvo (director), 1966. Rizzoli, Rialto Pictures.*

opinions. Only in 1971 was *The Battle of Algiers* distributed in France, but this was short-lived. With public demonstrations against the film's release from repatriated *pieds noirs*, war veterans and right-wing activists, cinemas were attacked, and at one venue protesters destroyed the film with sulphuric acid. When it was finally brought back in 1981, 'it was received with general indifference'.[63]

But in this case, a case in which a Jewish Italian film director seemingly sides with those who rebelled against the French, to great international acclaim, indifference is leavened with anger. Perhaps indifference is anger, an anger borne of a sense of the ungratefulness of the rebelling Algerians, who in the film are depicted as wishing to be free from those who think of themselves as bringing civilization. Perhaps also there is a sense of embarrassing disorientation, the kind that flashes across the conscience when one is caught doing something one professes to abhor. The persistence of rebellion leads a perplexed *pied noir* in one of the many crowd scenes to exclaim 'What do you want?' The drumming, shouting and ululating women mean as much to the *pied noir* and French military as the vision of Africans as undecipherable madmen on the forested shores of the River Congo meant to Marlow in *Heart of Darkness*.[64] The French soldiers and settlers are still incredulous that these featureless subjects may prefer a Muslim Algeria to a French Algeria. In showing that drugs, alcohol and prostitution, as well as the sexualization of women, are unwanted influences from the colonizer, Pontecorvo suggests that there is reason to the collective wish for independence. It is about not only political and economic control, but the rejection of a Western culture shown to be destructive. A traditional Muslim wedding is, itself, 'an act of war'.

The struggle for independence is captured in *The Battle of Algiers* through depictions of the motivations and tactics of the FLN, the French authorities, and settlers, whom the authorities are, above all, protecting. Each side uses terror, but in several verbal exchanges, such as that between the liberation fighter Larbi Ben M'hidi and Mathieu, the French colonel supervising the 'sweeps' on the Muslim population of the city, Algerian terror is revealed to be a response to French military rule. In this and other scenes, Pontecorvo renders Algerian retribution and retaliation intelligible, since it is against brute repression. This includes electric shocks, waterboarding, and guillotining of resistance fighters and the forced extraction of confessions, the planting of bombs by police in residential areas, and the attempted control of the mass media and banning of strikes, which all undermine any commitment to human rights. Torture was the nearest that resistance fighters got to the 'fair trial' promised by Colonel Mathieu.

As Daulatzai perceptively observes, '"Battle of Algiers" serves as a diagnostic, a parable, even an allegory of the moment.'[65] It shows that the French were willing to tolerate what was deemed intolerable a decade earlier, to retain control. The achievement of *The Battle of Algiers* was to depict the mangled and hallucinatory world of colonialism. Terror had become a response to terror. The process of colonization cements the position of the colonist as a compromiser, as someone who ultimately depends on the institutionalization of differential human rights, and indifference towards those deemed inferior. Pontecorvo's construction of moral equivalence between the Algerian men and women carrying out bombings of civilians in the 'European quarter' with French acts of mass imprisonment of liberation fighters, torture and beheadings underscores the incoherence of liberal Republicanism.

Perhaps this explains the vacillations between the banning, destroying and indifference to the film in France, and the sixty-year wait for the French government to admit torture. This came only in 2018 with President Emmanuel Macron's carefully worded admission of the torture and murder of the young French mathematician Maurice Audin, who was taken away from his wife and three children by French paratroopers in 1957.[66] He was 'tortured at the hands of Lieutenant Andre Charbonnier, who was nicknamed "the doctor" because he liked to use a scalpel on his victims'.[67] Before this time, the French government had fabricated a story about the disappearance of Audin, who was of course only one of thousands who were executed or killed *en masse*, like the Algerian protesters in Paris in 1961. The apology, however, simply stands alone, and is not linked to any criminal indictment of perpetrators or an apology for France's crimes as demanded by the Algerian government. In September 2018, at the height of Macron's concerns about colonialism, Algerian President Abdelaziz Bouteflika called on France to seek a 'pardon from the Algerian nation'.[68]

## Dehumanization

Its violence, intensity and international visibility made Algeria a centre for narratives and counter-narratives on colonialism. The fact that colonialism was justified in part by asserting fundamental human differences between Europeans and others gave struggles such as that in Algeria a heavily sociological dimension. When colonial subjects rebelled as they did in Algeria and throughout the world in the 1950s and 1960s, and official violence was used to suppress the tangible threats to imposed rule, images of the animality or sub-human nature of the colonized were invoked. The widespread belief among the French that Algerians were not sensitive to pain in the same way as they were[69] was a way to legitimate violence as government policy. If those upon whom it was exercised were somehow more brutish, hardened and psychologically less sensitive, then, like kicking a dog, the full force of the actions carried out against them was attenuated.

More than anyone else, Frantz Fanon keenly observed and analysed perceptions and representations of non-European subject populations, and how these affected both colonized and colonizer. He was distinctive as a writer in his almost total immersion in the colonial world. Raised in Martinique, a French Caribbean colony, and educated as a doctor in France, Fanon then worked as a psychiatrist in French Algeria. In his most famous book, *The Wretched of the Earth*, which was perhaps the literary counterpart to *The Battle of Algiers*,[70] Fanon writes of colonialism in general, but his most vivid observations come from his experiences in Algeria, also described in *A Dying Colonialism*. Although Fanon cannot be treated as an impartial historian of the Algerian War of Independence, he is a key figure in the sociological interpretation of colonialism and its intimate association with European constructions of race. As such, he is also central to understanding the ongoing human rights implications of colonialism.

While in France, Fanon saw another side of colonialism as he mingled with African and other students from French colonies. Instead of being treated as intellectuals or 'apprentices', as he had expected from his observations about status in French culture, black students were treated as inferiors. The French working class hurled racist abuse at them, while the middle classes patronized them with a mixture of praise and surprise at any perceived achievements. To Fanon, French people seemed incapable of treating people from colonial territories as respected equals. Indeed, as we shall discuss in more depth below, even the *harkis* – auxiliary soldiers and other employees of the security forces who had risked their lives for France – found that they were unwanted there.

Between Martinique, France and Algeria, Fanon received a varied picture of colonialism. He was always an involved observer who carried the courage of his conviction. He resigned after three years' medical practice in Algeria, and in his resignation letter to the Resident Minister, Fanon says that he could no longer be a party to the 'systematized dehumanization' under colonial rule, and frankly tells the Minister that he agrees with the Algerian insurgents. The violent events, he reasons, 'are the logical consequence of an abortive attempt to decerebralize a people'.[71] This exercise, like enslavement in the Americas, could only ever have long-lasting effects. While Tocqueville had thought that only God would obliterate the traces of slavery, Fanon believed that 'an entire generation of Algerians, steeped in collective, gratuitous homicide with all the psychosomatic consequences this entails, would be France's human legacy in Algeria … and in France'.[72]

This decerebralization occurred through the effects of colonialism on the psyche of those who were turned into objects of control and transformation. 'I was an object in the midst of other objects … sealed into that crushing objecthood', Fanon tells readers in *Black Skin, White Masks*.[73] Reminiscent of the more general existential theories of fellow psychiatrist and contemporary R. D. Laing, Fanon's work focused on the divided nature of the black self, which he calls a 'third person consciousness'.[74] This is a 'direct result of colonialist subjugation'.[75] In Laing's existential view, there are two ways of looking at the self – from inside one's own person and culture, and from outside by imagining what others see and think of you.[76] White people in European, North American and colonial societies, such as Algeria, are necessarily less attentive to how others perceive them, but among black and colonized people, Fanon detects a constant vigilance. Selfhood becomes part of a never-ending comparison with those who have so authoritatively asserted not only their superiority, but the qualities in people and cultures needed to attain that superiority. This is intensified by the dismissal of indigenous cultures with the 'burial of its local cultural originality'.[77] It is not hard to see how the marginalization, and sometimes eradication, of local traditions and institutions would, as Fanon suggests, lead to an inferiority complex. The most fundamental aspects of people's lives – such as births, marriages, deaths and the transmission of knowledge to succeeding generations – are entrusted to colonizers.

Fanon observes that, to solidify colonial control, the colonizers developed a political language of inferiorization, a special vocabulary directed towards black and colonized peoples. The image of Africans in the colonial mind, he argues, is as children. For example, when addressing colonized peoples, the colonial official or settler attempts to 'talk down' or speak in pidgin forms of the master colonial language. Much of *Black Skin, White Masks* concerns how self-proclaimed European superiority is received by black people, including in intercultural or interracial romantic relationships, which Fanon believes are indicative of broader relationships. Colonial baggage is brought to such relationships, making it hard for them to survive without the black partners 'whitening' themselves. This is necessary to escape the burden of inferiority. Fanon contends that 'the black man' has no ontological resistance because many of the sources upon which African customs were based were erased, as they were seen to conflict with 'civilization'.[78] With the constant undermining and destruction of indigenous cultural resources, the resistance and agency of the colonized person is compromised. The fatal step for a black person in Fanon's eyes is to internalize the idea of white superiority, and the belief that one's history and culture are of no value – but he does not fault those black people who succumb. He simply advocates resistance to internalization, and in part this is what may have driven him to support the Algerians so unconditionally in the War of Independence.

*The Wretched of the Earth* is a complement to *Black Skin, White Masks* in that Fanon puts the psychology of colonialism firmly in a sociopolitical frame. Colonial society, as he observed and experienced it, is not rational, but fragmented and fractured. Its legitimacy is premised on dehumanizing the dominated population. As with the silent, nameless 'Arab' of Albert Camus' novel, a wilful and elaborately constructed ignorance of the colonized allows dehumanization to be achieved through failing to recognize the colonized person as a person. Fanon notes the zoological terminology often used to describe the colonized population. Seen in the police searches for FLN members in Pontecorvo's film, the *ratonnade* ('rat hunt') was in common parlance.

This imagery is repeated in literature set in colonial Algeria. For example, Yasmina Khadra's *The Angels Die* is about an Arab-Berber man called Turambo. Set between the two world wars, Turambo tries to beat the crushing poverty he was born into as he transits from being a shoeshine boy to working in a garage, and eventually on to an exhausted and brutalized boxer. When young Turambo ventures into the European quarter of Sidi Bel Abbes, a young French boy accuses him of a crime, although he has done nothing. A policeman is rapidly on the scene, beating him with a truncheon and calling him vermin. Deepening his non-human condition, he is instructed to 'go back to your kennel and stay there'.[79] Turambo valiantly but reluctantly tries to succeed by using his fists, strength and agility, but frequently ends up humiliated. He is always an object of some sort. The colonial world in both this novel and Fanon's works is a world of binaries – white/black, European/Native, advanced/primitive, developed/undeveloped – which is constantly reinforced in the language and administration of conquest. According to Fanon, 'Manicheeism goes to its logical conclusion and dehumanizes the native, or to speak plainly, it turns him into an animal. In fact, the terms the settler uses when he mentions the native are zoological terms. He speaks of the yellow man's reptilian motives, of the stink of the native quarter, of breeding swarms of foulness, of spawn of gesticulations.'[80]

In Fanon's view, the goal of this onslaught was the acceptance and internalization of the idea that colonial society was a superior and preferable way of living. 'In the colonial context', Fanon tells us, 'the settler only ends his work of breaking in the native when the latter admits loudly and intelligibly the supremacy of the white man's values'.[81] Once this occurs, colonizing becomes truly legitimate, because it has attained the 'consent' demanded of the social contract. This is, in part, because those who are accorded fewer, lesser or no rights, at some level, have been made to condone inequalities incumbent on their acknowledged inferiority. In Algeria, this was reinforced by the colonizer's more elaborate internal racial dichotomies, counterposing the good Amazigh and the bad Arab.[82]

## Women as a Colonial Bone of Contention

One means of 'breaking in' the Natives was to alter the role of women in Algerian society. If colonialism is to be effective, as Tocqueville had earlier hinted, colonized peoples must be made not only to see the superiority of the colonizer's ways of life, but to embrace them. Perhaps one of the most fundamental aspects of any society is the way in which gender operates, how men and women relate to each other, and what rights, obligations and duties each has, including the many overlaps there might be in such roles. One of the premises of this is that the traditions of dress, fashion and costume define a society's distinctiveness, and one of those in Algerian society is the wearing of the veil by women. Indeed, the veil is one of the signs of the distinctiveness of the Arab world. In Algeria, this is generally a white veil, which in his essay 'Unveiling Algeria', Fanon says was a 'bone of contention in a grandiose battle'.[83]

According to Fanon's observations, French plans to maintain control were focused upon dismantling the integrity and uniqueness of Arab society. It was, in effect, 'destroying the people's originality'.[84] The French did this by singling out women as channels for undermining social cohesion and making the population less capable of resistance and more receptive to becoming like the French. Hence, the veil was attacked as a symbol of 'sadism' and 'barbarism'. Through various discourses, the colonial institutions heaped judgements upon Arab society and Islam, and upon Algerian men for perpetuating the wearing of the veil and women for accepting it. The instilling of guilt was a major dynamic of these attacks. French social workers, charity workers and housewives descended into the 'Arab quarters' to assist.[85] This was expressed through military feminism, as Marnia Lazreg calls the policy whereby French armed forces attempted to spread a kind of European feminist ideology among Algerian women by constantly asserting that their roles in Muslim society were inferior to the roles French women attained.[86]

The French-controlled schools reinforced military feminism by teaching that the veil was inconsistent with democratic ideals. Teachers, as 'technicians for the advancement of retarded societies',[87] were to be engineers for cultural change. There were some 'successes', and some women were symbolically unveiled in French military-organized ceremonies before the international press.[88] Later, many of the same women, after being exposed to the 'liberation' touted by the French, placed the veil back on. To the Algerian woman, Fanon argued, this unveiling was a kind of rape. It was a parallel unveiling of her secrets and mystery, and it made her available for adventure and fantasy.[89] Literal rape was also a French tactic of colonial war. According to Lazreg, the French used it as a way of destabilizing the family, and, as well as violating women, it was designed to wound the dignity of Arab men and weaken resistance to colonialism.[90]

'The woman who sees without being seen frustrates the colonizer',[91] and one could add that it also upsets normative Western ways of seeing gender. The veiled woman is the opposite of the Western woman as depicted in John Berger's *Ways of Seeing*. Based on discussions of artistic and photographic representation in Western culture, Berger argues that women have been and remain objects of surveillance.[92] How a woman appears to men determines how she will be treated, so she must 'contain it and interiorize it'. According to Berger, to succeed or be considered worthy or successful in Western society, women need to turn themselves into objects – and most especially into an object of vision or sight.[93]

The 'emancipation' policies of the colonizers were not only attempts to make Algerian women similarly objects, but also a means of combatting the increasingly important roles women were playing in the revolutionary struggle. These were depicted in *The Battle of Algiers*, as well as memoirs such as that of Zohra Drif,[94] celebrated by that film. Women played very important roles in the planting of bombs, and in the logistical assistance of resistance fighters. Later, the revolutionary groups manipulated the veil as a means of struggle,[95] removing it and restoring it as a technique of camouflage. *The Battle of Algiers* depicts the flirtatiousness of French soldiers with unveiled Algerian women, but, as Khadra's novel shows, the French did not tolerate the reverse, as Turambo finds out when he goes to a dance with Irene, the daughter of the French boxing promoter. Before Irene is quizzed about Turambo's qualities as a lover, a *pied noir* partygoer addresses him in the third person: 'Arabs aren't allowed here.' He continues by making Turambo a genetic throwback that has 'only just got down from his tree'.[96] This is illustrative of the highly selective, gendered and sexualized French 'integration' policy of the time in which the novel is set.

## Nervous Conditions

The dangerous romantic involvement of the white woman with the black or Native man, under colonialism but also outside it, was, of course, of interest to Fanon. This was in part because it meant constantly struggling to withstand prejudice, but also the pressures to assume an identity one would normally shun. At the party in *The Angels Die*, Turambo is proffered wine several times, and courageously refrains. To refuse alcohol is a refusal to become an apprentice French person. For Fanon, the colonized person is not just a dominated person, but a person being told that they are or should be something other than what they thought they were: 'colonialism forces the people it dominates to ask themselves the question constantly: in reality who am I?'[97] This produces double consciousness: firstly, that one is a Native person with family, community, traditions and history; and secondly, in the Algerian context, that one is a fledgling French person whose qualities are to become a negation of their own histories and experiences. This contradiction can act as the context for high rates of social and psychological dysfunction, whose results Fanon saw in his work as a psychiatrist in Algeria. The nervous breakdowns, psychoses, alcoholism and violence he observed were mostly directly inwards or against other Algerians. When Algerians externalized their frustration towards the colonial source, this was often taken as symptomatic of pathology. 'They insult us and then they're surprised that we're hurt', Turambo's friend Sid in Khadra's novel tells him – 'as if we didn't have the right to an ounce of pride', he continues.[98]

But instead of seeing the distress in the colonized population as reactions to colonialism, liberal professionals saw only racial defects. Fanon quotes a 1950s French psychiatric textbook used in Algeria, in which the North African within its pages is 'essentially criminal, predatory, violent, impulsive, extreme, deceitful, persistently obstinate, mental puerility without the spirit of curiosity found in the Western child. He is insensible to shades of meaning, and Cartesianism and reason are foreign to him.'[99] Algerians are not possessed of rationality and conscience, and, by extension, are not constituted to experience feelings in the same way as Europeans. At a scientific level, the differences that French psychiatrists observed in Algerians were explained both culturally and biologically through notions of primitivity. Fanon quotes a psychiatrist from the World Health Organization who states that the African makes little use of the frontal lobes, and that the normal African is a 'lobotomized European'.[100]

France's appropriation of power and wealth reduced scores of Algerians to dependents who were forced to rely on colonizers for hand-outs of food and other necessities. As Fanon observes, this often turned them against each other as they competed for the favour of the colonial authorities: 'Every colony tends to turn into a huge farmyard, where the only law is the knife.'[101] Favoured Natives comprised a local collaborating elite operating as a buffer between the colonial authorities and the mass of the population. What outsiders see as internal factionalism and the fracturing of the local society is generated by the external manipulation and pressure from colonial authorities.

The result is a complex psychological double bind which Fanon discussed at some length in Black Skin, White Masks and The Wretched of the Earth. The double bind implies that, in forming their identities, the colonized, whether it be Algerians or Antilleans in Fanon's examples, must choose between their family and culture, which is associated in the colonizing society with the past, and European society, which is associated with the present and future. If the colonized person has a weak psychic structure, which is highly likely in the 'nervous condition' of colonialism, it can provoke guilt, neurosis and what psychiatrists see as mental illness. At this point, colonialism corrects the problems it creates. The victims it has spawned are offered aid – which is like someone administering the antidote to a person they had deliberately poisoned.

This nervous condition has been explored in the literature of writers from colonized territories in some depth. While Chinua Achebe's *Things Fall Apart* is the classic novel of the frictions and destabilization of Native societies under colonialism, Tsitsi Dangarembga's critically acclaimed *Nervous Conditions* takes its title from Fanon's words and illustrates how psychic and social fragmentation occur within an extended family in Rhodesia during the period of exclusive white-settler rule in the late 1960s. The success of the patriarch of the family, Babamukuru, was largely down to his application within the British educational system and his adoption of a European gendered disciplinarian approach ('Whatever he touched, he pushed') to Shona children at the local mission school. The teenage girl narrator, Tambu, although a beneficiary of her uncle Babamukuru, notes his fragility. His embrace of British manners separates him from her. He has been 'pushing up from under the weight of the white man' and become 'a deep valley cracked open'.[102] The family in the novel is a microcosm of the wider colonial society, split between good and bad Africans. In the end, some members of the family auto-colonize, and the adoption of a kind of *faux* Englishness sets them apart from their kin and community. As in other colonial tales, immersion into the language, assumptions and worldview of the colonizer is at first an opportunity, but works itself out as a loss of self and community, and often ends in attempted redemption through reconnection with the indigenous world.[103]

## Macron Tours Africa

Although sixty years in the past, formal colonialism still casts its shadow over French political and social life. Unlike most other elections in former colonial and settler-colonial states, the 2017 French election was notable in that prominent candidates addressed colonialism. The eventual winner Emmanuel Macron, François Fillon, a former Prime Minister and candidate, and the racist Marine Le Pen all mentioned French colonization of parts of Africa. Predictably, Le Pen stressed the positive nature of French colonialism in Algeria, Fillon argued that colonialism was motivated by the understandable desire to spread French culture, and Macron admitted that it was 'a war against humanity', but later claimed that his assertion was 'neither denial nor repentance'.[104] Reacting to nationalist criticism a few days later, Macron apologized, not to those against whom this war was waged, but to the *pieds noirs*.[105] Demonstrating Macron's extreme ambivalence about colonialism, when the South Pacific island colony of New Caledonia voted 56 per cent to 44 per cent to remain a colony of France, he asserted that the result was '"a sign of confidence in the Republic" and expressed his "pride that the majority of Caledonians chose France". All sides should "look to the future" knowing that "the sole victor is the peace process that New Caledonia has been undergoing for thirty years, it is the spirit of dialogue".'[106] The result mirrored the divisions on the island between French settlers and indigenous Kanak, and is a function of French suppression of the Kanak independence movement and support of the settlers on the island, which it annexed in 1853.

In the year he was elected, Macron toured North and West Africa, making speeches on the relationships between France and its former colonies. Instead of probing further into this 'war on humanity' on his tours, Macron omitted reference to it. In his orations and answers to questions, the war on humanity was consigned to the past, to which no reminders were necessary because it hampered focusing on the future. In Algeria, Macron responded to a young audience member who asked him about French colonization. 'You're 25?' the President said, 'but you haven't known colonisation! Why are you bothering me with this?'[107] By denying the questioner any legitimacy to her perceptions of the ongoing effects of colonialism, Macron's response updated Fanon's colonial psychiatry, situating the perception itself as invalid.

As if he needed to win an argument with imagined accusers, Macron was at great pains to clear France from any lingering impact on the many social, economic and human rights problems in Africa. One way to close off all speculations about the long-term effects of colonial occupation was first to rebuff the possibility of such effects, and then hammer home the point by asserting that the decolonized peoples are themselves responsible. Mixing patronization with censure at a G-20 summit in 2017, Macron asserted that 'Africa', as a kind of undifferentiated whole, suffered from 'civilisational problems'. He diagnosed the problems for the continent as entailing 'a more rigorous governance, a fight against corruption, a fight for good governance, a successful demographic transition when countries today have seven or eight children per woman'.[108] African problems, in his mind, were caused by long-standing deficiencies in Native populations which carried over after independence, as evidenced in incompetent government and rampant sexual licence. Whatever the 'civilisational problems' might have been, they were certainly not related to over a century of French colonization of more than 60 million people of North and West Africa.

A few months after the G-20 summit, in a two-hour speech to students and dignitaries at Ouagadougou University in Burkina Faso, Macron reaffirmed that colonialism should not affect relations between the two countries because neither he nor most of his audience were alive during colonial times.[109] Here, Macron also addressed the Burkinabe President, Roch Kaboré, in the familiar form, and, as critics pointed out, in a way that he would not address, say, the Chinese premier.[110] At the same time, Macron brusquely dismissed any notion of reparations, focusing instead on the benefits of capitalism, such as jobs and trade. During a TV interview in Ghana, 'Macron told a young Frenchwoman of Congolese origin that it would be "totally ridiculous" for France to "pay a subsidy, or recognise, or compensate for" colonialism.' Instead, he indicated that France was willing to contemplate 'reconciliation'.[111] During his trip to Algeria, which featured a walk-through of Algiers, Macron defensively upheld the integrity of France, refusing to apologize and advising 'young Algerians ... not to harbour grudges from the past but look to the future'. The past, he admitted, was characterized by crimes, but, as he said, he was 'not here to judge those in the past. There have been crimes and there were people that also did good things. Your generation must not allow this. It's not an excuse (to blame the past) for what is happening today.'[112]

Instead of remembering the past, especially human rights abuses, Macron framed contemporary French efforts on the African continent in this and other speeches as principally economic, stressing 'partnerships'. Added to the mix was an advocacy of crackdowns on corruption, which were represented as entirely internal and contemporary. Macron was also concerned with 'security', mostly defined by efforts to stem African migration to Europe. Part of the 'partnership' involved reinforcing the importance of the French language as a unifying factor, as Macron did in his hour-long address to an audience in Cameroon in 2018. Following from his Ouagadougou speech, which also dwelt on language, Macron urged his audience not to view French as a 'relic of a colonial power',[113] but instead argued that French could become the dominant language on the continent, especially when decoupled from colonialism in the popular imagination.[114]

An underlying message of Macron's post-election speeches was that remedying perceived deficiencies in Africa would involve both African amnesia and French assistance. This was also the view of his predecessor, Nicolas Sarközy, whose speech in Senegal a decade earlier was an attempt to direct blame for the various perceived failures of a whole continent away from colonialism and towards endemic internal deficiencies. Sarközy lamented the slave trade and some aspects of colonialism, indicated that they required apology, but insisted that the

French also did good and that Africa's own leaders were responsible for many of the troubles of Africans today. Without irony or any specific examples, Sarközy depicted Africans as living in monotonous and unchanged societies, to which changes instigated through European dynamism were the remedy:

> The tragedy of Africa is that the African has not fully entered into history. The African peasant, who for thousands of years have [sic] lived according to the seasons, whose life ideal was to be in harmony with nature, only knew the eternal renewal of time, rhythmed by the endless repetition of the same gestures and the same words. In this imaginary world where everything starts over and over again there is no place for human adventure or for the idea of progress.[115]

## Algerians in France

Africans, and especially people of Algerian descent and other Muslims, have also been treated in France as barely human. While West and North African people have been in France a long time, some of the more recent presence relates to rights granted to men who fought for France as part of the Allied forces in World War II, as well as some 260,000 Arab and Imazighen *harkis* or *supplétifs* who assisted French efforts in the Algerian War of Independence itself. Although most Muslims were initially banned from going to France, after independence the government reluctantly allowed many *harkis* entry.[116] In 1962, 60,000 were taken to France, but many thousand others were discharged from their duties and left to their fate as traitors in Algeria. Some French officers illegally rescued 16,000 of their *harki* colleagues and arranged their passage to France, but any Algerian deemed to be in France unofficially could be immediately returned at the time.[117] Between 60,000 and 150,000 of them 'were tortured, mutilated, or killed by the Algerian population at large'.[118]

As anthropologist Vincent Crapanzano describes through moving testimonies of *harkis* and their families, they were sequestered for decades in transit camps in rural areas of France, subject to surveillance, privation and abandonment. The initial camps consisted of rows of tents where multiple families were deposited. The conditions in these, as described by Crapanzano's informants,[119] were harsh and inhumane. The camp at Rivesaltes, for example, 'was located on an unsheltered, arid windy plain with little vegetation, almost no trees, and therefore, no shade. In the winter, winds were glacial, in the summer torrid ... All the Harkis ... mentioned the freezing cold in unheated tents'.[120] Touring the abandoned camp at Rivesaltes with two *harkis*, Crapanzano describes their memories:

> As I walked through the ruins, the two Harkis pointed out where they had lived, telling me the barrack number ... where the showers had been (they were allowed one shower a week in the best of times); where the latrines were that were so dirty and smelled so badly that they preferred to go in the fields; where the clinic had been, the school, and the barber shop that one of the Harkis had opened ... At one point, the two men stopped and, looking across an empty field, told me in outrage that, during the first year of their parents' incarceration there, the camp authorities had hurriedly buried the scores of babies who had died in the harsh winter conditions in unmarked graves in the camp itself.[121]

The camp at Bias was 'an old prison and was surrounded by barbed wire and a high wall ... children as young as nine were taken from their parents without explanation. Most of them were taught a trade and put to work. Men that showed any sign of a rebellious nature were taken to a nearby psychiatric hospital, and those who returned were often broken shells of their former selves.'[122] Testimonies confirm severe inter-generational trauma and reveal frequent movement of families between camps, and the suppression of publicity about them by the French government. The camps closed in 1978 and, over time, *harkis* could settle in towns, and many relocated to industrial cities in the North of France. Many remained, however, marginalized and alienated from both the French population and the incoming Algerian and North African immigrant populations, whose histories were very different. In 2018, at the same time as making the cautious acknowledgement of French torture in Algeria, Macron granted the Legion d'Honneur to six former *harki* fighters and the co-founder of an association which fought for their rights, along with another nineteen who received the Order of Merit on 25 September, the National Harki Day, which was proclaimed in 2001 to recognize *harkis* contributions to France. These honours were accompanied by a €40 million support package for the *harkis* and their descendants.[123]

As a generic group, African, Asian and Caribbean French have been disproportionately disadvantaged in French society. Many Muslim migrants have been segmented into vast suburban housing estates called *banlieues*, in which unemployment rates of up to 40 per cent of the inhabitants have persisted into the twenty-first century.[124] Nicolas Sarközy infamously referred to French African youth protesters in the 2005 violent clashes following the deaths of two young *banlieue* residents at a power station, as they were fleeing from police, as 'rabble' or 'riffraff'.

Since the 1990s, the *banlieues* themselves have been widely perceived as a threat to French Republican universalism and have become zones of containment in a French version of civic stratification.[125] As van de Wetering states, 'many banlieue youths now live in a context in which they are in media, politics and public debate often stereotyped, categorized and stigmatized. They are perceived as a threatening, "abnormal", population, and are rarely approached as "normal French citizens".[126]

Muslim women's choices of clothing are likewise not seen as normal, as shown in the suppressing of various types of attire. This began in 1989 with the expulsion of three teenage students for refusing to remove their headscarves in a school in the industrial town of Creil. The expulsion was predicated on the principle of *laïcité*, the doctrine that schools be religiously neutral. Demonstrations by members of Muslim communities against this were met by unyielding defence of *laïcité* by the wider French public, including *Le Monde* and many French intellectuals.[127] After over a decade of suppressing the headscarf, in 2004 a law that banned students wearing it in French schools was passed. Other public debates were framed by many politicians and intellectuals in terms of the protection of Republican virtues against 'particularist, communalist Islam'.[128] This was apparent in the outrage expressed by French Interior Minister Gérard Collomb, and Marlène Schiappa, the Minister of Gender Equality, who respectively called the appearance of headscarved student leader Maryam Pougetoux 'shocking' and a 'manifestation of political Islam'. The 19-year-old Pougetoux had simply appeared on a TV debate about educational policy.[129]

In her ethnography of French Muslims, *The Republic Unsettled*, Fernando observes that Muslim women are constantly faced with a barrage of hostility towards simple displays of their visible differences. This is because acceptance of rights to difference – for example, girls wearing the headscarf in schools – is perceived as a weakening or betrayal of the universal rights enshrined in the principles of the radically secular French Revolution, and hence the core of French identity. The youth that Fernando worked with, however, did not necessarily demand a right to difference, and even preferred indifference to their culture, which would be, they maintained, no diminution of French Republican aspirations. The problem, however, is, as she points out,[130] that the colonial authorities regarded Muslims as inextricably attached to religion. Whereas Christianity, in the colonial mind, could be conceptually separated from the state and politics, Islam could not. Hence, because the headscarf was seen by French politicians as a matter of religion only, and not of individual conscience, it could not be protected by the European Convention on Human Rights,[131] and neither could the full Islamic niqab. In 2010, France banned concealment of one's face in public. This was challenged in 2018 when two French women who were fined for wearing the niqab took their case to the UN, and the Human Rights Committee ruled that this was a human rights breach, to which France was asked to respond.[132] Replaying French 'unveiling' of Muslim women in Algeria, France recently criminalized women in Islamic dress, with armed police forcing Muslim women on beaches to remove their body-covering burkinis in 2016, and, in 2019, women in the same attire in swimming pools in France were fined €35.[133] Insistence on secular uniformity extends also to the French settler government of Quebec, which banned public-sector workers from wearing religious symbols, specifically targeting the niqab in 2019.[134]

Stoler makes the point that, in the 1950s, France was trying to keep Algeria and Algerians part of France.[135] But Algerians in France today are, except for those in national sports or entertainment, often separate from it. This can, in part, be related to the French intolerance of Islam in colonial Algeria. The attempts to marginalize and discredit Islam and render it impotent, rather than to understand or enter dialogue, have had long-lasting effects that are visible in organized political anti-immigrant platforms,[136] as well as the laws prohibiting various types of Muslim attire.

## Post-independence Fallout

At the heart of the colonization of Algeria is a hypocrisy built into the practice of colonialism itself. Writing of French colonialism in West Africa – but applicable more widely – Conklin remarks that 'the French believed that their republican heritage imposed upon them not only a special obligation to uplift the oppressed of the earth materially ... but also a specific duty to defend the individual rights of man wherever they were threatened'.[137] The commitments to the principles of freedom were, Conklin maintains, what separated the French from other civilizing missions. However, this commitment was always fragile on account of resistance in the colonies, and because French belief in their unique superiority cast colonized peoples as inferiors to whom the extension of universal rights would always be compromised.

The idea that there were peoples that were less than human, or at least civilizationally inferior, was reinforced by 130 years of occupation of Algeria, and some of it was abetted by the invidious cultural comparisons of the Kabyle Myth. The Arabization of the post-independence institutions and national narrative of Algeria may have been partly a reaction to this, but more likely the post-independence leaders followed the same path as leaders across other African territories that were decolonized at mid twentieth century. That is, they constructed a national narrative based on the singularity of the nation, and in this case identified Arabness and Islam as expressing the essence of Algerian identity. The Arab leaders of the independence movement claimed the state acted in this way despite a powerful counter-discourse from what was known as the Berberist Crisis of 1949, in which Imazighen advocated ethnic pluralism as the defining feature of Algeria. Hence, the French technique of divide and rule was replayed in the institutions of the new state.[138] Until the early 2000s, this meant according no official recognition to languages such as the Amazigh language, Tamazigh, or to distinct ethnicities, as occurs across post-independence Africa. Even when Tamazigh was recognized in 2002, the state did not always provide schooling in it. Independence has also involved mirroring the suppression of certain Islamic practices in France – for example, by banning the niqab worn by Salafist women in Algerian schools and universities.[139] As reported by Amnesty International, forty-one people were arrested, and thirty-four of them detained for waving the Amazigh flag, and another twenty-two received one-year sentences for 'undermining national unity' by bearing the Berber flag in 2019.[140] Lorcin believes that the authoritarian Arabization is in part due to the absence of institutions to channel grievances and express opinions,[141] but if such institutions are absent in today's Algeria, they were certainly also absent under French colonialism.

At the first occasion on which the FLN were seriously electorally challenged – by the Islamic Salvation Front (SIF) in 1991 – the authorities annulled the election result in favour of the SIF, 'triggering a decade of civil war in which whole villages, districts, and targeted groups were massacred'.[142] This was followed by a military *coup d'état* in January 1992. About 700,000 people died in a civil war during the 'black decade' that lasted for most of the 1990s.[143] Martinez, in perhaps the most comprehensive account of the Algerian civil war attributes the conflict to a war-oriented *imaginaire* by which all sides, most prominently the military and Islamists, could gain politically and economically from violence.[144] While the reasons for the extreme violence of post-independence Algeria are manifold, acting upon assumed differential human qualities is an important context, which 'has been transformed in the post-colonial era into a historical memory of significance'.[145]

The Algerian state has not undertaken many correctives to colonial rule. While Macron was honouring *harkis*, Algeria was refusing to pay pensions to its own soldiers who had fought in the 'black decade', 20,000 of whom marched on the capital in protest in September 2018. They were met with tear gas and a huge police presence.[146] Similarly, while Macron has admitted torture, albeit over sixty years after the events,

Algeria has made no similar admission about its use of torture. Although there are elections, the Algerian state through successive governments remains authoritarian, with a heavy police and security presence almost everywhere. An activist was jailed for six months for posting a Facebook poster of himself holding a placard arguing that 81-year-old President Abdelaziz Bouteflika should not seek a fifth term in office in the 2019 election.[147] Despite suffering a stroke in 2013 and having rarely spoken in public since, Bouteflika was the longest-serving President after his mentor, the 'ruthlessly efficient' Houari Boumedienne.[148] While in office, Bouteflika presided over crackdowns on dissent of all kinds, including cultural and religious difference, with arrests of minority Muslim sect worshippers, and suppression and restriction of non-Muslim religions. Many Algerian Christians have been arrested and harassed under a 2006 Ordinance regulating non-Muslims,[149] and numerous churches have been attacked and closed by the authorities under the same law.[150]

Mass public demonstrations against Bouteflika's candidacy occurred prior to the election, resulting in numerous arrests, including of journalists protesting against state censorship.[151] However, Bouteflika's candidacy was approved 'with reservations' by the French intelligence services and France's ambassador to Algeria.[152] Significantly, while Macron was vocal about human rights abuses in Venezuela at the time, he was largely silent on the protests over Bouteflika's candidacy in Algeria, or indeed the role of the military in propping it up. Finally, after weeks of protest, Bouteflika withdrew his candidacy five weeks before the election, which was then cancelled and Bouteflika resigned. But mass protests demanding an end to autocracy continued as interim President Abdelkader Bensalah suppressed dissent, used mass monitoring techniques, and blocked news and social media outlets, and his government has refused to answer questions or be interviewed about these and other matters.[153]

Andrew Hussey writes, 'so-called democracy has made Algeria feel like a prison ... No one knows exactly when the last "war of liberation" ended. It is true that the rate of killing has slowed down, but nobody feels free.'[154] Fuelling the ubiquitous discontent in Algeria are the very high rates of unemployment – 26.4 per cent according to official statistics – among the burgeoning population of under-30s.[155] While many parts of Algeria today are tense, with the possibility of official violence ever present, the state has also not treated migrants, asylum seekers and refugees according to human rights ideals. A report by the Associated Press in 2018 alleged that Algerian authorities abandoned 13,000 people in the Sahara and that another 28,000 had been crammed into trucks and deported to Niger.[156] In recent years, over 3,000 sub-Saharan migrants a month have been put on forced walks in the desert in temperatures of 48 °C.[157] In 2018, Amnesty International issued another report detailing violent actions that the Algerian authorities carried out against migrants from sub-Saharan Africa.[158] These include non-recognition of asylum-seekers, and arrests of tens of thousands of migrants through house-to house searches, forcible expulsions *en masse* without any due process of law – sometimes to home countries in which their lives are in danger. Journalists have also revealed that Palestinian refugees, despite their 'special status' in Algeria, have been detained and criminalized.[159] The UN High Commission on Refugees (UNHCR) reported that 120 Syrians, Palestinians and Yemenis, some of whom were registered refugees, were detained, then deported to Niger, at the end of 2018,[160] and 20 of them were stranded in an inhospitable desert border region. The other 100 were unaccounted for. The Associated Press estimated that Algerian authorities had abandoned 13,000 would-be migrants in the desert over 14 months in 2017 and 2018.[161] The 200,000 Sahrawi refugees in camps at Tindouf have also been denied food and aid through Algerian government actions.[162] The UNCHR has labelled this situation an 'urgent humanitarian imperative'.[163]

All this raises the difficult problem of accounting for post-independence governments whose policies appear so antithetical to human rights ideals. There is no doubt that the Algerian government, along with those of many other former colonized territories, has adopted highly authoritarian rule, crony capitalism and official corruption. The convenient explanation from former colonial powers is that this either is caused by internal deficiencies or is an expression of a nascent developmental process that will in future improve. Perhaps, however, it has something to do with the war-oriented *imaginaire* Martinez identifies as the basis of the Algerian civil war in the 1990s.[164] That is, colonialism, like this conflict, operated in such a way that great gains of wealth and influence could be achieved through force. That certain people or peoples that were deemed obstacles to this were depicted as less than human might have only been an auxiliary – but, with time, less effective – justification. Eventually, violence along with political manipulation and intimidation becomes the main route to power, and equal human rights need not be a priority for the state.

The extent to which colonialism established the conditions for the human rights problems that are common in such territories cannot be pinpointed exactly. Many of the same forms of authoritarianism, theft and disregard for human rights that were apparent under colonial rule obtain in Algeria and other former colonies today. But, perhaps, an important factor lies in the palpable sense of all-round neglect and indifference that followed the departure of colonial masters. Writing of the corruption, poverty and lack of infrastructure in her native Antigua after the departure of the British, Jamaica Kincaid addresses her colonizers by telling them that 'all the laws that you know mysteriously favour you.

Do you know why people like me are shy about being capitalists? Well, it's because we, for as long as we have known you, *were* capital, like bales of cotton and sacks of sugar, and you were the commanding cruel capitalists.'[165]

Like Antigua, which was left with no waste disposal system by the British, colonial powers often neglected to clean up parts of the physical environment, leaving formerly colonized peoples to suffer the fallout. This was literally the case in Algeria through the legacies of nuclear tests. As journalist and scholar Francis Ghiles, remarks: 'The war of liberation did not end in 1962. French nuclear tests continued in the Sahara well after independence, thousands of "disappeared" Algerians never returned home and the French Army only gave its Algerian counterparts a map of the anti-personnel mines it had planted on the frontiers of Algeria in 2007.'[166]

France continued to test nuclear bombs in the Sahara in the 1960s, leaving spent plutonium and uncontained radiation, and estimates suggest that this affected from 27,000 to 60,000 Algerians who remain uncompensated. France's shift of nuclear bomb testing from the Sahara to its 'nuclear colony' French Polynesia also resulted in damage to the health of residents there, a small number of whom have been compensated.[167] With the assistance of Algerian elites, the fallout from French colonization remains.

# 5

# The Impossibility of Indigenous Human Rights

When we saw the pipelines being built that pushed this black fluid through, then we understood: this is what is coming to kill the world. The prophecy says that when the Black Snake comes, we will stand up and stop it ... we must stop destroying what gives us life.

LaDonna Bravebull Allard[1]

## Introduction

Native American prophecies such as that of the Black Snake predict the tragedies that would occur from the intrusion of invaders who acted without respect for the land or other people. A Zuñi prophecy foresaw the arrival of Europeans, and with it:

Cities will progress and then decay to the ways of the lowest beings. Drinkers of dark liquids [alcohol?] will come upon the land, speaking nonsense and filth. Then the end shall be nearer. Population will increase until the land can hold no more. The tribes of men will mix. The dark liquids they drink will cause the people to fight amongst themselves. Families will break up: father against children and the children against one another ... Maybe when the people have outdone themselves, then maybe, the stars will fall upon the land, or drops of hot water will rain upon the earth. Or the land will turn under. Or, our father, the sun, will not rise to start the day. Then our possessions will turn into beasts and devour us whole. If not, there will be an odor from gases, which will fill the air we breathe and the end for us shall come. But the people themselves will bring upon themselves what they receive. From what has resulted, time alone will tell us what the future holds for us.[2]

Some Pueblo prophecies suggest that there will be a time when the whites will have destroyed so much of the land that they will not be able to live on it anymore and the land will be returned to Native peoples. According to Stuart,[3] it is mainstream opinion among traditional Pueblo leaders that the 'wasteful ways, weak communities and economically based class system' of the USA will not survive, and only indigenous peoples with long-term cultural continuity will be able to endure. These prophecies all emphasize that it is not just the disrespectful ways in which nature is treated that result in catastrophe, but aggressive removal of land from common humanity.

For settler colonialism, a delicate balance needed to be struck between removing peoples with collective attachments to land, and doing so in ways that could be seen as consistent with liberal principles. In North America, one mechanism for such a balance was the assertion of a right to private property. An important precondition for this was to universalize the assumption that land is a material entity that can be cordoned off from a wider natural environment and owned individually. Indigenous peoples, while loosely recognizing territories for specific uses, and holding various natural features sacred, had nothing approximating the European idea of the right of private property in land.

This, however, may be a moot point, since they were deemed in both colonial and Enlightenment thought to be 'savages', who did not qualify as holders of any pre-existing rights, including what Europeans believed could be owned. With only some tortuous disquisitions by European jurists and philosophers to soften the blow,[4] indigenous peoples were inserted into a colonial legal system which enabled settler colonization to proceed through the exercise of property rights for colonists. In Australia, for example, Britain assumed that the lands were empty, or *terra nullius*, and therefore implanting white settlers on Aboriginal lands was entirely legitimate. The Aboriginal peoples who were supplanted under this doctrine were considered to be without ownership rights. *Terra nullius* was not limited to Australia. It was apparent either formally or as a default position during the expansion of Europe in the Americas. Although there were some juridical and legislative limitations, colonization proceeded by making lands available for settlement through violence, disease, forced removal or the destabilization of indigenous communities. In the process, Europeans invoked the authority of God and philosophical principles, and they made laws to make their ownership rights absolute.[5] This can be seen in the legal doctrines that formed the basis of international law, propounded first in crude form by English Puritan settlers in seventeenth-century New England, who based their entitlement on both the Bible and claims that agriculturists had unique ownership rights. These justifications were fortified by John Locke's conception of the origins of private property, and subsequently by doctrines from legal scholars, such as Emmerich de Vattel and William Blackstone, that reinforced Locke's premises.

The initial extension of the settler state beyond the thirteen English colonies was driven by the Jeffersonian view that settlement of new lands was a democratic right of Americans and the territorial basis of an 'empire for liberty'. Similarly, when considering the post-Independence expansion of the states of Virginia and Maryland, Thomas Paine, author of the canonical human rights text *Rights of Man* in 1791, situated the 'vacant western territory' as 'the common right of all'.[6] By 'all', it is clear that he meant European settlers. These views were premised to varying extents on Locke's assertion that 'improvement of the soil' was sufficient to remove common indigenous lands into private English settler hands. According to Locke's *Two Treatises of Government*, labouring on common land conveyed private property to the labourer. Since Indians did not, in his erroneous view, improve the soil or labour on it, they had no private property rights save in the animals they killed.

This arbitrary but convenient lever of dispossession predicated European rights to private property of lands of 'savages' upon Godly prescription. 'God', Locke tells us, 'who hath given the World to men in common, hath also given them reason to make use of it to their advantage and convenience'.[7] To use it, and be consistent with the Biblical injunction to 'go forth and multiply' – the command from Genesis – Christians must apply labour. All of this, and the individualistic orientation implied by the injunction, involves adopting private property. Locke insisted that indigenous peoples had no property rights *per se* since they were in the state of nature, while Europeans had moved beyond it. Therefore, in the absence of any strictures against violence, duress could be a legitimate way of turning over lands to colonists so they could exercise the private property rights they had earned through toiling the land. Borrowing from Schmitt, Agamben observes that Locke's assertion that the New World was a state of nature made it a juridically empty space in which anything and everything is possible. By being labelled a state of nature, North America became a state of exception.[8] Only after the assertion of settler sovereignty over this state of nature and its inhabitants do the liberal principles of the social contract and allegiance to the 'rule of law' operate – but almost always, as we will see illustrated in this chapter, as a state of exception.

Following from declaring ownership rights over indigenous lands, colonists faced the problem of how to treat the people who were removed. Imperative among the powers the settler state claimed was that of conferring rights on indigenous peoples as subjects, thus providing liberal legitimacy to the original colonization. In this process, those regarded as colonized subjects were seen as having no appreciable cultural, political or legal norms that could be used as a basis of negotiation over land and rights, and, indeed, in the allocation of meaningful authority. Colonists may have recognized that indigenous peoples had some rights, but none of these was sufficient to prevent dispossession. As I argued in a previous work,[9] wilful ignorance of the indigenous inhabitants, and particularly towards their ideas about land and rights, characterized much of the colonization of North America. Colonists insulated themselves from indigenous ideas, since to dialogue with them over the legitimacy of colonization could have undermined colonization itself.

Consequently, there have been no meaningful processes by which colonizers and indigenous peoples agreed on the cultural frameworks through which the administration and disposition of lands, resources and power would occur. This is mainly because the host societies of indigenous peoples were largely excluded from using their laws, norms, customs and institutions for deciding on the rights of different parties. In the absence of any equal intercultural dialogue, the rights of indigenous peoples were diminished, dismissed and excluded through design. Indigenous peoples were never meant to be self-determining, but to be recipients of selected rights that could be exercised or easily annulled or ignored. Perhaps the most powerful method of effecting land dispossession was the imposition of the liberal principle – deeply offensive to many indigenous peoples even today – that land can be owned. Many indigenous leaders, orators and spokespeople have refused to concede this basic premise of the American treaty system, including the Shawnee leader Tecumseh and the Sauk chief Black Hawk.[10] The basic absurdity of individual or state ownership of land is recorded in studies of twentieth-century Canadian land claims conflicts in which indigenous protagonists are put in positions in which they have to acknowledge that land can be owned or lose all their land, which by default becomes 'Crown land'.[11]

## The Non-rights of Indigenous Peoples

Unlike the stories of American slavery or colonial Algeria, the entanglement of colonists with indigenous peoples became principally about establishing permanent settler control over land. This was the intention of the French in Algeria, but it failed as a settler state for many reasons, not least of which was the fact that Algerians outnumbered French settlers. With successive waves of mass European migration to North America, an economy based for several centuries on African slavery, and continual depletions of the numbers of Native Americans, an exit for the colonists was never a remote possibility, as it was for the *pieds noirs*. Colonial dominion required both literally removing indigenous peoples, and administering the diverse groups spread out over an immense landmass.

A well-rehearsed process in the literatures of 'Westward expansion', land was gradually transferred from indigenous peoples to Europeans as settlement proceeded across the continent. In an oft-cited phrase, Tocqueville remarked that 'it is impossible to destroy men with more respect for the laws of humanity'.[12] These 'laws of humanity' conveyed rights to settlers enabling dispossession and disconnection of Native peoples from their lands and ways of life. Tocqueville observed the cruelty of this when he witnessed part of the Trail of Tears, involving the forced expulsion of Choctaw Indians from their homelands to an area across the Mississippi in the 1830s. In fact, the legitimacy of the eviction of them and other groups comprising the 'Five Civilized Tribes' at that time derived from a sleight of hand by Supreme Court Chief Justice John Marshall, who, in *Cherokee Nation* v. *Georgia* in 1831, sympathized with the Cherokee plea to retain their lands after Georgia had attempted to transfer them to miners and settlers, but ruled that the Court was not the appropriate tribunal for it to be resolved. In effect this allowed President Andrew Jackson to pass the 1830 Indian Removal Act that precipitated the Trail of Tears. Further enabling dispossession, Marshall's opinion in the case featured a unilateral declaration of state authority over Native Americans. Rejecting the notion that Indian tribes were equivalent to foreign nations, he contended:

> They [American Indians] may, more correctly, perhaps, be denominated domestic dependent nations. They occupy a territory to which we assert a title independent of their will, which must take effect in point of possession, when their right of possession ceases. Meanwhile, they are in a state of pupilage; their relation to the United States resembles that of a ward to his guardian. They look to our government for protection: rely upon its kindness and its power; appeal to it for relief to their wants; and address the president as their great father.[13]

This is based, as Marshall admits, on a mere assertion that indigenous peoples and their land are under the authority of the USA. Before this, Marshall declared that 'Indian territory' was within the United States through treaties, such as that of Hopewell in 1785, yet this treaty only notes – along with many other provisions – that the Cherokee are under the protection of the USA. One of the supreme ironies of American democracy, Tocqueville observed,[14] was that American Indians had also been dispossessed through trickery and bribery, including both the perpetual bad faith in negotiations by the Federal government and, more immediately, through strategic usages of firearms, alcohol, money and other goods that undermined indigenous social cohesion. The reformer and novelist Helen Hunt Jackson's *Century of Dishonor*, published in 1881, showed that the bad faith Tocqueville had observed east of the Mississippi was reproduced in treaty after treaty since then. As she detailed, the US authorities broke humanitarian law as well as the government's own laws in their dealings with numerous tribes.[15] In fact the USA violated every treaty it signed with Native groups.[16]

In many ways, these violations were integral to the heroic process by which European 'pioneers' spread themselves across the land. The liberal, modernizing nation could only realize its self-appointed destiny through removing the indigenous obstacles. In Frederick Jackson Turner's influential frontier thesis written at the end of the nineteenth century, for example, the Native Americans are situated as backwards, sometimes useful, but essentially rightless inhabitants of a land destined for others. 'Colonial settlement is for economic science what the mountain is for geology', Turner asserts, 'bringing to light primitive stratifications'.[17] The primitive stratifications he had in mind were in the process of being buried under more advanced layers of society that only the Euro-Americans could bring. Significantly, Turner regarded the Native territories as 'free land' of 'inanimate nature'. Although treaties and other agreements were often concluded, Turner's assumption that the land is 'free' tacitly admitted that treaties were signed merely to pacify Indians. While treaties were regarded as elements of the 'rule of law', it was clear that even the indigenous rights conceded in them were not meant to be respected.

Foundations of US Indian policy can be traced to the Declaration of Independence, which declared rights for land speculators, warning that Britain had allowed 'savages' to impede such rights. Moreover, 'He [Britain] has excited domestic insurrections amongst us, and has endeavoured to bring on the inhabitants of our frontiers, the merciless Indian Savages whose known rule of warfare, is an undistinguished destruction of all ages, sexes and conditions.' The Declaration is an assertion of autonomy from Britain and a licence to confront 'merciless Indian Savages' without interference. Washington, Jefferson and several other Founding Fathers were land speculators, and Jefferson had strenuously argued against British restrictions on the colonists in appropriating Indian land. As 'British policy violated settler conceptions of liberty in several ways',[18] conflict with the Crown circled around the right to dispose of indigenous territories. Jefferson ends the Declaration with a call for the right of the colonists to form free and independent states, giving the settlers a kind of *faux* indigeneity as 'free' settlers who are citizens, as opposed to the oppressed 'subjects' of the monarchy. The US Constitution functioned as a human rights document to empower settlers to encamp themselves on indigenous lands. It mentions Indians directly only twice: excluding them from taxation and, importantly, from political representation; and giving powers to Congress to regulate trade with them.[19]

Significantly, Jefferson also applied himself to cartography, beginning by sketching out the Ordinance of 1784 that created several Western territories for colonization. In the Ordinance of 1785, he did this by using mathematical methods, schematically organizing the land into grids of 1 square mile, and drawing boundaries by using longitude and latitude. The Northwest Ordinance of 1787 built on these precedents to grant settlers the liberty and freedom guaranteed by the American Revolution. In the words of one scholar, 'it became the preeminent text in American settler thought'.[20] Jefferson's appropriation of indigenous territories enlarged considerably with the Louisiana Purchase from Napoleon in 1803. For under $15 million, Jefferson negotiated the acquisition of all of what was designated as Louisiana, including lands to the west of the Mississippi not claimed by Spain. Jefferson dispatched Captains Lewis and Clark to explore this vast area before it had been purchased. After introducing smallpox, which would go to kill some 25,000 Native Americans in 1837 alone,[21] Lewis and Clark paved the way for over 100,000 white fortune-seekers in the first few decades after the expedition. Lands within the Purchase would provide for future European settlement, as well as for Southeastern Indians after the removals of the 1830s. Jefferson therefore prepared the scene for white colonization and the violent removals under Andrew Jackson. He had already condoned white squatting on indigenous lands, constantly rebuffing Native American protests by referring to them as children and insisting they adapt to Anglo-Saxon farming.[22] When land transactions occurred in the Southeastern USA in the early nineteenth century, 'sometimes hundreds of acres of land were traded away for a few gallons of alcohol'.[23] This would have been a violation of the Trade and Intercourse Acts passed from the 1790s to the 1830s to prohibit private acquisition of Indian lands.[24]

The Louisiana Purchase transferred indigenous lands from one colonist to another. Neither France nor Spain, which had previously claimed these lands, had any type of cession from indigenous peoples. Both countries had given land grants to settlers, and had allowed land speculators and squatters onto the lands. As if this vast territory was devoid of humans, indigenous peoples were not involved in the deliberations between Jefferson and Napoleon that transferred their lands to the US government. Assuming *terra nullius*, Jefferson had already assured Chickasaws, as early as 1805, that there were lands to the west of the Mississippi, 'unoccupied by any red men'.[25] Although there were anti-squatting laws in addition to the Trade and Intercourse Acts, Federal authorities were reluctant to enforce them, making US sovereignty reliant on *terra nullius*.[26]

The lengthy chapter of his *Notes on the State of Virginia* devoted to 'Aborigines' provided a foretaste of Jefferson's *terra nullius* view of North America. He notes that, although Indians have only a very loose structure of government and no written laws, they constitute a well-ordered society and 'crimes are very rare among them'.[27] He adds that their contacts with Europeans have had a devastating effect on their ways of life, especially due to losses of their land, but also due to the introduction of alcohol and epidemics of infectious disease such as smallpox. Despite their violent onslaughts on American Indians, Jefferson defends settlers by claiming that the land was taken fairly, and many settlers have 'proofs of purchase' from 'voluntary sales'.[28] Jefferson vigorously endorsed the original English colonization by Sir Walter Raleigh, and cites the Lockean rationale of 'improvement of the land' as one of the justifications for the increasing settlement of Virginia,[29] also adding Divine mandate to fortify Euro-American privilege: 'Those who labour in the earth are the chosen people of God.'[30]

Jefferson was also a chronicler of the gradual disintegration of Indian societies, hastened, as he notes, by a loss of language, and for some tribes the extinction of all their members, who had been moved off the land as whites poured westwards. While his writings show that he was rhetorically despondent about the destruction of indigenous societies, as with slavery, Jefferson did nothing to stop it. By contrast, he made Herculean efforts on behalf of the European settlers. Universal human rights were never Jefferson's goals, and nor were they the founding principles of the American state. Rather, a whole series of exceptions and gradations of rights were built into laws and policies that smoothed the paths to Euro-American occupancy of the continent. The treaty was the primary instrument used for this purpose.

## American Treaties

While the preambles to most treaties unilaterally asserted the authority of the USA to enter such agreements, American officials were never above using force if Indians did not agree to the terms of treaties. Tocqueville quotes Congressional records to show that the right to take Indian lands by 'the sword' was always left open. Treaties were simply the humane alternative.[31] The sword, however, often remained unsheathed since non-enforcement of treaty obligations often allowed settler violence to take its course as a powerful tool of dispossession. The process was further facilitated by many indigenous groups already being depleted by European diseases, alcohol and the adulteration of local ecosystems.

By the close of the nineteenth century, after wars, massacres and relocations, Native Americans had been removed from most areas of desired white settlement. Federal Indian policy then shifted to finding ways to assimilate them by confining them to reservations, a policy also pursued in Canada. Reservations were presented by Congressional advocates as forms of social progress, with farming, Euro-American schooling and wage labour accruing to Indians who lived settled lives within defined boundaries. But when Indians resisted such moves, they were often relocated, sometimes *en bloc*, to other areas not immediately needed for white settlement. One example is the 'Navajo Long Walk' which entailed the expulsion, via a Presidential Executive Order, of the entire tribe away from their lands in what is now Northeast Arizona to Bosque Redondo in New Mexico in 1864. Some years after their return, Navajos complained that the Indian Agent used 'threats and coercion to make us sign numerous papers of which we have no knowledge whatsoever'.[32] This was after the signing of the 1868 Navajo Treaty which enabled Navajo to return to their homes under more stringent regulations. The treaty negotiations were tainted by the US official, General William Tecumseh Sherman, exaggerating the land base for their new reservation, and by general Navajo incomprehension while they were suffering extreme hunger and despair at Bosque Redondo.[33]

One of the most dramatic instances of removal after this followed the 1872 Modoc war. The conflict occurred after Modocs returned from their relocation to the Klamath Reservation in Oregon, which was created by treaty to allow white emigrants to travel unimpeded through their lands. Rejecting life on the reservation and unhappy with US non-compliance with several of the terms of the treaty, many Modoc families returned to their territories, and dug into the Lava Beds area of Northern California. They had many successes against numerically superior US Army attempts to return them to the reservation, but were eventually defeated. Writing only a few years after the war, Stephen Powers describes the tragedy: 'They fought with unparalleled heroism for their homes', Powers writes, 'but were crushed by superior power; and their fallen chiefs were held to a stern and awful accountability to laws which they had no hand or voice in making, and whose spirit and substance had been so wantonly violated by the conquering race as by themselves'.[34] While atrocities were committed by both sides, after a military trial of the leader of the Modocs, Kintpuash, he and other supposed collaborators were hung, decapitated and their heads sent to the Army Medical College in Washington, DC.[35] Modocs deemed hostile were deported almost 2,000 miles away to the Quapaw Reservation in Oklahoma in 1873, where their descendants remain. Others were placed on the Klamath Reservation. Although the Modocs had 'no hand or voice' in making any of the laws or policies to which they were subject, the overwhelming confidence of the 'conquering race' that their own methods were universally legitimate over-rode all else.

The dishonest treatment of the Modocs was of a piece with general Indian policy in California after it had been annexed from Mexico in 1848. In 1851, Federal commissioners were dispatched to negotiate treaties with Natives throughout the state. This resulted in eighteen treaties, by which Indians surrendered their claims to occupancy of most of the state in return for reservations, livestock, clothing and farming equipment.[36] Under the terms of the treaties, indigenous peoples were required to recognize the sovereignty of the USA over all their lands and place themselves under the protection of the USA as wards of the state. At the time when they agreed to this condition, Anglo settlers, miners and farmers also under protection of the US government had reduced many Indians to starvation and desperate poverty, which was addressed by forcing a land cession in exchange for assistance. Afterwards, it was revealed that the commissioners only spoke to a fraction of the tribal leaders in California, and these individuals were not empowered to cede the huge swathes of land designated in the treaties. Despite the massive cessions, the California state legislature strongly objected to the treaties, even though the Federal commissioners had deemed most of the reservation lands worthless. State legislators maintained that treaties would 'deprive whites of all their improvements, discoveries and hard-earned acquisitions'.[37] Hence, California politicians lobbied against the ratification of the treaties and advocated that Indians be removed from the state entirely. In 1852, the US Senate rejected the treaties secretly and had the deliberations classified for fifty years. The result was to open all Indian lands for white settlement, and this precipitated the genocide of California Indians.[38]

By the early twentieth century when the immediate effects of treaties, forced removals, massacres and genocide had abated, life on reservations across the country was proving unhappy and demoralizing. Numerous Native spokespeople commented on the duplicitous quality of the system of rights designed to apply to them. Chitto Harjo,[39] a Choctaw who took complaints to a Senate investigating committee in 1906, complained of the failure of the USA to fulfil its numerous treaty obligations, beginning before the Trail of Tears and involving the dishonouring of treaties signed before and after removal in the 1830s. Arthur Parker, a well-known Seneca archaeologist, spoke about the legitimacy of the treaties themselves at the Society of American Indians in 1918. 'How were the Indians to know', he said, 'that the treaties they signed were documents that contained verbiage that could be construed differently from what they understood?'[40] Even when the verbiage was vaguely comprehensible, the government did not enforce the conditions applying, leading Parker to ask, rhetorically, whether 'when you sign your name to a document you are bound to perform what the document says'.[41] Harjo pointed out that American Indians had fought for the Union in the Civil War, and Parker observed that great numbers had served the USA in World War I, yet their loyalties were no guarantees that the state would honour its commitments to them. In the early twentieth century, the Nakota writer and activist Zitkala-Ša refers to 'America's Indian Problem' as arising from the 'barbaric rule of might' and the 'legal disability' of the American Indian, which enabled 'this inheritance of somebody's loot'.[42]

Treaties assumed that the American state had the authority to bind indigenous people to its authority unilaterally. Effectively denying indigenous sovereignty, the treaty is a tool of a racial contract. Many treaties were signed under duress, and without any understanding of indigenous patterns of political authority, representation and, indeed, law. Moreover, the US government violated the treaties, which were couched in solemn and binding language such as 'as long as waters run and the grass shall grow'.[43]

## The Roads to Standing Rock

These duplicities are crucial contexts for the often difficult conditions in which many indigenous peoples live in the USA, and form the backdrop to contemporary human rights concerns. The Standing Rock example that I narrate here is only one – albeit highly visible – illustration of ongoing exceptions to universal human rights.

The completion of the Dakota Access Pipeline (DAPL), built and owned by Energy Transfer Partners (ETP), was legitimated under the authority of a 2017 Executive Order made by a President with financial stakes in the pipeline and the oil refinery. Resting upon centuries of colonial land-confiscation practice, the sanctioning of the pipeline denies the Sioux and other indigenous groups rights to their lands and waters. This is in part because the USA has already contravened its own laws, and the facts created by such violations massively favour ETP and its shareholders. The Executive Order of a deeply transactional President is descended from the original transaction of the Louisiana Purchase between Thomas Jefferson and Napoleon Bonaparte. Stanley Vestal, who remains one of the most perceptive commentators on the Sioux and the Hunkpapa leader Sitting Bull, describes the original deal:

> Twenty odd years before Sitting Bull was born, a hard-up Corsican adventurer sold most of the Sioux country to a Virginian doctrinaire for a substantial sum in cold cash. Neither of these gentlemen had ever laid eyes on the lands they haggled over, and the Sioux had never heard of them. Yet, by the convenient fictions of European diplomacy, Sitting Bull's country was thereafter considered to belong to the United States, the remainder being ceded by the British. It was as though the King of Siam should sell Texas to the Grand Lama, merely because certain Siamese gentlemen had visited Texas and thought they might like it.[44]

France's claims to these indigenous lands were based on fur trader and explorer René-Robert Cavelier, Sieur de La Salle, claiming 'Louisiana' for France at the end of the seventeenth century. This included all territory drained by the Mississippi River from Canada to the Gulf of Mexico. From this foundation, the American state claimed Sioux lands, and the Sioux were dispossessed of them through at least nine different Acts passed by the American Congress and treaties that were signed with them.[45] The bizarre character of American claims to control Sioux lands was underlined in the actual moments in which Captain Lewis, through a translator with limited knowledge of the Lakota language, referred to French and Spanish 'fathers' to the Sioux, who had handed the land to seventeen different 'fathers' representing the seventeen US states at the time. After Lewis had distributed gifts as a sign of good faith in this contorted explanation of dispossession, the Sioux remonstrated, and when they did Lewis tried to intimidate them by firing an airgun into the sky.[46]

A first treaty at Fort Laramie in 1851, with the eight Plains groups including the Sioux, was made necessary because of their staunch resistance to white encroachment. Although the Sioux were militarily highly skilled, the treaty was negotiated when disease and hunger had taken a huge toll on them. Wagon trains full of gold-seekers, Mormons and land-hungry emigrants had stormed across their lands bringing cholera, smallpox and measles. Death and cultural disruption in many Plains societies, especially in 1848–9 when there were massive smallpox outbreaks, followed, and treaty negotiations took place in this atmosphere.[47] The 1851 Treaty involved the USA in negotiation with eight separate tribal groups over an agreement written in English and containing barely translatable words, concepts and assumptions. To represent the Sioux, the US commissioner appointed a chief called

Stirring Bear, a man who resolutely protested his unsuitability for authority over an entire people.[48] The frequent practice of the Americans appointing representatives or spokespeople from the Native American party, ubiquitous in the historical records, amounted to a kind of indirect rule through 'paper chiefs'.[49] Such impositions undermined the Native American decentralized, voluntary and consensual forms of leadership and decision making, and thus enabled the USA to dictate the terms of negotiation for the indigenous side.

The 1851 Treaty was for the Plains nations to allow emigrant trains through lands which were guaranteed to them, in exchange for annuities of $50,000 per year for ten years and peace with the US government. The treaty confirmed their ownership of lands in the Dakotas, Wyoming and Montana. However, the Senate refused to ratify the treaty, which, under Article 5, also delineated 60 million acres of Plains Indian territory for their exclusive use without forfeiting any other claims they may have had outside these boundaries.[50] White encroachments, protected by the US military, on lands covered by the treaty soon made it hard for the indigenous signatories to exercise the rights they had agreed to. For example, after massive white encroachment, the Cheyenne and Arapaho, both parties to the treaty, were driven out of their lands in Colorado to a small parcel of insignificant lands on the Arkansas River. Even a government report on this relocation admitted that 'what had been taken by force must be retained by the ravisher, and nothing was left for the Indian but to ratify a treaty consecrating the act'.[51]

After multiple unauthorized settler invasions, a second Treaty of Fort Laramie in 1868 guaranteed the 'Great Sioux Reservation'. This included all the land in South Dakota west of the Missouri River, and unceded (but undemarcated) hunting territories in Montana, Wyoming and Nebraska, into which no white was permitted entry without consent. A clause in the treaty stipulated that these unceded lands would be available to the indigenous groups 'so long as buffalo may range'. Conveniently, as this was unfolding, bison, the main food source of the Plains Indians, were being reduced, by white hide hunters and by Native Americans induced into commercial hunting, from an estimated 50 million animals that originally roamed the Plains to less than 1,000.[52] In what Hubbard[53] calls an act of genocide, hunger became a powerful additional force in diminishing indigenous rights to their lands. The slaughter of the bison was calculated to pressure the Plains Indians to abandon their lands, since without animals they would have less reason to inhabit the territories. General Philip Sheridan, present at the signing of the 1868 Treaty, objecting to the buffalo clause, chided that the best sportsmen of England and the USA should be invited to the Plains to end any wrangling once and for all.[54] However, there was little need to do this because conditions created by the US government and its settlers, such as degradation of the bison ecology and large-scale hide hunting, would ensure that Plains peoples would not be able to sustain themselves and would have to move off their lands and into agencies, and then reservations.[55]

The 1868 Treaty was couched in condescending language depicting Native Americans as in need of 'civilization', and was characterized by clauses designed to induce the Sioux to abandon their migratory lifestyles in favour of Euro-American farming. With this treaty, the US selected one chief – Spotted Tail – to speak for all the Brulé Sioux, something he had no authority to do. Other Sioux chiefs who were either amenable to government gifts – such as the Hunkpapa Gall – or considered 'friendly' – such as the Oglala Red Cloud – were also designated. Not all the Sioux were party to it – most significantly, the influential leaders Sitting Bull and Crazy Horse, who both believed whites to be dishonest. They and their followers took no part in the treaty, and were not, under their own customs, bound by it.[56] Throughout the negotiations, the Sioux party was not fully informed about the documents they signed. The US agents made much mention of gifts, rations and protections, but little about the lands they had to surrender.[57] Indeed, subsequent Sioux recollections of the treaty indicated that they understood that it was a peace treaty exchanging peace for the removal of forts and settler outposts, but there were numerous Articles in it which provided subtle pretexts for future dispossession, as Ostler has shown.[58] The treaty granted numerous types of assistance to the Sioux, including schooling, medicine and farming supplies, but land was by far their most important consideration. Hence, the stipulation in Article XII of the treaty that any cession of the reservation lands established for them – which could be held collectively – required consent of three-quarters of the adult males.

James Welch maintains that 'like all treaties negotiated between the United States government and the tribes, this one was broken almost immediately and repeatedly'.[59] Within three months, the US War Department declared Indians in their own unceded hunting territories 'hostile' and to be under the exclusive control of the military.[60] This was the exact opposite of what was specified in the treaty – whites were unauthorized to settle, occupy or travel through these lands without Indian consent under Article XVI. A short five years after the treaty was ratified by Congress, another serious violation occurred. The Black Hills, which are sacred to the Sioux, and covered under the 'Great Sioux Reservation' boundaries established under Article II as the same as pertaining to the 1851 Treaty, were confiscated after the President and Army commanders Sheridan and Sherman authorized a secret expedition led by General George Custer to find gold there. The discoveries opened the way for a massively profitable Gold Rush, the founding of boom towns such as Deadwood, and huge influxes of white settlers. The violation of the treaty by the US government was deliberately triggered by members of the party occupying the Black Hills and, on the authority of President Grant, the withdrawal of US troops that were dispatched to ensure that incursions such as this should not occur.[61] These actions, in effect, unilaterally extinguished indigenous ownership of these lands,[62] and deprived the Sioux of lands not only sacred to them, but important for hunting, gathering and forest resources. The legitimacy of this cession rested on a Special Commission which elicited 10 per cent of the male population to sign up to release the Black Hills and abrogate the 1868 Treaty by which the Sioux Nation had 'absolute and undisturbed use and occupation' of the lands mentioned above. As noted earlier, these could not be alienated except by a vote of three-quarters of the adult male population.

The ensuing Great Sioux War of 1876, of which the defeat of Custer at the Battle of Little Bighorn was a part, was provoked by US violations of the 1868 Treaty. The Sioux were eventually defeated, and railroad, mining and other business lobbies persuaded Congress of the inevitability of further breaking the 1868 Treaty.[63] The US government formalized the confiscation through the Black Hills Act of 1877, which permanently exiled the Sioux from their lands, again without the required three-quarters majority vote. The US Army supported this endeavour, in part to create a 'military colony' in the Black Hills, and eventually the Dawes Act of 1887 was implemented and this transferred lands in severalty to male household heads, 180 acres to each head of household. The excess was sold off to white settlers for 50 cents an acre before the allotments to the Sioux were made, hence both undervaluing and diminishing Sioux lands further.[64] The terms of the 1868 Treaty and this end result were completely unrelated to each other, signifying that the American mechanisms to recognize rights within America's own self-asserted authority structures were in fact ways to invalidate these same rights.

Indeed, the ignoring of the 1868 Treaty and the diminishing of the 'Great Sioux Reservation' was a stated objective of Federal government policy.[65] Subsequently, the Sioux Act of 1888 created the six Sioux reservations that are in existence today.[66] This was highly manipulative, and built upon the deceitful land losses of the Dawes Act. The placing of Sioux on reservations stipulated in the Dawes Act required consent, and, to induce it, many financial and other benefits were offered to Indians for parting with their lands. The inducements worked because, as Utley observes, 'the technique was to bury Indians under mountains of words while working behind the scenes to lure individuals away from the influence of the chiefs [who mostly opposed allotment]'.[67] Through dividing the people, the Commission set up to negotiate allotment, led by General Crook, eventually got the required signatures in 1890, and threw open Sioux lands for white settlement even before the lands were surveyed. This coincided with a bad winter, crop failures, hunger, starvation, epidemics and fatalities of 45 a month in a population of 5,550 at Pine Ridge alone.[68] The benefits of signing up for allotment were not sufficient to alleviate these catastrophes.

The process of dispossession continued in the 1940s when the USA sequestered Sioux reservation land (and the homes on these lands) for six dam projects on the Missouri River. The Pick–Sloan Flood Control Act empowered the Army Corps of Engineers (ACE) to run the dams and maintain authority over the Missouri river system. Again, the 1868 Treaty covered this territory. The Sioux along the river were not consulted and the Act 'condemned Indian lands without the approval of tribal councils or the secretary of the interior, and it failed to cooperate with tribal representatives even in those cases when Congress mandated it to do so'.[69] As Nick Estes points out, the Act only authorized the building of dams. It did not 'expunge Indigenous jurisdiction, treaty rights or water rights'.[70] The lands promised by treaty were then subjected to eminent domain powers, and damages for land, but not loss of water, were issued to people removed from their homes to make the area ready for flooding. The transfer of Sioux lands to ACE in this way, therefore, violated the 1868 Treaty as well as the Supreme Court decision of 1908 known as the Winters Doctrine, which holds that 'tribes retain senior, reserved rights to water flowing through the originally defined boundaries established by treaty, statute or executive order'.[71]

These dams were made to control floodwater, but also to benefit mostly non-Native consumers and recreational sports enthusiasts. Damming resulted in the loss of 550 acres of prime reservation lands, including wetlands, whole forests, as well as the loss of infrastructure and the removal of 900 families not only from their homes,[72] but from lands to which they had intimate, enduring connections. In the official accounts of the dam projects, the relocations of the Sioux were depicted as something akin to a mere engineering problem.[73] In turn, the wetlands which were the natural sponges of the ecosystem, were removed by damming, paradoxically making floods more likely in the future. This is because climate change-induced increases in precipitation in the Great Plains, and specifically the Missouri River basin, raises river water levels that can burst the banks, with no natural terrain to absorb water that the dams increasingly cannot control. This means that some of the water bodies under which DAPL traverses, which were supposed to provide water-based recreation and prevent floods, are now subject to regular flooding. According to ACE, sixty-two levees had been breached across the Midwest in March 2019, leaving a 'Swiss cheese' infrastructure.[74]

Following Sloan–Pick, entire communities were relocated because of initial flooding from the dams, mostly to far less desirable reservation lands, or even off-reservation. The subsistence agricultural economies that had been functioning well along the river were suddenly destroyed and transformed to cash and wage labour economies. Most of the plants, wildlife and commercial timber on the Crow Creek and Lower Brulé Reservations disappeared.[75] The Sioux ways of life along the river were terminated, in large part because of the loss of access to water. While the tribes were compensated, they received considerably less than the value of their losses from the US government,[76] and many tribes are still contesting the value of their losses. The flooding inundated cemeteries and burial sites, causing human remains to float to the surface.[77] Sometimes, family members did not become aware that known burials had surfaced 'until workers accidentally excavated two of them and dumped the remains into the dam embankment'.[78] As late as 2015, volunteers were still discovering and reburying Sioux remains displaced by the flooding.[79] This augments many other acts of desecration of indigenous remains and sacred sites that would occur with DAPL.

## 'This Is Like a War Crime'

As we saw earlier, the Sioux have a prophecy of a Black Snake that extends itself across the land and imperils all life, beginning with the water.[80] This Black Snake is interpreted by Sioux activists and their allies as being incarnated in the serpentine 1,172-mile DAPL, a 30-inch diameter steel tube that will carry 450,000 gallons of highly flammable oil from the Bakken and Three Forks fields in North Dakota to a terminal in Illinois.[81] Estimated in 2019 to cost $3.9 billion, it crosses the 'Great Sioux Reservation', which, as we saw, was massively diminished through the government violating its own agreements, manipulating the Sioux and inducing starvation, and then selling indigenous lands to settlers through the reservation allotment process.

The first proposed DAPL route in 2014 would have run the pipeline 10 miles from Bismarck, the North Dakota state capital. The town, which is 92 per cent white, was opposed to it, but authorities there did not have to make an objection because ACE ordered the re-routing out of concerns for leaks into the local Bismarck water supply.[82] The new route is a short distance from the Standing Rock reservation, crossing the Missouri River and going 90 feet underneath Lake Oahe, one of the ten largest lakes in the USA, created in the early 1960s by flooding from the most ecologically damaging of the Pick–Sloan dams on the Missouri River. It supplies water to the Standing Rock reservation and other locations.

DAPL carries grave health and ecological risks. The legal team acting for the Standing Rock Sioux alleged that the companies building the pipeline engaged in shoddy construction, lax safety standards and underestimation of risks,[83] a significant one being from leaks under Lake Oahe. In December 2016, Barack Obama's last full month in office, the ACE stopped the construction under the lake and mandated a thorough environmental review or, failing that, a re-routing of the pipeline. Subsequently, a legal opinion that environmental and indigenous rights concerns needed to be addressed before the pipeline proceeded was authored by Interior Department Solicitor Hilary Tompkins. ACE logged their intent to do a complete environmental study, against opposition by Republican congressmen from North Dakota, on 18 January 2017. The review was also to consider the tribe's water, land and treaty rights. This was then reversed on President Trump's second day in office, 23 January, when he signed an Executive Order to proceed with the DAPL and Keystone XL pipelines without considering either indigenous rights or environmental hazards. To enable this, and without any word of explanation, the Department of the Interior withdrew a 35-page legal opinion that concluded there was 'ample legal justification' to prevent DAPL from crossing a reservoir near the reservation.[84] On 8 February, ACE formally announced permission for the easement giving access under the lake.[85]

As with oil pipelines elsewhere,[86] contamination of water and wider local ecologies is a real possibility. Using official data on pipelines, the Center for Biological Diversity maintains that 'since 1986 pipeline accidents have spilled an average of 76,000 barrels per year or more than 3 million gallons. This is equivalent to 200 barrels every day.'[87] The Center also lists 500 fatalities in the USA from pipeline accidents since 1986. In 2017, a total of 210,000 gallons of oil leaked from the Keystone Pipeline in South Dakota. The spill occurred near the lands of the Sisseton Wahpeton Sioux. According to the South Dakota Department of Environment and Natural Resources' website, this was the third pipeline spill in the state that year. Another came in April 2017, when about 84 gallons of crude oil leaked from the DAPL in Spink County.[88] From 2010 to 2016, Sunoco Logistics, the ETP subsidiary company operating DAPL, had 200 pipeline leaks,[89] and altogether ETP and its subsidiary have amassed over 800 violations of environmental codes and $15 million in fines. Between 2010 and 2017, 'ETP and its affiliated companies released more than 41,000 barrels of hazardous liquids causing more than $100 million in property damage', according to data from the US Pipeline and Hazardous Materials Safety Administration.[90] Opposed in the courts by the Standing Rock tribe, the 2019 application to increase the capacity of the pipeline from 570,000 to 1.1m barrels a day, if approved, will vastly increase the risk of leaks.[91]

These risks and the violation of their lands mobilized the Standing Rock community to oppose DAPL. Opposition was based partly around the serious ecological problems of pipelines and the climate-change implications of fossil fuel extraction. Writer, scholar and Native rights activist Winona La Duke estimated that the money spent on DAPL, with the parallel Enbridge Line 3, 'could erect 580 two-megawatt wind turbines, install 716,000 five-kilowatt systems on that many homes, and retrofit another 283,000 homes for efficiency'.[92] Instead of baking the planet, as she put it, this would provide more sustainable energy security. Equally important is that the current-day Sioux are inheritors of treaties that did not cede the land where DAPL is built, and the sacred qualities of the land make it something like a living text that cements cultural and inter-generational continuity.[93] DAPL literally tramples on cultural heritage, passing through or over about 380 archaeological sites and burial grounds,[94] many of which were destroyed in the process according to Standing Rock spokespeople.[95] The land and waters which are violated by DAPL are also sacred for other groups, such as the Mandan. Their legends hold that they emerged into the world there, and their famous Okipa Sun Dances were held at the same location.[96]

The movement of protesters called Water Protectors (see figure 5.1) developed as three main encampments on a strip of land adjacent to the construction of the pipeline. Some of these lands were on the Standing Rock reservation. Others were on lands that had, through treaty violation, passed to the Federal government, and then to ACE, who had sold them to ETP in order for them to build the pipeline. Led by Lakota from the Standing Rock reservation, the three camps – Oceti Sakowin, Sacred Stone and Red Warrior – brought together the largest single gathering of Native Americans since the battle of Little Bighorn in 1876, and reunited the seven nations of the Sioux people.[97] Crowds of up to 10,000 people gathered at the protest site over 10 months in 2016 and 2017.[98] It also attracted non-indigenous people, including local landowners and ranchers, and supporters from all over the world.

On the long weekend from 19 to 22 November 2016 that I was volunteering at Oceti Sakowin camp, with students and faculty of the University of Wyoming American Indian Studies programme, there were about 6,000 people camping there. Most were indigenous and united in the revulsion at environmentally and socially damaging corporate extractive projects on indigenous lands. They were resisting the violation of lands whose meaning extends back in time; places where burial and sacred sites have been dug up; rivers and lakes from which water is sourced, abundant in fish, waterfowl and animals. This is one of many

**Figure 5.1** *Water Protectors assembled on Backwater Bridge being opposed by militarized police and National Guard troops in armoured vehicles, 21 November 2016.*
*Source: photograph by Øyvind Ravna.*

pipeline projects attracting substantial resistance to the adulteration of indigenous lands. Around the same time, and following DAPL, there have been protests at other pipeline sites by coalitions of indigenous and other groups. These include actions against Enbridge line 3 bringing tar sands oil through northern Minnesota, Enbridge line 5 which transports oil through unceded indigenous lands in Michigan, and the Bayou Bridge pipeline in Louisiana, as well as several locations of the Keystone XL pipeline.

In August 2016, the Governor of North Dakota declared a state of emergency and called in the National Guard. When I arrived, the security personnel facing the Water Protectors consisted of heavily militarized police, marksmen with high-powered rifles, private security guards, counter-terrorism agents from the TigerSwan company hired by ETP, and aerial surveillance by drones, aircraft and helicopters. I estimated there to be about fifty police vehicles at any given time, in addition to multiple armoured vehicles and Humvees, some cruising over sacred lands at Turtle Island, across from the protest camps. The armaments used included a high-powered water cannon, which was deployed against Water Protectors on the night of 21 November when it was −6 °C. Saturation with cold water in the extreme cold led to instant hypothermia in many of the Water Protectors that night. I could only look on as the medical tents at Oceti Sakowin, where only about 10 per cent of the volunteers were medically trained, treated 167 casualties; 26 people had to be taken to hospital in Bismarck. Altogether, about 300 people required medical treatment – including Sophia Wilansky, a 21-year-old recent graduate of Williams College who had part of her arm blown off by a concussion grenade. She had eight hours of surgery immediately afterwards, and has needed five operations in total.[99]

Security forces arrayed against the Water Protectors used high-velocity rubber bullets, concussion grenades, tear gas, tasers, mace (often sprayed from an armoured vehicle), flares and LRADS (long-range acoustic devices) that transmit high-pitched sounds capable of inducing hearing loss. Snipers with live ammunition were camped out on the hills overlooking the Oceti Sakowin camp. I witnessed the use of non-lethal weapons, and heard frequent loudhailer threats to 'use munitions to affect arrests' of anyone guilty of 'criminal trespass'. The latter could be precipitated by walking onto the Backwater Bridge, where the police had established a crude barricade composed of concrete slabs and burnt-out National Guard trucks. Water Protectors frequently gathered on the bridge, a public structure, where they were at times met by the various 'munitions', including being fired on with rubber bullets or chemical sprays at point-blank range. One of the Arapaho students in our party had to make several trips to a medical tent to be seen by a variety of volunteers trained to respond to chemical weapons. He was suffering from rubber-bullet wounds, tear-gas inhalation and the effects of pepper spray.

The protection of the pipeline entailed a fusion of public and private security. The mainstream NBC media outlet reported what many Water Protectors at Oceti Sakowin camp were saying: a mysterious unmarked plane was jamming signals so that witnesses could not disseminate what they saw, heard and felt.[100] This was supplemented by drones and a helicopter used by ETP to surveil Water Protectors and jam mobile phone signals. Subsequently, more armaments were deployed. In December 2016 and January 2017, reports and photographic evidence showed Avenger surface-to-air missile launchers pulled into place, and people at prayer, journalists and medics were targeted 'strictly for observation of ungoverned encampments to help protect private property and maintain public safety', according to the Morton County Sherriff's Department.[101] Water Protectors alleged that even the river level had been lowered by altering the dam controls, to prevent them using boats to reach the construction site. This sounds like the USA is in a state of war with indigenous people. As I walked away from the scene on Backwater Bridge on 21 November, I heard a young Native woman tell her friend, 'This is like a war crime.'

## A Permanent State of Exception

The notion of states of exception was articulated by Carl Schmitt and, more recently, developed by Giorgio Agamben.[102] It refers to circumstances in which the state maintains authority through reserving the right to act in secret, and to 'deviate from the ... common law in a case of emergency, in the interests of the maintenance of the state and of public tranquility and security'.[103] The American and other states' relationships with indigenous populations are characterized by a permanent state of exception. Both the USA and Canada demand the extinguishing of the pre-existing sovereignty of indigenous groups through some written document they produce, and these are reinforced by subsequent passage of laws applying to the indigenous groups. This usually entails more laws, the ignoring of agreements, and refusal to enforce agreements or executive actions, so that many of the rights applicable to indigenous groups can be nullified.

The state of exception is particularly entrenched in the case of the Sioux because the original assertion of settler-state sovereignty, as we have seen, was made through the sale of purloined indigenous land. If American state ownership over indigenous lands could be obtained this way and sovereignty proclaimed by assertion alone, then it is a short step to making the Bill of Rights inapplicable to indigenous peoples, as was indeed the case at Standing Rock. The actions that I described deter the exercise of rights covered in the first ten Amendments to the Constitution to lawful protest and free speech. The suppression of speech and the circulation of imagery contradict the freedom of expression enshrined in the First Amendment, a freedom already violated in the past by the banning of indigenous spiritual practices, and the appointment of Christian zealots as Federal agents responsible for reservation administration, to Christianize.[104]

Freedom of speech was violated very directly at Standing Rock by ETP operating an unmarked plane to jam internet and mobile phone signals to prevent the dissemination of information and images about the conflict. Supplementing this is the deterrence of free speech and lawful protest through the official violence described above. When Water Protectors have contested the excessive use of force to counter protest, they have been rebuffed. For example, the FBI denied Sophia Wilansky the return of shrapnel from her arm to use as evidence to support her lawsuit against North Dakota police, despite a written agreement between Wilansky's father and the FBI to release the materials 'in a timely manner'.[105] More widely, the suppression of free speech occurred through the criminalization and redefinition of protest, along with FBI investigations of Water Protectors on terrorism charges.[106] Altogether, 836 arrests of activists were made in southern North Dakota over a six-month span beginning in late 2016. Of those, only 26 were convicted of a crime,[107] and many were arrested on the rarely used charge of 'civil disorder', used in the past to suppress social movements such as the American Indian Movement. On a single day in October 2016, 141 arrests were made.[108] Evidence to support the charges was frequently supplied directly by ETP, showing collusion between the company and police. ETP hired TigerSwan to gather intelligence on those contesting DAPL, and their evidence, including allegations that Water Protectors were terrorists and jihadists, was used by Morton County Sheriff's department to justify more intense levels of official violence.[109] *The Intercept* revealed that: 'More than 100 internal documents leaked to The Intercept by a TigerSwan contractor, as well as a set of over 1,000 documents obtained via public records requests, reveal that TigerSwan spearheaded a multifaceted private security operation characterized by sweeping and invasive surveillance of protesters.'[110]

Prison sentences for some Water Protectors were 36–57 months in length, with a man from Pine Ridge receiving 3 years for simply setting a small fire near the police barricade.[111] People who disseminated information about the conflict, such as journalists and film makers with Press passes, were especially targeted for arrest.[112] For example, on 1

February 2017, Laguna Pueblo journalist Jenni Monet was arrested while interviewing Water Protectors who were setting up a new camp. All 76 of the interviewees and the journalist were arrested for criminal trespass and inciting a riot. They were held for 30 hours without charge.[113]

The criminalization of free speech has been introduced in many states through anti-protest legislation relating to sites of 'critical infrastructure'. In North Dakota, Representative Bill Tveit, one of the sponsors of such legislation, called it without irony a 'landowner rights bill'.[114] In early 2019, eight states introduced template legislation, formulated by the right-wing American Legislative Exchange Council, to impose steep criminal penalties for protest against oil and gas infrastructure projects, under the justification of national security.[115] According to the American Civil Liberties Union (ACLU), twenty pieces of legislation designed to limit the right to protest have been introduced since 2017, with success for bills in Oklahoma and Tennessee, and the two Dakota states.[116] By 2019, North Dakota had passed four anti-protest bills, ranging from increased fines for trespassing on private property to punishment for wearing a mask in any public forum without written permission. Another bill would make pipeline projects exempt from normal public disclosure rules and seal records permanently.[117] As DAPL was built into other territories, the protests continued, and in 2018 thirteen people faced five years in prison under new anti-protest laws in Louisiana.[118] Such protest in the vicinity of an oil pipeline is a felony in the state, punishable by up to five years in prison, and in Texas such trespassing is also a felony carrying a two-year prison sentence and a fine of up to $10,000.[119] With the Federal government actively working with local officials to hide records and deny public records requests regarding plans for future pipeline protests, it is also evident that the suppression of information in order to shut down rights to free speech and protest is well under way.[120]

The only possible relief from this seemingly endless cycle of human rights violation is from the judiciary, but it is a component of the state committing the violations. Despite this, several legal efforts have been made and are ongoing. These challenge the legitimacy of various aspects of DAPL, although the pipeline is already now complete. Lawyers, activists, NGOs and regulatory bodies have questioned whether ACE adequately consulted the Standing Rock tribe. They have also sought judicial reviews of whether the 1st and 14th Amendment rights were violated by police and TigerSwan during the conflict, and whether authorities imperiled life and excessively burdened the Standing Rock tribe by closing off a main road between the reservation and the town of Bismarck. Additionally, ACE has been pressed to release documents on the environmental impact of DAPL, and TigerSwan have been charged with operating illegally in North Dakota.[121] Various configurations of Sioux tribal governments are actively taking part in these legal challenges. At the same time, an unsuccessful countersuit was launched by ETP against various groups of Water Protectors.[122]

While the current conflict over the siting of DAPL on lands guaranteed to indigenous peoples requires an engagement with colonial histories, courts have generally not advocated the reopening of arguments about past actions. Thus, judiciaries have not addressed the original and ensuing duplicities that enabled DAPL to be an issue in the first place. Instead, only *post-hoc* compensation has been offered. For example:

> In 1980, in the *United States v. the Sioux Nation of Indians*, the Supreme Court ruled that Congress had acted in bad faith. The courts set fair compensation for the Black Hills at $102 million. It is estimated that the settlement's value has appreciated to $1.3 billion today. The Sioux, however, will not accept this payment. They contend that they do not want the money. What they want is their sacred Black Hills back. In addition, Sioux leaders argue, $1.3 billion, based on a valuation of the land when it was seized, represents only a fraction of the gold, timber, and other natural resources that have been extracted from it.[123]

As in various cases referred to the Indian Claims Court, and more recently through the Land Distribution Bill, whereby violations of treaty were remedied by the depositing of funds that indigenous groups could claim in compensation, there is no option to reverse the original violations of rights.[124] Besides this, exceptions to universal rights were either built into the laws themselves or activated in the implementation of executive actions of eminent domain. For example, when ACE assumed control of lands along the Missouri River after the dam building, it did not negotiate with the affected reservations in any meaningful way, but sought compensation deals with white farmers on a case-by-case basis. Indian reservations were compensated via tribal governments, rather than the individual indigenous allotment holders whose lands were flooded.[125]

The starkest conclusion one could reach is that the exercise of Sioux rights to their lands, and to block the pipeline on lands illegitimately confiscated from them, is itself illegitimate because many human rights do not apply to Native Americans. The same conclusion was reached in the *Dann* case, originally heard in the Supreme Court in 2002, in which the Western Shoshone filed suit against the US violation of the Treaty of Ruby Valley of 1863, in which extensive lands in what was then Nevada Territory were granted to them, and which did not contain any land cession. The USA argued that the land had subsequently been appropriated through 'general encroachment', a hitherto unknown legal concept, and attempted to remedy the situation through the Indian Claims Commission. The case also went to the Inter American Court of Human Rights and was commented on by the UN Committee on the Elimination of Racial Discrimination (CERD). In 2006, CERD reported that the 'gradual encroachment' doctrine is contradicted by 'the fact that the Western Shoshone peoples have reportedly continued to use and occupy the lands and their natural resources in accordance with their traditional land tenure patterns', and the Indian Claims Commission procedures 'did not comply with contemporary international human rights norms, principles and standards that govern determination of indigenous property interests'.[126] In this case, the invention of the construct 'gradual encroachment' legitimated treaty violations and thereby ruled out significant remedy for human rights violations.

When Native Americans have sought enforcement of treaties and complained about the bad faith of the state, the American judicial system has continually rebuffed them. This was done decisively in the Supreme Court case *Lone Wolf* v. *Hitchcock* in 1903, in which the Kiowa contested the enforcement of the Treaty of Medicine Lodge Creek of 1867 – specifically, that land cessions had to be approved by three-quarters of the adult members of the tribe. Since land cessions had been unilaterally made by the government after the signing of the treaty, *Lone Wolf* was petitioning against government fraud. However, the Supreme Court in effect nullified the treaty by asserting that Congressional plenary powers exculpated the government for the violation of the treaty when proposed land cessions did not elicit requisite tribal approval. *Lone Wolf* states that 'plenary authority over the tribal relations of the Indians has been exercised by Congress from the beginning, and the power has always been deemed a political one, not subject to be controlled by the judicial department of the government'.[127] Congress therefore 'summoned absolute legislative power unrestrained by constitutional limitations or judicial review'.[128] It is clearly stated in the judgment that even tribal property is under the ultimate authority of Congress, and can be confiscated without compensation, and is therefore not covered by the 5th Amendment of the Constitution.[129] 'In other words', as Calloway puts it, 'Indians had no rights that Congress was bound to protect'.[130]

Under the ruling, Congress may abrogate an Indian treaty without the consent of the tribe. Indeed, denying such consent was the intent at the time, as numerous Congressmen remarked, backing up their argument by appealing to the concept of Native Americans as children or wards of the state whose property could not be left to their own disposal.[131]

*Lone Wolf* is still the law today, but it was held to be inapplicable to the compensation for the Sioux loss of the Black Hills in 1980 in *United States* v. *the Sioux Nation of Indians*. Significantly, this case did not pronounce on the legitimacy of the taking of the Black Hills, only the compensation for taking it.

The denial of the integrity of treaties, and therefore the human rights of indigenous peoples to their lands, is based on a set of state assertions which ultimately refer only to themselves. Absolute Congressional power over Native peoples is 'from the beginning', as boldly stated in *Lone Wolf*. Before that, Tocqueville observed this *a priori* assumption of the American state from records of the Committee on Indian Affairs in 1830: the 'fundamental principle, that the Indians had no right, by virtue of their ancient possession, either of soil or sovereignty, has never been abandoned either expressly or by implication'.[132] This does not mean, however, that contestations over treaty rights, and indeed rights to land such as those on which ETP is encamped, cannot be reviewed, as these are subjects of the upcoming Supreme Court case *Carpenter* v. *Murphy*, involving jurisdiction on lands guaranteed by treaty to the Muscogee Creek but not formally 'disestablished' by the USA.[133] Furthermore, the Sioux and their legal team have continued to contest the legal, environmental and cultural ramifications of DAPL – which doubled its operating capacity in 2019 – in the courts.

## The Impossibility of International Indigenous Human Rights

Despite these adversities, there are scholars who optimistically claim that indigenous peoples are today active agents wielding power through local councils, tribal assemblies and even corporations. If we confine ourselves narrowly to a legal analysis of indigenous rights, it can appear as though the global story is one of gradual progress towards the formal recognition of indigenous human rights. Looked at through court cases, legislative acts and government policies over the last fifty years or so, concrete gains can be identified, and the United Nations Declaration on the Rights of Indigenous Peoples (UNDRIP) of 2007 could provide international validation of these rights. While UNDRIP is important, it is non-binding and it must be incorporated into state laws. From the point of view of indigenous peoples, these laws are, of course, imposed laws. Sometimes, immense cultural differences separate those who are allegedly making 'claims' for human rights and state authorities. These differences pertain to the fundamentals of the processes themselves, including very different epistemological assumptions about human relationships, culture–nature relationships, and over the very concepts of rights and law that may apply to land and resources.

Although various national and international laws offer recognition of indigenous rights, they still presume that states will honour, implement and enforce them. If indigenous peoples' human rights reside in non-binding international and binding domestic legal arenas, reversals of treaty violations, land confiscation and ecologically disastrous extractive activities on what little land indigenous people have left seem remote.

One obvious reason for the pessimism is that indigenous peoples remain as colonized peoples. A 2016 report to the Human Rights Council by the Special Rapporteur on the Rights of Indigenous Peoples, Victoria Tauli-Corpuz, flagged the militarized attacks on indigenous peoples at Standing Rock within a list of similar violent reactions to indigenous human rights claims by states such as Russia, Honduras, Philippines and Colombia. Tauli-Corpuz believed that this was part of a 'global crisis' symbolized by the 200-or-so murders of indigenous and other defenders of land rights and environmental protection around the world.[134] The irony is that the UN is the major institutional forum in which indigenous voices can be heard, but, despite the existence of the Permanent Forum on Indigenous Issues in New York, the UN cannot breach state sovereignty to implement indigenous peoples' human rights. States can, of course, be guided by international laws and standards, such as Article 27 of the International Covenant on Civil and Political Rights, which has been in force since 1976, and the ILO Convention No. 169 of 1989, both of which established rights for indigenous and minority communities in respect of their unique ways of life. But none of this amounts to anything other than moral persuasion.

Questions which are of importance to indigenous peoples are almost all connected with denials of their sovereignty. These include concerns over land confiscation; forced relocations; forced assimilation; militarization of landscapes; prohibitions against indigenous religious, linguistic and cultural practices; and compulsive bad faith of states. While UNDRIP and other international legal instruments affirm various indigenous human rights, and have been used successfully in some court cases around the world,[135] there are no enforcement provisions. ILO No. 169 specifically indicates that the term 'peoples' shall have no standing in international law, and UNDRIP features a final Article that clearly affirms the sovereignty of states, a proviso which in effect entrenches the exceptions to indigenous human rights. As hard hitting as Tauli-Corpuz' HRC report is, its contents will be received by many governments indifferently, if at all, and this is why the kind of resistance offered by the Standing Rock tribe and its allies offers such hope for change.

# 6

# Decolonizing Human Rights

## Introduction

Interspersed throughout these chapters are three broad observations. Firstly, formulations of what later became universal human rights largely did not apply to colonized and enslaved people. The universal took shape and life through the exceptions. Although some citizens of colonizing and enslaving states might have been uncomfortable about them, these exceptions were not seen to invalidate universalism because the people subject to exceptions were regarded as having qualities that placed them outside human universality. Secondly, after slavery abolition acts and decolonization, human rights became more prominent within state legal systems, but exceptions remained, and formerly colonized and enslaved peoples' human rights were contoured by attitudes and policies rooted in colonialism. Thirdly, because indigenous peoples have been not decolonized, the original exceptions to human rights upon which state sovereignty was based have maintained themselves, and further exceptions, exclusions and violations have been extended.

As colonialism and slavery have re-emerged as current focuses of scholarship, cultural production and political activism, the stratified nature of human rights is increasingly exposed. The bland legalism and soothing reassurances of liberal progress obscure the structural continuities from the past, revealing a colonialism of human rights. Therefore, in concluding, I argue that there is a need to decolonize human rights in terms both of bringing colonialism and slavery more centrally into discussions of human rights and by concrete actions. I suggest that this can be addressed by making the exceptions to liberal universalism the centre of human rights discussions, but more crucially through actions of reparative justice and indigenizing law. These are at least partial antidotes to the suffocating parochialism of human rights and the Western legal theory it is encased within.[1] Firstly, it is helpful to look at some context that might help with understanding the confusions over human rights.

## Colonial Disorientation and Redemption

Indigenous and colonized peoples reflect Europe back to itself. This was apparent at the outset when the violent assaults of early European colonizing expeditions and settlements resulted in Native populations rapidly declining.[2] In these spaces of death, and amid peoples they believed to be inferior and strange, colonial agents could find themselves destabilized. Their violence often mimicked the primitivity and madness they ascribed to the Native. This occurs in what Michael Taussig called the 'epistemic murk' of colonialism.[3] Although European colonists had clearly defined ideas as to what separated them from those whom they were subjugating, violence and terror created an indefinable landscape in which the separateness of the indigenous and the European could not be preserved. To assert their dominance, colonists mirrored the barbarism that they projected onto those they dominated, and, as Taussig shows, this was obvious in places where Native populations were inducted into lucrative resource-extraction projects. Heroic masculine exploration narratives that Taussig cites, as well as more famous ones such as Henry Morton Stanley's *In Darkest Africa*, show the disorientation of steadfast and righteous commitment to imperial missions alloyed to large losses of Native life.

The many incidences of colonial disorientation are echoed vividly in literature such as George Orwell's 'Shooting an Elephant'. It is a short story in which the natives of a colonial outpost in Burma insist that the British administrator who narrates the story kill an elephant that allegedly had an attack of 'must' and charged into the village. The colonial officer accedes to their requests and acts out the authority assigned to him by both Britain and the native subjects themselves. He doesn't want to execute this cruel authority – it is against his better judgement – but he ends up emptying a rifle into the head of a beautiful animal that was peacefully munching grass. Describing himself in the third person, Orwell's colonial administrator shares with Conrad's Kurtz in *Heart of Darkness* – who was 'hollow to the core'[4] – the feeling of becoming 'a sort of hollow, posing dummy'. He continues: 'for it is the condition of his rule that he shall spend his life in trying to impress the "natives", and so in every crisis he has got to do what the "natives" expect of him. He wears a mask, and his face grows to fit it.'[5] The disorientation in Orwell's and Conrad's protagonists is brought on by the conflicted selves generated by the colonial enterprise, which – as Kurtz, who lived with a 'crop of unextinguishable regrets', realized – was being carried out by 'unsound method'.[6]

Carl Jung felt something of this when he visited Taos Pueblo in 1925 and spoke with Ochwiay Biano, the chief of the Pueblo. Such was the chief's clarity that Jung remarks: 'I was able to talk with him as I have rarely been able to talk with a European.'[7] Biano tells Jung that 'whites always want something; they are always uneasy and restless. We do not know what they want. We do not understand them. We think that they are mad.' Overcome by emotion, Jung then reflects:

> It was enough. What we from our point of view call colonization, missions to the heathen, spread of civilization, etc., has another face – the face of a bird of prey seeking with cruel intention for distant quarry – a face worthy of a race of pirates and highwaymen. All the eagles and other predatory creatures that adorn our coats of arms seem to me apt psychological representatives of our true nature.[8]

Seen through the experiences of indigenous people such as Biano, Afro-descended peoples and the formerly colonized, no articulation of human rights can be conceptually separated from the unreason and predation of Europe.

In this context, what then are the functions of human rights? Perhaps one of them is to reassure those who want to think well of their nations and histories, and perhaps also those who have been these states' victims. As Susan Sontag tells us of photographs of atrocities in distant places, 'we feel we are not accomplices to what caused the suffering. Our sympathy proclaims our innocence as well as our impotence.' The declaration of sympathy is also a setting aside of 'how our privileges are located on the same map as their suffering ... and may be linked to their suffering.'[9] Open acknowledgement of links between privilege and suffering are instead dislodged as focus shifts to amelioration through human rights, instead of culpability and reparation.

Nevertheless, unless digital capitalism completely erases and edits history à la 1984, this uneasiness will persist. In his Ebony magazine article of 1965, 'The White Man's Guilt', James Baldwin maintains that to the white a black person is 'a most disagreeable mirror'.[10] Even though whites have largely written the history of the USA, they know that even this history does not flatter them, for it is evident in the 'things you have bought with the flesh you have sold'.[11] At the turn of the twentieth century, W. E. B. Du Bois made a similar point. In perhaps the most important chapter of *The Souls of Black Folks*, 'Of Our Spiritual Strivings', he begins with reflecting on the 'Negro problem' and his own position within it. Du Bois remarks that whites approach him as if to say, 'how does it feel to be a problem?'[12] The problem, of course, is what to do with those whose ancestors were captured, violated, raped and murdered by members of a group that professed allegiance to virtue, the integrity of which is tested by the mere presence of descendants of the enslaved. Updating Baldwin's observations, white visitors today regularly complain about plantation museums in the American South that concentrate on the role of enslaved African people in the building and maintaining of the ornate and richly decorated houses that they tour.[13]

In his talks in Britain in schools and other institutions, Barbadian social historian Hilary Beckles found 'shame, guilt and awkwardness', which 'conspired to produce the deafening denial and solemn silence that define the responses of the British nation'.[14] This extends also to discussions of race in general, and of the complex histories and ethnic mixes that comprise the population of contemporary Britain. 'It's the muting of the conversation', Afua Hirsch says in her reflection on the subject, continuing: 'the fact that we cannot in Britain today cope with exploring and accommodating these identities in a healthy way'.[15] The Afro-descended or indigenous person is not merely an emblem of a historical wrong, but part of a group that is a surviving embodiment of crimes. Not all such people today are suffering, and many have done well in the largely materialistic terms approved within contemporary capitalist societies, but gaping inequalities remain. These inequalities have resulted in massive transgenerational privilege, national wealth and global power for the beneficiaries.

Therefore, we can ask whether human rights are an attempt to moderate, or disguise, predation. If we admit that predation and *differential* human rights are inter-related, since both are involved in European colonial missions, then we return to the question of what human rights represent.

## Human Rights under Titanic Inequalities

If human rights are at some level a rhetorical amelioration of guilt induced by realizations of racial exceptions, they increasingly are situated in contexts of diminishing potential to be supported and realized. This is because contemporary societies mirror colonial and slave societies to the extent that extreme inequalities are normalized by powerful institutions and governments. As a result, resort to guilt is attenuated. Capitalism, the economic shell within which contemporary human rights operates, is a vehicle for the perpetuation of vast inequalities. David Cole points out that:

> Today, the twenty richest Americans have more wealth between them than the bottom half of the US population – some 152 million people. In 1979, CEOs of America's most successful businesses earned, on average, about thirty times as much as their workers. By 2013, they earned almost three hundred times as much. And in the thirty-year period from 1979 to 2008, the top 10 percent of Americans received 100 percent of the benefits from growth in income, while the incomes of the bottom 90 percent fell.[16]

These national inequalities are reproduced even more starkly between nations and regions of the world. Organizations such as the OECD and Oxfam have drawn attention to this. In 2017, Oxfam argued, at the World Economic Forum at the Swiss resort of Davos, that the wealthiest eight people in the world owned more wealth than the bottom half of the global population of 3.5 billion. Even Crédit Suisse pointed out that the wealthiest 1 per cent of the world own more than all the rest put together. Huge swathes of the world population own nothing. As Lessenich has observed in discussing these claims,[17] although these statistics are often dismissed by financial organizations and liberal economists who still maintain the master narrative of ever increasing global prosperity and gradual development of the Global South, it is uncontestable that global inequality exceeds national inequalities. Overall global inequality, he argues, is more extreme than nation-states with the most unequal income distributions.

If human rights and democracy are bound together, at a certain level of inequality, democracy cannot exist except in eviscerated form, pared down to ballot boxes and referenda, many of which are of dubious integrity. The link is broken. The liberal state merely presides over these inequalities, and its dependence on legitimation from corporations means that its policies facilitate continuing deep inequality. The 'rule of law' simply legitimizes ever increasing across-the-board inequalities, with vast segments of national populations having little investment in the idea that human rights will alleviate their sufferings.

The 'titanic inequalities' Patrick Deneen[18] describes in his critique of liberalism reflect titanic differences in access to rights – but, more fundamentally, the right to have rights and the right to invalidate rights.

Non-universal human rights are not some recent ideological backlash of racist and nationalist populism sweeping through Western liberal countries – they were enshrined in 'liberalism's founding text',[19] John Locke's *Second Treatise on Government*. Locke shows that the commonwealth or political society that emerged with the mythical social contract would be a world of inequalities, enlarged further through the advent of private property, which Locke conceived as obtaining by original right through labour and cultivation of the soil on common lands. Through money, the advent of which was needed to transfer and expand property, as well as commodities of all kinds, the empire of private property could expand. Once societies such as those of the largely egalitarian indigenous groups were replaced by Protestant-Ethic capitalism in English North America, the path was clear for the vast extension of structured inequality to occur through settler colonialism.

Thus, it is not just that private property expands inequality, it is that racial exclusion from the right to property amounts to an *a priori* condemnation of such groups to the far margins of liberal society. Locke imagined indigenous peoples to subsist in the most rudimentary ways on infinite lands of 'waste', lacking even the comforts of the English peasant – 'And a King of a large fruitful Territory there feeds, lodges, and is clad worse than a day Labourer in England.'[20] In his view, if American Indians transformed into farmers and saw themselves and nature as commodities, they would experience social elevation. Emergence out of the precarious 'state of nature' was part of a grand historical movement that American Indians would be forced to join. 'In the beginning all the World was America', Locke proclaimed, following it with 'for no such thing as *Money* was any where known'.[21] The future envisioned by liberalism was one of cultural homogeneity, and inequality within it. '*Money*' went to those who obtained property.

At least one of the links between democracy and human rights was broken from this founding principle of liberalism, whereby money was constituted to replace communal co-operation as a basis for inevitable social evolution. We know also that liberalism spawned the capitalist economy, which, with industrialization, ensured that property was a function of capital rather than shared historical attachments to community and land, as practised by both indigenous peoples and European peasants. Marx argued in *The Grundrisse* that capitalism precipitated the destruction of these feudal attachments, replacing them with an interdependence of producers and owners of capital bound together solely by monetary exchange. Exchange therefore became an amoral global bond, and reduced people to seeing others only in terms of their usefulness. In Marx's view, this alienated people not only from each other – since people were reduced to competing individuals – but from themselves, since the products of their labour were appropriated by capital. Hence, 'individuals by following their pure self-interest realise their social, or rather general, interest [and] this means merely that they exert pressure upon one another under the conditions of capitalist production'.[22]

## Disavowing Human Rights

The perplexing co-existence of a global capitalist amorality of vast inequalities with the morality of universal human rights is edging towards resolution as liberal Western governments openly reject international human rights norms applying to their or their allies' policies or governmental personnel. In this way, possibilities for state actions or legislation to diminish such rights have proliferated. For example, pro-Brexit campaigners and politicians in Britain were motivated by the desire to be free from the European Convention on Human Rights, which was brought into UK domestic law with the 1998 Human Rights Act. It covers issues such as employment, religious freedom, social security, inquests and freedom of the press,[23] which will no longer apply when Britain departs the EU. In 2018, the UK Parliament specifically voted not to import the European Charter of Fundamental Rights – which pronounces on institutional respect for social, political and economic rights – into UK law after the exit from the EU.[24] In 2015, then Prime Minister David Cameron secretly changed the ministerial code to make international human rights laws less explicitly binding on officials. This was challenged in court but the activists contesting it lost the case, with the May government arguing that the changed code should still apply.[25] The UK government has also announced plans to exonerate its soldiers unilaterally from historical allegations of breaches of international human rights laws,[26] and it continues to supply lethal military arms to states on its own human rights priority list. These sales amount to £12 billion, or about one-third of the British arms sales.[27]

Calling it a 'cesspool of political bias', the USA withdrew from the UN's HRC in 2018, largely over criticism of Israel's killings of civilians in Gaza and the Occupied West Bank.[28] Claiming self-defense, Israeli Prime Minister Benjamin Netanyahu, who was facing corruption and bribery charges at the time, asserted that the HRC is hypocritical and has no legitimacy because of its report condemning Israel's killing of civilians in Gaza.[29] Britain's Foreign Secretary Jeremy Hunt announced, in 2019, that Britain would oppose every measure in the HRC specifically condemning Israel's actions and labelled the UN body 'disproportionate and discriminatory'. Hunt also apologized to British Jewish leaders for Britain's capping of Jewish immigration to Palestine in 1939.[30]

In June 2018, President Trump openly called for the abandonment of a principle enshrined in the Bill of Rights: due process of law, for immigrants at the US–Mexico border.[31] Often through Executive Orders, Trump has sought to reverse many of the human rights protections in laws and policies going back to the Constitution. These include attacks on civil and voting rights – comprising also of dissolving a commission investigating the integrity of voting systems – rolling back restrictions on police actions, the reversing of protections for disabled people and sexual minorities, and eliminating similar protections for workers and immigrants. Despite all this, Nikki Haley, then the US ambassador to the UN, insisted that 'the United States will continue to be a world leader in calling for human rights for all people and in calling attention to mass atrocities'.[32] This assertion is baffling, but may be more coherent if human rights are redefined to eliminate certain kinds of protections, which is what the US administration subsequently attempted to do.

Less than a year after this, Secretary of State Mike Pompeo announced support for the global gag rule preventing the USA from supporting any NGO involved in campaigns against sexual violence that might endorse abortions, regardless of the contexts in which conception might have occurred, and this extended to a threatened veto of a Security Council resolution on sexual violence in conflict zones where rapes are common.[33] Pompeo's statement was framed as an endorsement of human rights, and this has been extended in his Commission on Unalienable Rights, chaired by lawyer Mary Ann Glendon. In the context of Pompeo's concerns that 'rights claims are often aimed more at rewarding interest groups and dividing humanity into subgroups', the Commission will address these questions: 'What are our fundamental freedoms? Why do we have them? Who or what grants these rights? How do we know if a claim of human rights is true? What happens when rights conflict? Should certain categories of rights be inextricably "linked" to other rights?'[34]

At the same time, the USA refused to comply with routine UN human rights monitoring from Special Rapporteurs and independent experts over potential human rights violations such as police brutality, capital punishment and the separation of migrant children from their families at the US–Mexico border.[35] National Security Adviser John Bolton threatened economic sanctions if the ICC took actions against American military personnel alleged to be involved in human rights abuses in Afghanistan. 'We will', Bolton said 'ban its judges and prosecutors from entering the United States. We will sanction their funds in the US financial system, and we will prosecute them in the US criminal system. We will do the same for any company or state that assists an ICC investigation of Americans.'[36] A few months after Bolton's speech, the USA revoked ICC Special Prosecutor Fatou Bensouda's visa to travel to New York. The Trump administration, however, is not unique since the combination of both proclaiming reverential allegiance to human rights and violating the same rights claimed to be embraced has been a hallmark of US foreign policy since the early twentieth century. As Grandin observed of US interventions in Latin America, the USA 'so openly championed martial virtue and violence as the best way to spread human rights'.[37]

It is not surprising then, that a recent poll surveying people in twenty-eight countries showed that, while people believe that universal human rights are important, large numbers do not perceive them as being enjoyed equally. Only four in ten people in Britain, France and the USA thought that everyone in their country enjoyed the same basic rights.[38] Zeid Ra'ad al-Hussein, the former Director of the HRC, predicted the collapse of the UN itself because of the ordinate control of states, especially the five permanent Security Council members.[39] Their power often makes appeals to, and enforcement of, human rights on grounds other than state security, geopolitical strategies and commerce impossible. Hussein's successor, Michelle Bachelet, complained that budget cuts caused by states not paying their dues on time was already negatively influencing the ability of the HRC to monitor compliance with human rights standards, especially in the areas of children's rights, civil and political repression, discrimination against women, torture and racial discrimination.[40]

I have alluded to only some of the most glaring gaps between the promise of alignment to liberal values and human rights and the policies and actions of Western states. Even though Western publics, opposition politicians and judicial reviews may raise alarms, a 'political culture of bad faith'[41] is now openly expressed in political discourses. These are evident when state officials make claims that are obviously contradicted by actions and policies. For example, close diplomatic ties between the American and British governments and Saudi Arabia can be seen to condone a monarchy that ruthlessly suppresses internal dissent, stringently polices cultural and gender expression, and executes vast numbers of prisoners every year. Externally, its bombing of Houthi militia in Yemen has created a humanitarian crisis. To admit openly that the arms sales from Britain and the USA are more important than human rights, and even human life, is to expose the hypocrisy. Hence, supplementary justification is required. Here is an example from UK Foreign Secretary Jeremy Hunt:

Britain's history and our values require us to play our part in making a constructive difference in the Middle East – and our unique links in the region mean that we have the ability to do so. Our strategic relationship with Saudi Arabia and the United Arab Emirates allows us the opportunity to influence their leaders. Since becoming foreign secretary last July, I have paid two visits to both countries.

We could, of course, decide to condemn them instead. We could halt our military exports and sever the ties that British governments of all parties have carefully preserved for decades, as critics are urging.

But in doing so we would also surrender our influence and make ourselves irrelevant to the course of events in Yemen. Our policy would be simply to leave the parties to fight it out, while denouncing them impotently from the sidelines.

That would be morally bankrupt and the people of Yemen would be the biggest losers.[42]

This is just one illustration of apparent hypocrisy being rhetorically reasoned away. Hunt does this by avoiding any specific details, keeping British actions vague ('strategic' can, of course, mean anything) and not mentioning the grounds for any putative condemnation of Saudi Arabia and its Gulf allies, which likewise are autocracies. First, there is the appeal to 'Britain's ... values', which are tacitly assumed to be virtuous. Then the dilemma is sketched out, but in such a way as to avoid describing any meaningful context. Finally, condemnation of Britain's arms sales is dismissed as 'morally bankrupt' because the munitions Saudi Arabia uses are assumed – and only by ignoring evidence – to be for the betterment of the people of Yemen, rather than for bombing civilian populations in a proxy war against Iran, which backs the Houthi militia in Yemen. Hunt reinforced this in his unsuccessful candidacy for Prime Minister, indicating that the 'strict licensing system' was sufficient and that he was 'happy for British manufacturers to benefit' from arms sales to Saudi Arabia.[43] According to the NGO Save the Children, this war has caused the death by starvation of 85,000 children; and 16 million people, half the national population, is threatened by starvation.[44] As Robert Worth observed: 'During two weeks of reporting in September [2018], I saw suffering on a scale I have rarely seen anywhere: overcrowded hospitals full of skeletal, starving children; makeshift camps of displaced people begging for handouts, many of them with war wounds; child soldiers on almost every street.'[45]

A similar logic has been used by British and American administrations for several decades. Violations of human rights, such as assassinations, military attacks in which civilian populations are known to be victims, torture, detention without trial, open rejection of the Geneva

Convention and secret renditions, are permissible to pre-empt what are predicted to be far worse outcomes, either 'strategically' or otherwise. A doctrine known as 'lesser evil' emerged in this context as a tenet of Western liberalism, a current of opinion and political strategy which maintains that the violation of certain codes of democracy and human rights is preferable to respecting rights supposedly guaranteed to certain populations. 'Unlawful combatants' detained at Guantánamo Bay and subject to torture, or Palestinians in Gaza and the Occupied Territories subject to assassinations and collective punishment, would fall under this doctrine.[46] The 'lesser evil' approach works by homogenizing the populations in question, rather than treating them as individuals with human rights. This is done in order to protect what is represented as national security through the suspension of laws and the violation of human rights. For example, the Authorization to Use Military Force resolution passed by the US Congress shortly after the 9/11 attacks provides Executive powers to carry out actions normally prohibited by the US Constitution and the commitments of the USA to international law.[47] On occasion, such practices have even been considered human rights measures, as, for example, when a British court ruled so in 2007, with the indefinite detention of a man in Iraq.[48]

Given the obvious distaste among liberal states for abiding by human rights standards, especially when they compromise 'strategic' considerations, perhaps what is needed are more open discussions of bad faith. If Western liberalism, and former colonial and slave states that embody it, were brought more centrally into human rights conversations, ways to address ongoing injustice could be more honestly discussed. Although not without difficulties, one possibility is reparative justice. This is crucial because, unlike most liberal human rights discourse, reparative justice recognizes that the crimes of the past have continuous expressions – both for the perpetrators, who within the same hegemonic process permanently enriched their societies, and for the victims who were thereby impoverished for generations. Reparations offer possibilities for decolonizing human rights by addressing the foundational exceptions to human rights themselves.

## Reparative Justice

While many descendants of enslaved and colonized peoples are concerned with remembering the past, state politicians are more insistent on suppressing, denying, forgetting and urging descendants of crimes of colonialism to 'move on'. Representatives of states, as well as other institutions such as corporations, shipping companies, banks and universities, that benefitted from slavery and colonialism can simply indicate that the people who undertook the practices now deemed abhorrent are long dead, and little meaningful justice can be applied so long after the crimes. Furthermore, because these atrocities occurred or were instigated in the past, those whose present wealth, status and superior rights are attributable to slavery and colonialism can hold up their hands and claim that they cannot rectify the past. What they sometimes do, however, is make symbolic changes that recognize the abhorrence while incurring no dent in their wealth and prestige. In fact, such symbolic initiatives may enhance prestige, and possibly wealth, without any alteration of the structural inequalities and states of exception that evolve from colonialism and slavery.

Universities have been at the forefront of efforts to address these histories. Higher-learning institutions were beneficiaries of colonialism and slavery through bequests and legacies derived from the ownership and sale of enslaved Africans going back to the seventeenth century. Within the last decade, due to black activists and students and their allies, many institutions have recognized their benefits from slavery. One of the first was the Ivy League institution Brown University (see figure 6.1), whose main benefactors were four brothers after whom the university is named. They owned ships that transported enslaved people from West Africa to the Americas. In 2003, a major report from the university recommended that the institution:

> (1) tell the truth about its historical ties to slavery, and include this in freshman orientation, (2) create a slave trade memorial, (3) set up an academic centre for the study of slavery, (4) maintain high ethical standards in university investments, (5) expand opportunities at Brown for those disadvantaged by slavery, and (6) set up a fund to help educate the children of Rhode Island, the state in which the university is located.[49]

The Center for the Study of Slavery and Justice which evolved out of this report was mandated to pursue research questions such as:

> What were the conditions on the ships used to bring slaves to America?
>    What kinds of knowledge – political, religious, agricultural, artistic and otherwise – did enslaved people create?
>    What were the links between slavery and present-day phenomena like racial profiling and human trafficking?[50]

In 2016, Georgetown University also recognized its debt to enslaved Africans. It took similar steps to acknowledge, apologize for, and provide

**Figure 6.1** *Slavery Memorial at Brown University by Martin Puryear, installed in 2014.*
*Source: photograph by Warren Jagger.*

some measure of recompense for the benefits it derived from slavery, particularly the sale of 272 slaves in 1838 to rescue the university from debt. This included the delivery of an apology to some of the descendants of the enslaved people by the university president and a Jesuit priest. A *New York Times* editorial referred to this as 'learning from its sins'.[51] More recently, Georgetown students voted to increase their own tuition fees to make reparations to descendants of families sold by their university.[52]

Several other universities in the USA, one in Scotland, and both Oxford and Cambridge have taken steps to recognize the benefits they received from slavery. Glasgow University discovered that up to £198 million in today's value had been donated in the nineteenth century by people who had profited from the slave trade.[53] The University of Bristol estimated that 85 per cent of the wealth used to found the university came from slavery.[54] Whether these acknowledgements lead to concrete reparative measures or simply specified scholarships and renaming of buildings is unclear, as is indeed any continuation of reparations for these crimes. In 2019, the Southern Baptist Theological Seminary, whose founders owned fifty enslaved people, categorically refused to offer any reparations to a historically black college founded by slaves.[55] The momentum, however, is not with the Southern Baptists, as increasing numbers of institutions connect public history with reparative justice. One of the most ambitious of these is the Global Curatorial Project's 'In Slavery's Wake' which is directed by the Smithsonian National Museum of African American History and Culture and the Center for the Study of Slavery and Justice at Brown University, with partner institutions in Africa and Europe.[56]

American universities not only benefitted from slavery – many are located on indigenous lands procured through the 1862 Morrill Act, which provided land grants of parcels of 'Federal lands' to establish universities and colleges, originally in the Union states. The lands in question were seized from indigenous peoples and used as the capital to invest in higher education to promote the transmission of knowledge in the areas of industry, agriculture, science, liberal arts, military tactics and Christianity. Given that many of the land-grant universities have turned into thriving businesses, obtaining vast profits and paying their management, sports coaches and some of their teachers and researchers extremely high salaries, it is notable that there have been few public acts of recognition or reparation. The indigenous peoples whose lands were taken – through duplicitous treaties, violence and simple assertion of state sovereignty – provided the capital for their founding, and by extension for the expansion not only of the universities but of American capitalism. Instead, organizations such as the Association of Public and

Land Grant Universities, and academic commentators on these institutions, have largely been celebratory, ignoring the colonial origins of their highly successful universities.[57]

Also missing from current initiatives is any consideration of the ongoing impacts of slavery on African societies. Although there were internal forms of slavery and a slave trade across Africa, the loss of millions of people to the Atlantic slave trade and disruption of complex and interdependent social orders has been a prime determinant of the overall poverty and trauma, compounded by formal colonialism, of African peoples. However, attempts have been made at the international level to encourage nations that participated in the Atlantic slave trade to see their actions as crimes against humanity and as matters relevant to the present status of Afro-descended peoples in the Americas and Europe. As we know, enslavement enhanced the economies of Europe, even those such as the Scandinavian countries that simply supplied materials for imperial ventures, Greece which built ships, and Switzerland, whose banks financed parts of the slave trade.[58] The British merchant bank Baring Brothers was particularly important in supplying a 'revolving credit line' to the Bank of the United States for purchases of Africans, land and infrastructure for slavery. This credit was redeemed through cotton and other products of slave labour exported to England.[59]

Although it was not the only factor, the wealth generated by enslaved Africans provided an impetus for the Industrial Revolution in Britain from the end of the eighteenth century onwards.[60] In his analysis of 'primitive accumulation', Marx pointed to the role of colonialism and enslavement as key factors in the establishing of industrial capitalism. He argues that colonial powers 'all employ the power of the State, the concentrated and organised force of society, to hasten, hot-house fashion, the process of transformation of the feudal mode of production into the capitalist mode, and to shorten the transition'.[61] In Volume I of *Das Kapital*, Marx is adamant that the atrocities committed by Britain, Portugal, Spain, France and the Netherlands were in the service of trade, and hence the further accumulation of capital: 'The discovery of gold and silver in America, the extirpation, enslavement and entombment in mines of the aboriginal population, the beginning of the conquest and looting of the East Indies, the turning of Africa into a warren for the commercial hunting of black-skins, signalised the rosy dawn of the era of capitalist production.'[62]

According to historian Calvin Schermerhorn, by 1860 enslaved people created about 19 per cent of the national wealth, and slave-produced cotton accounted for 57 per cent of US exports.[63] Similarly, French Caribbean slave colonies produced enormous wealth for France. By the 1780s, this consisted of about half of Europe's sugar and coffee, three-quarters of which France re-exported, and about a million French people's employment depended on the colonial and slave economies.[64]

Since national economic prosperity and individual enrichment undoubtedly transmitted lasting economic success and private inter-generational enrichment for enslaving nations, it is reasonable to suggest that not only recognition, but recompense, is needed. Several economists have estimated the amount of lost wages of enslaved black workers in the USA to be between $6.5 and $10 trillion in 2014; and the losses due to labour market discrimination between 1929 and 1969 at $1.2 trillion.[65] The need to address the harms done by the Atlantic slave trade was the message of the 1993 Abuja Proclamation, issued by the First Pan-African Congress on Reparations. It read in part:

> Fully persuaded that the damage sustained by the African peoples is not a 'thing of the past' but is painfully manifest in the damaged lives of contemporary Africans from Harlem to Harare, in the damaged economies of the Black World from Guinea to Guyana, from Somalia to Surinam ... what matters is not the guilt but the responsibility of those states and nations whose economic evolution once depended on slave labor and colonialism, and whose forebears participated either in selling and buying Africans, or in owning them, or in colonizing them.[66]

The deliberations at Abuja included discussion of Lord Anthony Gifford's report, 'The Legal Basis of the Claim for Reparations', which argued for reparations to be issued under international law. The paper situated plantation-slave systems as crimes against humanity and proposed that all Africans and the African diaspora have suffered the consequences of these crimes. One of Gifford's propositions is that 'the claim would be brought against the governments of those countries which promoted and were enriched by the African slave trade and the institution of slavery'.[67] The move to enter dialogue with Britain on this basis, following from Abuja, was attempted at the World Conference on Racism, Discrimination, Xenophobia and Related Intolerance in Durban, South Africa, in 2000. However, the Blair government strenuously resisted any consideration of reparations. Representing Britain, Baroness Amos argued that, because slavery and the slave trade were under British law and backed up by the authority of Parliament, they could not be crimes against humanity. Hence, enslaved peoples were literally *Homo sacer*. When then confronted with the historical and legal evidence that they were, the British delegation adjusted its argument, holding that because this all happened a long time ago, it was too remote for reparations.[68]

Thus far, only undertakings of recognition, and not commitments to reparative justice, have been forthcoming from states that enslaved

Africans, and such states have not been willing to treat their own prosperity and the impoverishment of former slave territories as connected and, hence, relevant today. In a visit to Ghana, the state on the territory from where British traders took many captives, former Prime Minister Tony Blair expressed his sorrow for slavery and the slave trade to Ghanaian President John Agyekum Kufuor.[69] Significantly, he stopped short of an apology, which, although it could have connoted culpability, need not have, as President Macron's apology to Josette Audin, the widow of tortured and murdered pro-liberation activist Maurice Audin, showed.[70] Although Macron apologized for France's systematic torture in Algeria, this was not linked to any concrete reparative justice and France has vigorously opposed assuming any meaningful reparations for its enslavement of Africans and its colonizing of Algeria and elsewhere. This is true of not only Macron's position, as we saw in chapter 4, but also that of his two predecessors Hollande and Sarközy.[71]

British Prime Minister David Cameron tried a different tack in a state visit to Jamaica in 2015, when he met with Prime Minister Portia Simpson-Miller. After being met by protesters demanding reparations and being asked to address the issue by Simpson-Miller, Cameron said slavery was 'abhorrent in all its forms' and insisted on 'moving on' from 'this painful legacy'. Instead of reparations, Cameron announced £25 million to build a prison to house Jamaican nationals incarcerated in the UK, and a £300 million 'development package' to be shared around the Caribbean.[72] This was subsequently revised, with claims by the British ambassador in Jamaica that it 'wasn't clearly articulated among the stake-holders'.[73] Drawing attention to persistent poverty, familial dysfunction and underdevelopment in Jamaica and other Caribbean islands, the CARICOM organization established a reparations committee, and prominent scholars such as Hilary Beckles and Verene Shepherd have called for Britain to 'clean up its colonial mess' and negotiate with them on reparations, because Britain's state-authorized system of enslavement must be judged to be an internationally wrongful act that denied fundamental human rights on a massive scale.[74] Beckles cites various means by which concrete figures for the economic, social and psychological losses to Caribbean nations could be arrived at, and ends by connecting past human rights violations with current trauma and disadvantage: 'the mass poverty in towns and villages, widespread illiteracy, dysfunctional family structures, and rampant ill health in the form of endemic diabetes and hypertension are contemporary expressions of the horrors of slavery that targeted black persons'.[75]

When formerly colonized peoples have brought past atrocities to the attention of leaders of former colonial powers, their concerns have likewise been diminished. On the centenary of the Jalianwalla Bagh, or Amritsar massacre, in which troops under the command of Acting Brigadier General Reginald Dyer killed up to 300 Indians and injured as many as 1,200, the British envoy merely signalled his 'regret', and Prime Minister Theresa May said the killings were a 'shameful scar'.[76] Neither indicates that these murders were part of a general pattern of colonial violence. Rather, they are consigned to being aberrations within an assumed benign history. Such reactions do not invite any serious reflection on the wrongdoings of the British authorities, and their relevance to people in India and Britain today. Neither is there reflection on the actual atrocities themselves: how they happened, who was involved, how the British government authorized them, and how they might be more than a 'shameful scar' for descendants of these colonial actions.

Similarly, slavery was of course a system of forced commodity production, but to speak of it only as such, as Blair and Cameron did, signals a kind of distancing that obscures wider histories of the rape, whipping, imprisonment, torture and hanging of women, and the shooting, lashing, imprisonment and torture of men. Slavery is an institution in which captives in their hundreds were thrown overboard in the Atlantic, sometimes just to collect insurance payments.[77] To go beyond the bland and emotionless reactions of British officials, reparations need to be taken seriously. How reparations could be defined is, of course, difficult, and complexity has been one of the reasons cited by colonial states such as Britain for refraining from any serious engagement with the issue. This relates to identifying who should receive reparative justice – is it individuals or groups? Alternately, should nation-states like all of those of the Caribbean, which were initially sites of colonial genocide and then plantation slave colonies, receive recompense from Britain and other slave states?

Beckles points to the precedent of retroactive justice through the Nuremberg trials, which ruled that the state of Israel was to be issued with reparations from Germany. One could also add that reparations from Germany to the victors in World War I were ordered through the Treaty of Versailles. While the genocide of Hereros and Namas in German South West Africa (now Namibia) was also recognized as part of a pattern of German military atrocities, instead of reparations being ordered for the victims, a new mandatory system of colonization came into effect through the Covenant of the League of Nations, whereby the Union of South Africa took over German South West Africa. Other reparations were issued retroactively to selected populations in the twentieth century. In 1988, for example, $20,000 each was given to 100,000 surviving Japanese-Americans who had been locked in internment camps in the USA during World War II. Confirming the structural embeddedness of racial exceptions to human rights, it is hard to ignore the fact that reparations have been applied only to European populations, or nationalities such as the Japanese, deemed to already be 'developed' in European cultural evolutionist terms.

The UN has also made the case for considering reparations for African-Americans. In 2016, the HRC's *Report of the Working Group of Experts on People of African Descent on its Mission to the United States of America* observed the persistent discrimination against African-Americans and racism within the American system of justice as linked to prior histories of enslavement:

> Despite the positive measures, the Working Group remains extremely concerned about the human rights situation of African Americans. In particular, the legacy of colonial history, enslavement, racial subordination and segregation, racial terrorism and racial inequality in the United States remains a serious challenge, as there has been no real commitment to reparations and to truth and reconciliation for people of African descent.[78]

The practicalities of making reparations is a matter of intense debate with predictable gulfs between the idea that too much time has elapsed for any meaningful recompense, the linked opinion that today's whites are not responsible for the crimes of the past, and the position that the longstanding discrimination and disadvantage of Afro-descended peoples is a result of enslavement. It can and has been argued that no clear delineation of who should be compensated can be made. Despite some of these difficulties, for states and institutions to do nothing or only make symbolic gestures simply reinforces the selective application of rights.

Although reparations have been raised before, they were debated in the US Congress in 2019. Because the crime of slavery was the foundation for a continued assault on the human rights of African-Americans, without reparative justice, appeals to human rights from the USA and other enslaving nations are incoherent. Reparations acknowledge grave wrongdoing that is not only inconsistent with commitments to human rights, but an admission that the crimes of the past have had continuing effects on the descendants of the populations involved. To a certain extent, reparations underline the absurdity of the liberal concepts of equality and universality of human rights. As Ta-Nehisi Coates maintains in his seminal essay on reparations, 'the idea of reparations threatens something much deeper – America's heritage, history, and standing in the world'. He continues: 'Reparations would mean the end of scarfing hot dogs on the Fourth of July while denying the facts of our heritage. Reparations would mean the end of yelling "patriotism" while waving a

Confederate flag. Reparations would mean a revolution of the American consciousness, a reconciling of our self-image as the great democratizer with the facts of our history.'[79]

Coates' observations hold also for the position of the European colonial states, none of which has moved towards reparative justice for the territories from which they so richly benefitted. This is despite the fact that these states – most prominently documented for Britain – handsomely compensated enslavers for their loss of 'property in men', and did this in part by reasoning that it was the equivalent to the compulsory purchase of land. Although there were debates in Britain about compensation, these were primarily surrounding the form of it, not the principle.[80] Indeed, the British government bent over backwards to accommodate the interests of those who owned enslaved people, making minute calculations according to the value of land in terms of its productivity and of different categories of slaves. Those who simply owned slaves but not land were compensated much less.[81]

To allow human rights to be linked to concerns of long-term social and political processes, Western states would have to make reparative justice apply to the broader crimes of colonialism. Most immediately, Britain and France, as well as other colonizing states, would have to take complaints about their actions during colonial rule seriously and comply with international laws. A glaring example of this is Britain's defiance of the 2019 ICJ advisory opinion, and the subsequent UN General Assembly vote, that within six months the Chagos Islands should be returned to the residents Britain forcibly evicted in the early 1970s so it could lease out their islands to the US military. The Labour Party shadow Foreign Secretary Emily Thornberry expressed the hypocrisy of rejecting the ICJ ruling when she stated:

> [Britain] claims to believe in a world order based on rules and rights, yet time and again, it shows by its actions that it has total disregard for both ... The International Court of Justice has given a clear and unambiguous opinion in respect of the Chagos Islands, which the UN General Assembly will soon endorse, and it is simply not good enough for the Tory government to say that because they disagree with that legal opinion, they are entitled to ignore it.[82]

Indeed, by November 2019, Britain had not met the six-month deadline for decolonization. Sadly, reparative justice in this case would now have to factor in how the damage caused by the US military activities could be cleaned up, and how this island, now containing huge volumes of plastic in its lagoons, could be viable for the Chagossians. Thus far, the UK has only committed to a $50 million support package and 'heritage visits', which allow Chagossians to spend time on what it denotes as 'the Territory'.[83] In order for human rights to be gradually divested of the glaring exceptions charted in this book, colonial powers would have to engage in reparative justice and decolonize remaining territories.

## Indigenizing Law

Reparations to indigenous peoples for their losses of land, people and culture have not been discussed seriously, and their colonization continues as state sovereignty goes largely unquestioned in the institutional orders of international and national human rights. Continuing violations are enabled by the mandatory use of laws of the state. Instead, as many indigenous scholars and activists have suggested, a dialogue which would involve the use of indigenous values, customs and laws could help redress the ongoing human rights violations.

As we saw at Standing Rock, the act by which the US government asserted its laws and sovereignty over the Plains Indians was the 1803 Louisiana Purchase. Here, one European state, France, sold indigenous lands over which it simply asserted ownership to a colonial settler state. In this case, sovereignty was based on La Salle's mere assertion over a massive swathe of indigenous territory, as mentioned in chapter 5. Indeed, European legitimacy in occupying North America ultimately rests on layers of simple assertions. US and Canadian authority over indigenous lands can be traced to the advent of the British Empire, when Sir Humphrey Gilbert brandished a royal patent in what became St John's Harbour, Newfoundland, and was invested with a rod. Sir Humphrey returned to England with a slice of turf symbolizing British ownership. The right to decree laws was immediately put into effect and 'Her Majesty's ultimate right to the land was to be honoured and upheld.'[84] Based originally on the removal of a piece of soil, and extending further through other magical declarations and assertions, over 200 years later the North American settler states gave themselves rights to impose their laws on indigenous peoples.

In the context of Standing Rock, this proceeded through authorizing Euro-American settlers to establish homes on Plains Indian lands and to traverse them in search of lands farther west, belonging to other indigenous groups who were likewise victims of the original thefts. As we have seen, human rights violations are layered chronologically, one upon another, leading to the siting of the environmentally hazardous DAPL on lands and waters that are deeply enmeshed in Sioux identity and history, but over which jurisdiction falls to a state that achieved this through multiple duplicities. The Sioux have been situated as subalterns within a system of imposed law. This law allows the state to take decisive action to dispossess indigenous people who were not its citizens, not accorded rights within the society, and over whom authority could only be said to exist under a racial contract.

Similar dynamics play out in other contexts. For example, in the lands of the Innu peoples of Labrador-Quebec peninsula, Europeans first asserted their laws and sovereignty simply through docking on the coasts and sending missionaries to convert the Innu and Inuit peoples there. In 1752, Moravian missionaries took possession of indigenous land by carving King George III's name on a tree.[85] British and French, then Canadian, colonial occupation proceeded through further impositions such as the Royal Proclamation of 1763, drawing a border between French and English claimed territories of Innu lands; the attempted sale and then transfer of these lands from Britain to Canada soon after; and a string of unconsented-to Canadian policies such as the Indian Act, a treaty system and, most recently, a land claims policy, the end result of which is the massive diminution of Innu lands and the *de facto* extinguishment of indigenous ownership of lands they have occupied for millennia.[86] Like the USA, Canada also exerts hegemony by silently assuming a state of exception permitting unilateral alienation of lands inside and outside the land claims process. One of the most significant of these in the making of the Innu as subalterns is through placement of industrial projects such as the Muskrat Falls megadam on their lands before any land claims agreement has been concluded.[87] This renders the land claims merely symbolic, open to challenge only in state courts that are themselves exponents of state sovereignty.

These are just two examples that should make it clear that there is a need to problematize the 'rule of law' as the only means of both addressing the conflicts between the state and indigenous peoples and conceptualizing human rights. It is not only that state laws pertaining to indigenous peoples are intrinsically unjust because they contain exceptions, may not be honoured by the state and are administered deceptively, it is that they are based on rules and cultural assumptions of only one party to a conflict over land and sovereignty. One of the most important of these, entrenched in Western human rights themselves, is the assumption that human rights are principally individual rights provided by a procedure-bound state.

There is an urgent need to depart from this colonial model for ascertaining the human rights of indigenous peoples. For a start, it cannot be based on an assumption of the social contract. The Lockean social contract disconnects people from history, culture and collective experience and replaces these with an attachment to the state, but, for indigenous groups, it is to a state in which they can only be situated as subalterns. Moreover, the universal and timeless character of the social contract, meant to apply generically, crushes all alternatives to it, and this becomes a *raison d'être* of the colonizing state. By contrast, indigenous peoples never invented a social contract, or dreamt of a Lockean 'state of nature' so miserable and fractious that it drove people to seek to establish states. They never considered that certain ways of life invalidate full participation in society. Indeed, the ways in which both society, polity and community were considered differed markedly from European practice, and varied across North America – and, of course, beyond. In his discussion of the Anishinaabeg White Earth constitution which he helped to compose, Gerald Vizenor writes of indigenous government as linked to stories, histories and the natural world, flowing out of the *survivance* of peoples. 'Consent to traditional native governance', he writes, followed from 'totemic associations, public presentations of concepts and visions, and the common practices of communal reciprocity'.[88] In these undertakings, Native peoples envisioned democracy and liberty. Other North American peoples adhered not to governance and rights allocation through centralized permanent representative authority based on written laws, but to egalitarianism, respect for individual autonomy, and almost compulsory redistribution of resources.[89]

In this context, indigenizing law could be an important way to address the perpetual human rights violations made by states and corporations against indigenous peoples. There are already vestiges of this in international law, such as the UNDRIP, which was the product of decades of indigenous activism and state intransigence at the UN. The four Anglo-Saxon settler states – the USA, Canada, Australia and New Zealand – all voted against it, but some years later each ratified it. Comprising forty-six articles, UNDRIP holds states accountable for the 'universal' application of civil and human rights, and extends this to: limited rights to their own cultural and legal formations (Articles 5, 11, 12, 13, 24 and 34); collective rights (Article 2); self-determination and the freedom to determine their own political status (Article 3); the right not to be subjected to genocide or violence, including forcible removal of children (Article 6); and the right not to be subjected to forcible assimilation or relocation (Articles 8 and 10). Furthermore, states have a duty to consult in good faith and obtain free, informed and prior consent before implementing any policy towards them (Article 19), and to implement fair, independent and impartial processes acknowledging indigenous laws, traditions and customs to recognize indigenous land claims (Article 27).

While states are urged to enforce the declaration (Article 38), and several indigenous groups have already used the declaration in international courts to reverse losses of land and culture,[90] it is not binding, and Article 46 makes it clear that UNDRIP is in no way a challenge to state sovereignty. The problem remains that indigenous peoples must petition for the ultimate confirmation of their human rights by appealing to the institutional and cultural frameworks of their antagonists. The reciprocity Vizenor refers to as inherent to indigenous governance is rejected in international indigenous human rights in favour of the fictional social contract-derived authority of the state.

There are also traces of recognition of indigenous law in the 'Calls for Action' of the 2015 Truth and Reconciliation Report (TRC) in Canada. The TRC deals with forced residential schooling as an element of assimilation policies that occurred in Canada in the nineteenth and twentieth centuries, but was implemented across the colonial world. We may more accurately speak of these efforts as 're-education' since indigenous peoples already transmitted knowledge through education that is inherent in their rich repositories of knowledge, as embodied in storytelling, oral histories, travelling, hunting, fishing, gathering, farming and direct relationships between extended multi-generational family members. The report of the TRC makes it clear that the severing of these vital links between individuals, families and communities is not simply a historical episode, but has ongoing effects, and amounts to 'cultural genocide'. While the report does not call for reparations for crimes against humanity on the part of Canada and its colonial progenitors, Britain and France, it does contain ninety-four suggestions for actions and reconciliation. These are framed within an appeal to Canada to implement UNDRIP fully, and it includes a demand for Canada to provide for 'the recognition and integration of Indigenous laws and legal traditions in negotiation and implementation processes including Treaties, land claims and other constructive agreements'.[91]

While UNDRIP and the TRC contain important statements designed to recognize indigenous human rights, these remain within Western legal frameworks that presuppose settler-state sovereignty. Indeed, as Coulthard maintains for Canada,[92] colonial relations are reproduced by 'recognition' itself. To decolonize human rights, what is needed is not 'recognition' of indigenous cultures according to these assumptions, but the right of indigenous peoples to use their norms, customs, values and laws in dealings with states, and to bind states and settler populations by these elements of indigenous culture. Here, the deployment of indigenous customs and laws is important given that their unique forms of praxis and knowledge add to the possibilities for justice denied through state systems. In the wider global context of suppression of indigenous ways of life, Bacca has called 'for an attention to the right of indigenous peoples to think and speak in their own languages on all matters, including of course, the meaning and content of law, jurisprudence, jurisdiction, diplomacy, and rights'.[93] The continued use of imposed colonial law and master colonial languages risks further annihilation because cultural continuity – which can be interpreted as an international human right – requires use, respect and continued practice of indigenous laws and governance. In his study of Northern Arapaho cosmology, Jeffrey Anderson summarized this dilemma: 'The issues facing Arapaho people today are not comprehensible in generic political terms, such as self-determination and sovereignty. They are also neither comprehensible nor resolvable entirely within the categories, strategies, and relationships imposed by Euro-American knowledge, history and space-time.'[94]

This is so despite the fact, as Loretta Fowler makes clear in her earlier study of Arapaho political authority,[95] that the Arapaho system partly adapted the imposed political structures by integrating them to their own age-graded authority system. Nevertheless, the age-structured, yet consensus, orientation of the Arapaho, which parallels governance systems of other indigenous groups, is at extreme variance with Euro-American structures emphasizing absolute, permanent and binding political authority. Their resilient attachment to cultural continuities has made the Arapaho, as Fowler maintains,[96] free from the corrupting influences of imposed Euro-American political institutions affecting other indigenous groups that accepted imposed structures less reluctantly.

An important element of the decolonization of human rights is to affirm that laws or frameworks of common understandings of the world are transgenerational and refer to knowledge and norms formulated in the past, but which are binding on current generations. In many indigenous traditions – as incarnated in the Innu word, *tipenitamun* – sovereignty relates to responsibility to the land and animals.[97] Almost untranslatable, *tipenitamun* would be used to refer to one's belongings in the world, and this includes all that is out on the land, including the animals, fish, birds, trees, waters and, importantly, spirits. These are not belongings in the sense of being owned but belongings that must be respected, and, importantly when animals are killed, shared. The ultimate owners are the animal spirits.[98]

Additionally, *tipenitamun* implies activity, and cannot be taken as a passive noun. There can be no absolute ownership of land, because land is common to humans, non-human animals and other living things. The separation between people and the natural environment cannot be incorporated into governance because Innu are bound to all other life through a rich repository of stories and legends that mean that their actions on the land are never purely practical, but always cosmological.[99] Respect for all living things in Innu cosmology is imperative, and bad consequences are thought to follow disrespect. Hence, all living things, and especially animals, have agency and intentionality that affect humans.

This means that environmentally harmful projects such as mining, dams and extractive industry incarnate disrespect not only to the lands on which they are built, but to the animals, birds and fish whose migration is impacted. Exercises of Canadian sovereignty which ultimately legitimize energy and extractive projects, in effect, invalidate *tipenitamun*. This does not mean that there is no resistance or that Innu could not voluntarily agree to participate in such projects, but as Ross-Tremblay has argued, any indigenous action emerges from the production of cultural oblivion and amnesia by Canada. Current policies are layered upon histories of induced starvation, child removal, evangelization, relocation to reserve communities and imposed governance structures.[100]

One of the tragic effects of re-education policies as addressed by the TRC is that this link between people and their unique worldviews, of which their law is a part, was deliberately undermined. Indigenous autonomy was further weakened by the imposition of European-modelled political structures and the establishment of elected leadership. Many indigenous leaderships are funded by the state and established to operate as subsidiary mirror institutions under Canada's Indian Act, as I have observed of the Innu Nation of the Labrador-Quebec peninsula.[101] Incentives from the imposed electoral political systems can mean, as Haudenosaunee scholar Taiaiake Alfred points out, that 'the people who dominate in most Native communities and organizations today model themselves on the most vulgar European power-wielders'.[102] In the context of increasing opportunities for commercialization and privatization of indigenous lands, leadership positions can deliver important personal financial benefits. Leaders may therefore be incentivized and induced to cede land, culture and sovereignty by the state. Some North American indigenous leaderships further distance their communities from the enduring social relations that reinforce local systems of meaning, since money comes to mediate all relationships.[103] An ongoing protest over the passage of an oil pipeline through Wet'suwet'en territories in British Columbia shows how such a conflict can take shape when imposed leadership conflicts with existing traditional leadership. This involves the antagonism between the Indian Act band council authority, which operates according to Canadian political templates and which approved the pipeline, and the hereditary chiefs, who assert that the pipeline is a violation of their laws.[104]

Several indigenous groups have attempted to resist the move to imposed governance systems. For the Algonquin of Barriere Lake, Quebec, the use of their own political traditions rather than the imposed election-based band council system has been imperative. As Pasternak explains in her study of 'grounded authority' in the struggle between the Algonquins and the state, 'under indigenous law, the customary government is not just about governance between people but involves coexistence with the nonhuman world'.[105] Hence, indigenous governance would bring into play a wider span of considerations, including human obligations to nature. The Wet'suwet'en hereditary chiefs and their followers, like the Algonquins and White Earth Anishinaabeg who rejected the 'boilerplate constitutions' produced by the Bureau of Indian Affairs in the USA,[106] are asserting their own forms of governance as the precondition for recognition of their rights as indigenous peoples. The problem, however, is that, while Canadian courts have recognized indigenous laws, they are not bound by them, and regarding the Wet'suwet'en case, they have found ways to bypass them by justifying an infringement to various protocols such as the duty to consult, despite adverse court rulings.[107]

From having almost *carte-blanche* authority to confiscate unceded indigenous lands, from the 1970s onwards a series of decisions eroded Canada's ability to usurp such territory. In 2014, the *Tsihlqot'in Nation v. British Columbia* decision placed a further requirement on the state and corporations to establish consent from the relevant Aboriginal group to do this. This, however, does not amount to decolonizing Canadian law or human rights, and in its presumption of authority accords no importance to indigenous customs and traditions about land. Indeed, it amounts to a reinforcement of *terra nullius* because it affirms that the Crown's title is absolute, even though it was made simply by what Borrows calls 'empty incantation'.[108] So, as Val Napoleon points out, although 'Aboriginal Title' exists, and some indigenous laws are recognized by the state, these do not get transported into Canadian law. Indigenous property rights remain perpetually violable.[109] The *Tsihlqot'in* decision also begs the question of whom Canada needs to extract consent from, and under what types of political and legal assumptions? The default position is that consent will be granted by the elected leaders within the Canadian-template band council system, but, as Borrows maintains, indigenous law is something coherent and legitimate that could easily be identified and used in conflicts with the state.[110]

Indigenous governance depends on cultural continuity. This was expressed powerfully in a narration by Bernard Ominayak, chief of the Lubicon Lake Cree, in conversation with Mohawk anthropologist Dawn Hill-Martin in 1992:

I firmly believe, as long as we can hold on to our traditions or spirituality ... that's the direction to go, our land and our spirituality. As long as we have one we'll be strong enough to survive this process or attack on our people [of denying a land claim and building an extractive project on indigenous lands]. If they succeed in breaking us, it will be because they succeed in destroying our spirituality ... If there's one thing we can rely on, as we have seen through this mess, it's our ceremonies, the grandfather, our Creator. We have to remember that is where the power is. The government realizes that when you know who you are, or are strong in your identity, they [Natives] can be a powerful adversary, as history has shown us.[111]

Despite the ravages of imposed political authority, decolonization of human rights would need indigenous laws, customs and traditions to be brought into play, not so that they can be incorporated into state laws, but as legitimate in their own right and having force in dealings with the settler colonial state. Decolonization will have to entail recognition on the part of settler colonial states that their founding, and subsequent acts of indigenous dispossession, are empty incantation. Ways to use and appreciate indigenous laws will have to be found, and only then will human rights be shed of some of their colonial trappings.

Moreover, decolonizing human rights will mean discounting the authority of political leaders in Western liberal states such as Britain, the USA, France and Canada, not only because these are all states that are beneficiaries of ongoing denials of human rights along racial lines, but because they perpetually subordinate human rights to geopolitical power, trade and the preservation of inequality. Along with this, we will have to reject the many self-representations of liberalism that ignore the exclusions to its vaunted universalism. Instead, what are needed are fresh perspectives that bring the past into conversation with the present without being afraid to dent national vanities. As new generations of Afro-descended and indigenous scholars, activists and journalists and their allies become more vocal, we should be optimistic that human rights will not remain lodged in liberal frameworks that largely do not challenge the crimes of colonialism and enslavement.

# Notes

## Introduction

1 Rankine (2019).
2 Bennoune (2018).
3 Koskenniemi (2011: 114).
4 Reuters in Manama (2018).
5 Human Rights Watch (2018).
6 Landler (2018).
7 United Kingdom Government (2018).
8 United Kingdom Government (2019).
9 Bowcott and Borger (2019).
10 Vine (2011: 35–6); Weissbrodt and Bergquist (2006).
11 See, for example, Douzinas (2007: 9–26).
12 Hunt (1996: 30).
13 Sikkink (2017: 55–93); Barreto (2013: 17).
14 Orwell (1988 [1934]), (1957).
15 Mouffe (2013: 15).
16 A taste of this is contained in observations I make about a 'land claims' meeting between the leadership of Innu Nation and their Canadian advisers. See Samson (2003: 57–86).
17 Morris (2013: 159).
18 Durkheim (1973 [1890]).
19 Bentham (2011 [1975]).
20 Edelstein (2019: 194–6).
21 Erakat (2019: 31–2).
22 Wootliff (2018).
23 Shelley (2004: 102–6).

# 1 Non-universal Human Rights and Restlessness

1   Césaire (1955: 37).
2   Mazower (2009: 21, 53).
3   Mills (1997: 4).
4   See Mouffe (2013: 30–9).
5   Moore (1978).
6   Sen (2012: 10).
7   Mills (2017: 91–112).
8   Buck-Morss (2000: 844).
9   Kaisary (2012: 198).
10  Araujo (2017: 57).
11  Armitage (2012: 90).
12  Rousseau (1966 [1791]: 9–13).
13  Edelstein (2019: 128–30).
14  Mills (1997: 14–16; 2017: 29).
15  Locke (1965) [1689]: 325–44).
16  Cronon (1983: 55).
17  Todorov (2009: 15–16).
18  Conklin (1997).
19  Conklin (1998: 433–4).
20  Benton and Slater (2015: 140).
21  Loukaides (2007: 32).
22  Sweeney (2018).
23  Weber (1958 [1919]: 77–128).
24  Weber (1958) [1919]: 85).
25  Agamben (1995, 2005).
26  Agamben (2005: 2).
27  Marx (1978a [1843]).
28  Quoted by Langer (1969: 72).
29  Arendt (1968: 123–57).
30  Arendt (1968: 124).
31  Jackson (2007: 45, 109).
32  Quoted by Jackson (2007: 244).
33  Hanchard (2018: 70).
34  Gagarin (1982).
35  Hanchard (2018: 71, 105, 186).
36  Tully (2012: 11–12).
37  Cooper (2018: 58–62, 97).
38  Du Bois (1969b [1896]: 4).
39  Draper (2010: 87).
40  My simple calculation of £2.57 billion was made through this website: www.in2013dollars.com/uk/inflation/1834?amount=20000000. Using calculations that make different assumptions, Draper arrives at £13 billion and £76 billion: Draper (2010: 106–7).

41  Draper (2007: 78).
42  Draper (2007).
43  Draper (2007: 78).
44  Further detail is provided by the Legacies of British Slave Ownership project at University College London (n.d.). See also Draper (2018).
45  Mamdani (2012: 7).
46  Stokes (1959: xiii–xiv).
47  Mill (1975a [1859]: 16).
48  Mill (1975b [1861]: 281).
49  Stokes (1959: 69).
50  Garrett (1970 [1916]: 2, 26).
51  Geggus (1989: 1295).
52  Geggus (1989: 1296).
53  Hunt (1996: 26).
54  See Geggus (1989: 1304–5), Kaisary (2012).
55  Tocqueville (2001b [1841]: 111).
56  Morris (2016: 102–3).
57  Morris (2015: 60).
58  Morris (2015: 14).
59  United Nations, Human Rights, Office of the High Commissioner (2018a).
60  Equality and Human Rights Commission (2018).
61  Toh (2019).
62  Human Rights Watch (2019).
63  United Nations, Human Rights, Office of the High Commissioner (2017).
64  Jarvie (2018).
65  Walker (2018).
66  Benton (2006: 27).
67  Equality and Human Rights Commission (2018).
68  Spohn (2015: 53).
69  Stoler (2016: 133).
70  Fredette (2014: 43).
71  Mayblin (2014: 433).
72  Cooper (2018: 68, 75).
73  Horne (2006 [1977]: 33).
74  Cooper (2018: 75).
75  Lu (2017).
76  Mills (2017: 30).
77  Samson and Gigoux (2017: 45–52).
78  National Enquiry into Missing and Murdered Indigenous Women and Girls (2019).
79  Short (2016: 16–18).
80  Sassoon (1997 [1930]: 97).
81  Sassoon (1997 [1930]: 178).
82  Das (2018).
83  Schmitt (1996 [1932]: 48).
84  Arendt (1968: 267–304).

85  Arendt (1968: 270).
86  Arendt (1968: 290).
87  Apoorvanand (2019).
88  Macklin (2018).
89  Dettmer (2017).
90  Spencer (2019).
91  United Nations, Human Rights, Office of the High Commissioner (2019).
92  Bedi (2018); BBC (2019).
93  Arendt (1968: 271).
94  Mazower (2008: 581).
95  Snyder (2009).
96  Sebald (2001: 172).
97  Schmitt (1996 [1932]: 46).
98  Agamben (1995: 126–7, 122).
99  Agamben (1995: 131).
100 Among the many works on this subject, see Masalha (1997), Berda (2017), Erakat (2019).
101 Tehranian (2000: 824).
102 Singer (2002).
103 Buzan and Lawson (2015: 206).
104 Donnelly (1998: 20).
105 Sikkink (2017: 15).
106 McNeilly (2018).
107 Moyn (2010: 117).
108 Moyn (2018: 13).
109 Moyn (2018: 90).
110 Césaire (1955: 45).
111 Mazower (2009: 62–5).
112 Tocqueville (1945: 345).

## 2 The Uneasy Present of Colonialism

1   Kincaid (2018 [1988]: 15).
2   Kincaid (2018 [1988]: 31).
3   Deborah Cole (2018).
4   Sarkin (2011: 1).
5   Burke and Oltermann (2016).
6   Niezen (2017).
7   Mumbere (2018).
8   Swart (2008).
9   Mbembe (2015).
10  Gopal (2019: 454).
11  Dahlgreen (2016).
12  Evans (2018).
13  See Dresser (2009; 2016).

14  Staples (2019).
15  *New York Times* (2017).
16  In Moody and Small (2019).
17  Austen (2017), Martens (2018).
18  Smart (2018).
19  Little (2019).
20  Gray (2016).
21  Small (2017: 82–90).
22  Small (2017: 84).
23  Goddeeris (2015), Gerdziunas (2017).
24  Riding (2005), Louison (2019).
25  Hochschild (1999: 293).
26  Crowell (2018).
27  Ball (2016).
28  Robertson (2018).
29  Denson (2017: 17).
30  Eltis and Richardson (2010: 23).
31  Carillo (2018).
32  Ranson (2018).
33  Elkins (2005: x).
34  Cobain (2016: 107–8).
35  Klose (2013: 126).
36  Cobain (2016: 109–10).
37  Press Association (2013).
38  Elkins (2005: 313).
39  Stoler (2016: 74).
40  Cobain (2016: 130).
41  Sato (2017).
42  Cobain (2017).
43  Chrisafis (2018a).
44  Hochschild (1999: 294).
45  Lu (2017: 52–3).
46  Siddique (2018).
47  Lundin (2019).
48  Polonsky (2019).
49  Furness (2019).
50  Davis (2019).
51  Scobie (2019).
52  Cobain (2016: 107).
53  Gott (2011).
54  Obahopo (2017).
55  Haydn (2014), Weale (2016).
56  Buchan (2018).
57  Owen (2016).
58  Heath (2018).
59  Henley (2005).

60  Stoler (2016: 53).
61  Kassam (2017).
62  Truth and Reconciliation Commission of Canada (2015).
63  Ochoa O'Leary, Romero, Cabrera and Rascón (2012).
64  Johnson (2018).
65  Sogolo (1998).
66  Small (2017: 165).
67  Marsh, Siddique and Bannock (2018), Gentleman (2018).
68  Gentleman (2019b).
69  Gentleman, (2019a).
70  Gelder (2019).
71  Olusoga (2019).
72  See, for example, the 'closed extracts' of the British National Archives (n.d.), on Commonwealth Immigration.
73  Matthews-King (2018).
74  Jain (2018).
75  Wilkinson (2018).
76  Kwibuka (2019).
77  Berinzon and Briggs (2016: 342–3).
78  Massoud (2018).
79  Cairo Institute of Human Rights (2017).
80  Reuters (2018).
81  Agozino (2005: 125–6).
82  Mokone, Mosime, Quintal and Hlatshwayo (2019).
83  Salandy (2019).
84  Anderson (1998).
85  Chabrol (2018).
86  Cheeseman and Fisher (2019).
87  Fieldhouse (1986: 85).
88  Ndikumana (2015: 8–9).
89  Cooper (2018: 99).
90  Gassama (2008).
91  McArthur and Rasmussen (2017).
92  Osgood-Zimmerman, Millear, Stubbs et al. (2018).
93  Patnaik (2007: 122).
94  Lessenich (2019: 134).
95  Patnaik (2007: 116).
96  Patnaik (2007: 135).
97  Merriott (2017).
98  United Nations, Department of Economic and Social Affairs (UN DESA) (2009: 21).
99  United Nations (n.d.).
100 Baradaran (2018: 249).
101 Baradaran (2018: 249).
102 Lessenich (2019: 131–3).
103 Sumich (2018: 2).

104 Kottasová (2018).
105 International Labour Organization (2015).
106 Ish-Shalom (2006: 298).
107 Tsang (2018).
108 Deneen (2019: 65–7).
109 Ibhawoh (2014: 14).
110 Arendt (1968: 260).
111 McCool, Olson and Robinson (2007: 20).
112 Hansen (2013: 187).
113 Dubb (2019).
114 Wang (2012: 17–22).
115 Tomasky (2018).
116 Cole (2016).
117 Hall (2002: 27).
118 Mills (1956).
119 Miliband (1969).
120 Bulman (2018).
121 Kirby (2016: 21, 22).
122 Watters (2016: 107).
123 Syal (2018).
124 Withnall (2014).
125 Sitaraman (2017: 254).
126 See Mayer (2016), Lafer (2017), MacLean (2017).
127 May (2017: 189).
128 Frum (2018: 153–4).
129 Cited by Shear (2018).
130 Frum (2018: 104–21).
131 Frum (2018: 110).
132 Gstalter (2018).
133 Levitsky and Ziblatt (2018).
134 Wong, Schmidt and Sullivan (2018).
135 Levitsky and Ziblatt (2018: 127).
136 BBC (2018b, 2018c).
137 Sabbagh (2019).
138 BBC (2018a), Galdos (2018).
139 Schmidt (2018).
140 Shaw (2018).
141 Shane and Frenkel (2018).
142 Grandin (2006: 59–64), Rabe (2011).
143 YouGov (2014).
144 Tharoor (2016), Gopal (2017, 2019).
145 Ferguson (2004, 2011).
146 See Jack (2018).
147 Worley (2017).
148 Kunzru (2019).
149 Younge (2018), Kunzru (2019), Gildea (2019: 231–7).

150 Fanon (1963: 43).
151 Fagan (2019).
152 Equality and Human Rights Commission (2019).
153 Agerholm (2019).
154 Bright (2018).
155 Nolan (2019).
156 Reinbold (2017: 7).
157 Mubinde (1994: 149).
158 Mubinde (1994: 129).
159 Mamdani (2001: 10).
160 Rutazibwa (2019).
161 Mamdani (2001: 74–5), Rutazibwa (2019).
162 Mamdani (2009: 145–70, 271).
163 Epstein (2017: 39).
164 Epstein (2018: 81).
165 Epstein (2017: 47).
166 Human Rights Watch (2017).
167 Ibrahim (2016: 26).
168 Uddin (2017).
169 Lewa (2009: 11).
170 United Kingdom Mission to Human Rights Council Geneva (2018).
171 Foreign and Commonwealth Office (2018).
172 BAE Systems (2018: 59), Doward (2017).
173 Doward (2018).
174 United Nations (2018).
175 Tilianaki (2018).
176 Quoted by Mastracci (2018).
177 Shear (2019).
178 United Nations, Human Rights Council (2019).
179 Mann (2008: 3–4).
180 Kuo (2018), Millward (2019).
181 Madley (2016).
182 Stockel (2006).
183 Samson (2014, 2016).
184 Associated Press (2018a).
185 Gerster (2018).
186 Buncombe (2017).
187 Sanford (2005: 1–2).
188 Suleiman (2002: 523).
189 Walter (2017: 12).
190 Agamben (1995: 10).

# 3 Slavery and its Afterlives

1  Hurston (2018: 4).

2  Tocqueville (1945: 372).
3  Gilroy (1993).
4  Hurston (2018: 4–5).
5  Small (2015: 229).
6  Meier and Rudwick (1966: 28).
7  Eltis and Richardson (2010: 23).
8  Meier and Rudwick (1966: 34).
9  Eltis and Richardson (2010: 2).
10  Krikler (2012).
11  Du Bois (1969b [1896]: 128–9).
12  Meier and Rudwick (1966: 51).
13  Eichstedt and Small (2002).
14  Bidisha (2019).
15  Conrad (1994 [1902]: 83).
16  Jacobs (1987 [1861]: 28).
17  Jacobs (1987 [1861]: 35).
18  Finkelman (2015: 6–7).
19  Quoted by Diouf (2007: 19).
20  Lincoln (2001 [1858]).
21  Avalon Project (n.d.).
22  Texas State Library and Archives Commission (n.d.).
23  Nimako, Abdou and Willemsen (2014: 41).
24  Miller (1991: 1).
25  Commager (1978: 88–9).
26  Jefferson (1975: 4).
27  Jefferson (1975: 10).
28  Miller (1991: 14).
29  Jefferson (1975: 236).
30  Finkelman (2015: 193).
31  Jefferson (1975: 127–8).
32  Jefferson (1975: 568).
33  Dierksheide (2008: 187).
34  Douglass (1996 [1852]: 116).
35  Dierksheide (2008: 188).
36  Morgan and Morgan (2008).
37  Dierksheide (2008: 195).
38  Davis (2014: 114–19).
39  Jefferson (1975: 186).
40  Jefferson (1975: 190).
41  Jefferson (1975: 189).
42  Jefferson (1975: 193).
43  Jefferson (1975: 546).
44  Finkelman (2015: 131).
45  Baptist (2014: 6).
46  Du Bois (1969a [1903]: 54).
47  Woodward (1966: 23–4).

48   Higginbotham (2013: 63–4).
49   Woodward (1966: 43).
50   Woodward (1966: 19–20).
51   Woodward (1966: 54).
52   Accessed at http://chnm.gmu.edu/courses/122/recon/civilrightsact.html.
53   Gordon (2017: 102–3).
54   Levitsky and Ziblatt (2018: 91).
55   Woodward (1966: 51).
56   Berger (1968: 33).
57   Legal Information Institute (n.d.).
58   Rothstein (2017: viii).
59   Berger (1968: 76–7).
60   Woodward (1966: 99–100).
61   Rothstein (2017: xii).
62   King (2007: 4).
63   King (2007: 13).
64   Gordon (2017: 12).
65   Rothstein (2017: 43).
66   King (2007: 31).
67   Du Bois (1995 [1899]).
68   Drake and Cayton (1993 [1945]).
69   Gotham (2000).
70   Drake and Cayton (1993 [1945]: 184–7).
71   Clark (1965: 25).
72   Clark (1965: 27).
73   Clark (1965: 30).
74   Clark (1965: 34–5).
75   Woodward (1966: 100–2).
76   Stuntz (2011: 5).
77   Pinckney (2011: 33).
78   Sentencing Project (2013).
79   Flynn, Holmberg, Warren and Wong (2017: 117).
80   Sentencing Project (2013).
81   Steiker and Steiker (2015).
82   Walker, Spohn and DeLone (2000: 244–5).
83   Severson (2013).
84   Flynn, Holmberg, Warren and Wong (2017: 110).
85   Zimring (2017: 14–15).
86   Zimring (2017: 45, 49).
87   Winston (2019), Benner (2019).
88   Blow (2015).
89   Stolberg (2015).
90   Pérez-Peña (2015).
91   Poniewozik (2016).
92   Williams and Smith (2015).
93   Stack (2019).

94  Del Real (2019).
95  Eligon (2015).
96  Baradaran (2018: 249–50).
97  Schmidt and Apuzzo (2015).
98  Locke (2017: 302–3).
99  Romo (2018).
100 Locke (2017: 273).
101 United Nations, Human Rights, Office of the High Commissioner (2016).
102 Flynn, Holmberg, Warren and Wong (2017: 147, 149).
103 Flynn, Holmberg, Warren and Wong (2017: 148).
104 Cole (2016).
105 Cole (2016).
106 Cole (2017).
107 Flynn, Holmberg, Warren and Wong (2017: 153).
108 Sentencing Project (2016).
109 Wines and Fausset (2018).
110 *Nature* (2018).
111 Morrison (2016).
112 Passel and Cohn (2008).
113 Passel, Wang and Taylor (2010).
114 Flynn, Holmberg, Warren and Wong (2017: 64).
115 Flynn, Holmberg, Warren and Wong (2017: 67).
116 Boodry (2016).
117 Bloomberg View (2014).
118 Locke (2017: 45).

## 4 The Less Than Human

1   Cited by Horne (2006 [1977]: 55).
2   Horne (2006 [1977]: 54).
3   Daoud (2015: 3).
4   Daoud (2015: 120).
5   Daoud (2015: 32).
6   Daoud (2015: 13).
7   Stoler (2016: 133–49).
8   Stoler (2016: 141).
9   Quoted by Fleming (2003: 19).
10  Tocqueville (2001b [1841]: 236).
11  Tocqueville (2001a [1837]: 19).
12  Tocqueville (2001a [1837]: 23).
13  Camus (2013: 83).
14  Tocqueville (2001a [1837]: 17).
15  Fleming (2003).
16  Tocqueville (2001a [1837]: 22).
17  Tocqueville (2001a [1837]: 24).

18  Horne (2006 [1977]: 61).
19  Heggoy (1973: 192).
20  Conklin (1997: 20).
21  Le Sueur (2005: 23–31).
22  Le Sueur (2005: 27).
23  Lorcin (2014: xviii).
24  Lorcin (2014: 241).
25  Kiernan (2007: 374).
26  Lorcin (2014: 17).
27  Stora (2001: 2).
28  Fleming (2003: 6).
29  Radio France Internationale (2017b).
30  Kiernan (2007: 365).
31  Quoted by Alvermann (2013 [1960]: n.p).
32  Sessions (2011: 265, 308).
33  Bennoune (1988: 35).
34  Bennoune (1988: 44).
35  Stoler (2016: 100–2).
36  Bennoune (1988: 45).
37  Fleming (2003: 265).
38  Camus (2013: 43).
39  Crapanzano (2011: 57).
40  Vidal-Naquet (1963: 26).
41  Horne (2006 [1977]: 27).
42  Fleming (2003: 306).
43  Cole (2010: 112).
44  Lenze (2016: 18).
45  Aussaresses (2007).
46  Vidal-Naquet (1963: 50).
47  Horne (2006 [1977]: 120–1).
48  Surkis (2010).
49  Shepard (2006: 180–2), MacDougall (2006: 72).
50  Shepard (2006: 239).
51  Horne (2006 [1977]: 33).
52  Cooper (2018: 73).
53  United Nations (1960).
54  Le Sueur (2005: 186–8).
55  Klose (2013: 95).
56  Klose (2013: 120–1).
57  Klose (2013: 126).
58  House (2001), Ramdani (2018), Gildea (2019: 101).
59  Crapanzano (2011: 56).
60  Stora (2001: 138).
61  Horne (2006 [1977]: 537).
62  Harries (2007: 211).
63  Harries (2007: 205).

64  Conrad (1994 [1902]: 51).
65  Daulatzai (2016: xix).
66  Hussey (2018).
67  Ghiles (2018).
68  Ghanmi (2018).
69  Klose (2013: 94).
70  Daulatzai (2016: xvi).
71  Fanon (1964: 53).
72  Quoted by Gibson and Beneduce (2017: xiii).
73  Fanon (1952: 77).
74  Fanon (1952: 78–9).
75  Fanon (1952: 13).
76  Laing (1960).
77  Fanon (1952: 14).
78  Fanon (1952: 78).
79  Khadra (2016: 65).
80  Fanon (1963: 43).
81  Fanon (1963: 43).
82  Lorcin (2014: 242).
83  Fanon (1965: 36).
84  Fanon (1965: 37).
85  Fanon (1965: 38).
86  Lazreg (2008: 145–52).
87  Fanon (1965: 41).
88  Lazreg (2008: 150), MacMaster (2009: 121–44)
89  Fanon (1965: 43).
90  Lazreg (2008: 154–60).
91  Fanon (1965: 44).
92  Berger (1972: 46).
93  Berger (1972: 47).
94  Drif (2017).
95  Fanon (1965: 61).
96  Khadra (2016: 282).
97  Fanon (1963: 250).
98  Khadra (2016: 172).
99  Fanon (1963: 299–300).
100 Fanon (1963: 300).
101 Fanon (1963: 308).
102 Dangarembga (1988: 64).
103 Samson (2019).
104 Chrisafis (2018a).
105 Sessions (2017).
106 McDonnell (2018).
107 Baldit (2017), Bock (2017).
108 Dearden (2017).
109 Viscusi and Gongo (2017).

110 Bock (2017).
111 Radio France Internationale (2017a).
112 Chikhi and Irish (2017).
113 Smith (2017).
114 *Journal du Cameroun* (2018).
115 Africa Resource (n.d.).
116 Shepard (2006: 239).
117 Van der Schyff (2010: 56).
118 Crapanzano (2011: 17).
119 Crapanzano (2011: 120–1).
120 Crapanzano (2011: 121).
121 Crapanzano (2011: 122).
122 Van der Schyff (2010: 57).
123 Chrisafis (2018b).
124 Stoler (2016: 131).
125 Stoler (2016: 133–4).
126 Van der Wetering (2017: 5).
127 Gildea (2019: 171–3).
128 Fernando (2014: 70).
129 Alami (2018).
130 Fernando (2014: 139–40).
131 Fernando (2014: 168).
132 United Nations, Human Rights, Office of the High Commissioner (2018b).
133 Quinn (2016), Blagburn (2019).
134 Reuters in Montreal (2019).
135 Stoler (2016: 131–2).
136 Lorcin (2014: 233).
137 Conklin (1997: 102).
138 Fois (2016).
139 Blidi (2018).
140 Amnesty International (2019b), France 24 (2019).
141 Lorcin (2014: xiv).
142 Lorcin (2014: xv).
143 Stora (2001: 234).
144 Martinez (2000).
145 Lorcin (2014: 254).
146 *The New Arab* (2018).
147 Amnesty International (2019a).
148 Lenze (2016: 24).
149 Freedom House (n.d.: 13–14).
150 Grira (2019).
151 *North Africa Journal* (2019).
152 *Middle East Monitor* (2019a).
153 See Committee to Protect Journalists (2019).
154 Hussey (2014: 256).
155 Ahmed (2018).

156 *Middle East Eye* (2018), Zandonini (2018).
157 *Middle East Monitor* (2019b).
158 Amnesty International (2018).
159 *North Africa Post* (2018).
160 United Nations High Commission on Refugees (2019).
161 *Middle East Monitor* (2018).
162 Babas (2018).
163 Chikhi (2019).
164 Martinez (2000).
165 Kincaid (2018 [1988]: 36).
166 Ghiles (2018).
167 Magdaleno (2015), Gildea (2019: 115).

## 5 The Impossibility of Indigenous Human Rights

1   Quoted by Estes (2019: 45).
2   Pueblo of Zuni (1972: 3).
3   Stuart (2000: 186–7).
4   See Keal (2003).
5   Samson and Gigoux (2017: 50–1, 146–7).
6   Paine (1987 [1780]: 126).
7   Locke (1965 [1689]: 328).
8   Agamben (1995: 36–7).
9   Samson (2013).
10  Dahl (2018: 68–9).
11  See Brody (1981: 97), Cruikshank (1998: 17), Samson (2003).
12  Tocqueville (1945: 369).
13  Prucha (1975: 59).
14  Tocqueville (1945: 369).
15  Jackson (1965 [1881]).
16  Wunder (1994: 34).
17  Turner (1961: 43).
18  Dahl (2018: 30).
19  Wunder (1994: 19–20).
20  Dahl (2018: 25).
21  Vestal (1934: 186).
22  Keller (2000: 53–4).
23  Keller (2000: 55).
24  Prucha (1962: 216–19).
25  Keller (2000: 61).
26  Weaver (2003: 75).
27  Jefferson (1975: 134).
28  Jefferson (1975: 135, 136).
29  Jefferson (1975: 184).
30  Jefferson (1975: 21–70).

31  Tocqueville (1945: 369).
32  Quoted by Bailey and Bailey (1986: 32).
33  Kessell (1981: 261–7).
34  Powers (1976 [1877]: 266).
35  Madley (2014: 117).
36  Heizer and Almquist (1971: 68).
37  Heizer and Almquist (1971: 70).
38  Madley (2016: 168).
39  Harjo (2015 [1906]).
40  Parker (2015 [1918]: 29).
41  Parker (2015 [1918]: 29).
42  Zitkala-Ša (2003: 155).
43  Andrist (1964: 8).
44  Vestal (1934: 185–6).
45  Neville and Anderson (2013: 237).
46  Ostler (2004: 19–20).
47  Ostler (2004: 33).
48  Vestal (1934: 203–5).
49  Vestal (1934: 217).
50  Neville and Anderson (2013: 238).
51  Quoted by Andrist (1964: 74).
52  Welch, with Stekler (1994: 67).
53  Hubbard (2014).
54  Andrist (1964: 133).
55  Ostler (2004: 57).
56  Welch, with Stekler (1994: 66, 75).
57  Utley (1963: 41).
58  Ostler (2004: 48–51).
59  Welch, with Stekler (1994: 69).
60  Vestal (1932: 110).
61  Ostler (2004: 61).
62  Welch, with Stekler (1994: 93), Slotkin (1998: 330).
63  Slotkin (1998: 325–31).
64  Welch, with Stekler (1994: 265).
65  Utley (1963: 48–52).
66  Welch, with Stekler (1994: 265).
67  Utley (1963: 53).
68  Utley (1963: 57).
69  Lawson (2009: 41).
70  Estes (2018: 144).
71  Estes (2018: 144).
72  Neville and Anderson (2013: 247).
73  Lawson (2009: 44).
74  Smith and Swartz (2019).
75  Estes (2018: 152).
76  Capossela (2001–2: 154), Lawson (2009: 65).

77  Capossela (2001–2: 159).
78  Lawson (2009: 64).
79  Bengal (2018).
80  Estes (2018: 14).
81  Rucker (2014).
82  Estes (2018: 41).
83  McCauley (2016).
84  Hill (2017).
85  Almasy (2017).
86  Finer, Jenkins, Pimm, Keane and Ross (2008).
87  Center for Biological Diversity (n.d.).
88  Egan (2017), Cuevas and Almasy (2017).
89  Estes (2018: 44).
90  Di Savino and Kelly (2018).
91  Faith (2019).
92  LaDuke (2019).
93  La Pier (2016).
94  Estes (2018: 43).
95  Native News Network (2016).
96  Grossman (2017: 189).
97  Estes (2018: 2).
98  Grossman (2017: 189).
99  Nicholson (2019).
100  Newcomb, Medina, Saliba, Euronews and Sottile (2016).
101  Axe (2017).
102  Agamben (1995, 2005).
103  Schmitt (2014: 13).
104  Wunder (1994: 33).
105  Montemayor (2018).
106  Levin (2017).
107  Hagen (2019).
108  Levin, Woolf and Carrington (2016).
109  Hopper (2019).
110  Brown, Parrish and Speri (2017).
111  Ladybud (2017), Associated Press (2018b).
112  Brown (2017).
113  High Country News (2017).
114  Dura (2019).
115  Horn (2019).
116  Rowland and Eidelman (2017).
117  Von Bernuth (2019).
118  Zanolli (2018).
119  Mirza and Clapp (2019).
120  Sykes (2019).
121  Horn (2018), Hasselman (2018), Brookings Register (2018).
122  Cama (2019).

123 Zotigh (2018).
124 See Clemmer (2009).
125 Estes (2018: 154).
126 United Nations (2006).
127 Quoted by Prucha (1975: 202).
128 Echo-Hawk (2013: 113).
129 Singer (2002: 38).
130 Calloway (2013: 238).
131 Hoxie (1984: 155).
132 Tocqueville (1945: 369).
133 Trahant (2019).
134 United Nations (2018).
135 Samson and Gigoux (2017: 159–74).

## 6 Decolonizing Human Rights

1   See Barreto (2013: 3, 13).
2   See global examples in Samson and Gigoux (2017: 38–74).
3   Taussig (1987: xiii).
4   Conrad (1994 [1902]: 83).
5   Orwell (1936: 95).
6   Conrad (1994 [1902]: 100, 89).
7   Jung (1965: 247).
8   Jung (1965: 248–9).
9   Sontag (2004: 91).
10  Baldwin (2018 [1965]: 41).
11  Baldwin (2018 [1965]: 49).
12  Du Bois (1969a [1903]: 43).
13  Brockell (2019), Emerson (2019).
14  Beckles (2013: 5).
15  Hirsch (2018: 22).
16  Cole (2018).
17  Lessenich (2019: 127–35).
18  Deneen (2019: 3).
19  Deneen (2019: 136).
20  Locke (1965 [1689]: 339).
21  Locke (1965 [1689]: 343).
22  Marx (1972 [1953]: 131).
23  See Wagner (2019).
24  Kentish (2018).
25  Taylor (2018).
26  Greene (2019).
27  McVeigh (2018).
28  Borger (2018).
29  Lazaroff (2019).

30  Harpin (2019).
31  Rogers and Stolberg (2018).
32  Haley (2018).
33  United States Department of State (2019), Human Rights Watch (2019).
34  Pompeo (2019).
35  Pilkington (2019).
36  Al Jazeera (2018b).
37  Grandin (2006: 53).
38  Ipsos Public Affairs (2018).
39  Al Jazeera (2018a).
40  Cumming-Bruce (2019).
41  Koskenniemi (2011: 151).
42  Hunt (2019).
43  Milmo and Vaughan (2019).
44  Save the Children (2018), Worth (2019).
45  Worth (2019).
46  Weizman (2007: 251).
47  Chemerinsky (2006).
48  Koskenniemi (2011: 66).
49  Brown University (n.d.).
50  Brown University (2019).
51  Collins (2018).
52  Hassan (2019).
53  BBC (2018d).
54  University of Bristol (n.d.).
55  Kobin (2019).
56  See National Museum of African American History and Culture (2019).
57  See la paperson (2017: 29), Stein (2017).
58  Small (2017: 40).
59  Schermerhorn (2018: 76).
60  Eltis and Engerman (2000).
61  Marx (1978b [1867]: 436).
62  Marx (1978b [1867]: 435).
63  Schermerhorn (2018: 1, 2).
64  Geggus (1989: 1291).
65  Vinik (2014).
66  Abuja Proclamation (1993).
67  Gifford (2000: 17).
68  Beckles (2013: 195–6).
69  BBC (2007).
70  Chrisafis (2018a).
71  Forsdick (2015).
72  BBC (2015a, 2015b).
73  Loop Jamaica (2019).
74  *Jamaica Observer* (2018), *The Gleaner* (2019), Shepherd (2018).
75  Beckles (2013: 171).

76  Associated Press (2019).
77  Shepherd (2018: 22).
78  United Nations, Human Rights Council (2016).
79  Coates (2014).
80  Draper (2010: 85, 113).
81  Draper (2010: 104–5).
82  Quoted by Bowcott (2019).
83  Foreign and Commonwealth Office (2019).
84  Evans (2017: 34–5).
85  Gosling (1910: 252).
86  Samson (2016).
87  Samson (2018).
88  Vizenor and Doerfler (2012: 12).
89  Samson (2013: 69–79).
90  Samson and Gigoux (2017: 171–4).
91  Truth and Reconciliation Commission of Canada (2015).
92  Coulthard (2014: 15).
93  Bacca (2017).
94  Anderson (2001: 38).
95  Fowler (1982: 3).
96  Fowler (1982: 275).
97  See the discussion of Innu *tipenitamun* in Ross-Tremblay (2019: 34–5).
98  Thanks to George Rich of Natuashish for explaining *tipenitamun* to me.
99  Henriksen (2009: 17–18).
100 Ross-Tremblay (2019: 31–5).
101 Samson (2001).
102 Alfred (1999: xvi).
103 Anderson (2001: 227).
104 Bellrichard (2019).
105 Pasternak (2017: 89).
106 Vizenor and Doerfler (2012: 18).
107 Hamilton (2019).
108 Borrows (2015: 723).
109 Napoleon (2015: 878), Samson (2014: 264–7).
110 Borrows (2002).
111 Hill-Martin (2008: 100–1).

# References

Abuja Proclamation (1993), Accessed at: www.shaka.mistral.co.uk/abujaProclamation.htm.

Africa Resource (n.d.), 'The Unofficial English Translation of Sarközy's Speech'. Accessed at: www.africaresource.com/essays-a-reviews/essays-a-discussions/437-the-unofficial-english-translation-of-Sarközys-speech?showall=&start=2.

Agamben, Giorgio (1995), *Homo Sacer: Sovereign Power and Bare Life*, translated by Daniel Heller-Roazen, Stanford University Press.

Agamben, Giorgio (2005), *State of Exception*, translated by Kevin Attell, University of Chicago Press.

Agerholm, Harriet (2019), 'Grenfell Council Spends More Than £90k on Bosses' Bonuses', BBC, 23 March. Accessed at: www.bbc.co.uk/news/uk-47540281.

Agozino, Biko (2005), 'Crime, Criminology and Post-Colonial Theory: Criminological Reflections on West Africa', in Ali Wardak (ed.), *Transnational and Comparative Criminology*, London: Taylor & Francis, 117–34.

Ahmed, Hamid Ould (2018), 'Algeria Blighted by Youth Unemployment Despite Recovering Oil Prices', Reuters, 12 September. Accessed at: www.reuters.com/article/algeria-economy/algeria-blighted-by-youth-unemployment-despite-recovering-oil-prices-idUSL5N1VY41A.

Al Jazeera (2018a), 'Human Rights Chief Expresses Fear over Possible UN "Collapse"', 20 August. Accessed at: www.aljazeera.com/news/2018/08/human-rights-chief-expresses-fear-collapse-180820191255377.html.

Al Jazeera (2018b), 'Full Text of John Bolton's Speech to the Federalist Society', 10 September. Accessed at: www.aljazeera.com/news/2018/09/full-text-john-bolton-speech-federalist-society-180910172828633.html.

Alami, Aida (2018), 'The College Student Who Has France's Secularists Fulminating', *The New York Times*, 1 June. Accessed at: www.nytimes.com/2018/06/01/world/europe/maryam-pougetoux-islam-france.html.

Alfred, Taiaiake (1999), *Peace, Power, Righteousness: An Indigenous Manifesto*, Don Mills, Ontario: Oxford University Press.

Almasy, Steve (2017), 'Dakota Access Pipeline: Army Issues Final Permit', *CNN*, 9 February. Accessed at: https://edition.cnn.com/2017/02/07/politics/dakota-access-pipeline-easement-granted.

Alvermann, Dirk (2013) [1960], *Algeria*, translated by Brian Currid and Jeremy Gaines, Gottingen: Steidl.

Amnesty International (2018), 'Forced to Leave: Stories of Injustice Against Migrants in Algeria'. Accessed at: www.amnesty.org/download/Documents/MDE2895122018ENGLISH.PDF.

Amnesty International (2019a), 'Algeria: Activist Jailed for Holding Anti-President Placard', Press Release, 7 February. Accessed at: www.amnesty.org.uk/press-releases/algeria-activist-jailed-holding-anti-president-placard.

Amnesty International (2019b), 'Algeria: 41 Arrested for Carrying the Amazigh Flag as Authorities Crack Down on Freedom of Expression', 5 July. Accessed at: www.amnesty.org/en/latest/news/2019/07/algeria-41-arrested-for-carrying-the-amazigh-flag-as-authorities-crack-down-on-freedom-of-expression.

Anderson, Benedict (1998), 'From Miracle to Crash', *London Review of Books*, 16 April. Accessed at: www.lrb.co.uk/v20/n08/benedict-anderson/from-miracle-to-crash.

Anderson, Jeffrey (2001), *The Four Hills of Life: Northern Arapaho Knowledge and Life Movement*, Lincoln: University of Nebraska Press.

Andrist, Ralph (1964), *The Long Death: The Last Days of the Plains Indian*, New York: Collier Books.

Apoorvanand (2019), 'The New Citizenship Bill and the Hinduisation of India', Al Jazeera, 12 January. Accessed at: www.aljazeera.com/indepth/opinion/citizenship-bill-hinduisation-india-190110141421871.html.

Araujo, Ana Lucia (2017), *Reparations for Slavery and the Slave Trade: A Transnational and Comparative Study*, London: Bloomsbury.

Arendt, Hannah (1968), *The Origins of Totalitarianism*, New York: Harcourt Inc.

Arendt, Hannah (2018), *Thinking Without a Banister: Essays in Understanding, 1953–1975*, New York: Schocken Books.

Armitage, David (2012), 'John Locke: Theorist of Empire?' in Sankar Muthu (ed.), *Empire and Modern Political Thought*, Cambridge University Press, 84–111.

Associated Press (2018a), 'Canada Parliament Declares Myanmar Treatment of Rohingya Muslims as Genocide; Human Rights Observers Laud Move', 21 September. Accessed at: www.firstpost.com/world/canada-parliament-declares-myanmar-treatment-of-rohingya-muslims-as-genocide-human-rights-observers-laud-move-5231391.html.

Associated Press (2018b), 'Dakota Access Protester Gets 3 Year Federal Prison Sentence', 28 September. Accessed at: https://apnews.com/226afb89a3454e618510d62b0161d331.

Associated Press (2019), 'British Envoy Regrets 1919 Colonial Massacre of Indians', 13 April. Accessed at: https://apnews.com/3c5963d8269e424aa6b5fe5146b76c24.

Aussaresses, Paul (2007), '"Do You Think I Enjoy This?"' in William Schulz (ed.), *The Phenomenon of Torture: Readings and Commentary*, Philadelphia: University of Pennsylvania Press, 137–8.

Austen, Ian (2017), 'Canada, Too, Faces a Reckoning with History and Racism', *The New York Times*, 28 August. Accessed at: www.nytimes.com/2017/08/28/world/americas/canada-john-a-macdonald-kingston.html.

Avalon Project (n.d.), *Confederate States of America – Georgia Secession*. Accessed at: http://avalon.law.yale.edu/19th_century/csa_geosec.asp.

Axe, David (2017), 'National Guard Deploys Missile Launchers to Dakota Access Pipeline to "Observe" Protestors', *Daily Beast*, 17 January. Accessed at: www.thedailybeast.com/national-guard-deploys-missile-launchers-to-dakota-access-pipeline-to-observe-protestors.

Babas, Latifa (2018), 'Customs in Mauritania and Algeria Impose Strict Regulations on Sahrawis in the Tindouf Camps', 31 October. Accessed at: https://en.yabiladi.com/articles/details/70484/customs-mauritania-algeria-impose-strict.html.

Bacca, Paolo Ilich (2017), 'Indigenizing International Law from an Inverse Legal Anthropology', *Naked Punch*, 13 May. Accessed at: www.nakedpunch.com/articles.

BAE Systems (2018), *Annual Report*. Accessed at: https://investors.baesystems.com/~/media/Files/B/Bae-Systems-Investor-Relations-V3/PDFs/results-and-reports/results/2018/annual-report-2018.pdf.

Bailey, Garrick, and Roberta Glenn Bailey (1986), *A History of the Navajos: The Reservation Years*, Santa Fe: School of American Research Press.

Baldit, Étienne (2017), 'VIDÉO – En Algérie, Macron s'étonne qu'un jeune de 25 ans "l'embrouille" avec la colonisation', *Le Lab Politique Europe 1*, 6 December. Accessed at: https://lelab.europe1.fr/video-en-algerie-macron-setonne-quun-jeune-de-25-ans-lembrouille-avec-la-colonisation-3513299.

Baldwin, James (2018) [1965], 'The White Man's Guilt', in James Baldwin, *Dark Days*, London: Penguin, 41–50.

Ball, Edward (2016), 'At Last, a Black History Museum', *New York Review of Books*, 24 November. Accessed at: www.nybooks.com/articles/2016/11/24/smithsonian-black-history-museum.

Baptist, Edward (2014), *The Half Has Never Been Told: Slavery and the Making of American Capitalism*, New York: Basic Books.

Baradaran, Mehrsa (2018), *The Color of Money: Black Banks and the Racial Wealth Gap*, Cambridge, MA: Harvard University Press.

Barreto, José-Manuel (2013), 'Decolonial Strategies and Dialogue in the Human Rights Field', in *Human Rights from a Third World Perspective: Critique, History and International Law*, Newcastle: Cambridge Scholars Publishing, 1–43.

BBC (2007), 'Blair "Sorry" for UK Slavery Role 2007', 14 March. Accessed at: http://news.bbc.co.uk/2/hi/uk_news/politics/6451793.stm.

BBC (2015a), 'David Cameron Rules Out Slavery Reparation during Jamaica Visit', 30 September. Accessed at: www.bbc.com/news/uk-34401412.

BBC (2015b), 'UK to Build £25m Jamaican Prison', 30 September. Accessed at: www.bbc.com/news/uk-34398014.

BBC (2018a), 'Cambridge Analytica: The Data Firm's Global Influence', 22 March. Accessed at: www.bbc.co.uk/news/world-43476762.

BBC (2018b) 'Fake News "Crowding Out" Real News, MPs Say', 29 July. Accessed at: www.bbc.co.uk/news/technology-44995490.

BBC (2018c), 'Electoral Commission "Misinterpreted" Vote Leave Expenses, Court Rules', 14 September. Accessed at: www.bbc.co.uk/news/uk-politics-45519676.

BBC (2018d), 'Glasgow University "Benefitted from Slave Trade Profits"', 16 September. Accessed at: www.bbc.co.uk/news/uk-scotland-glasgow-west-45539706.

BBC (2019), 'Assam NRC: What Next for 1.9 Million "Stateless" Indians?' 31 August. Accessed at: www.bbc.co.uk/news/world-asia-india-49520593.

Beckles, Hilary McD. (2013), *Britain's Black Debt: Reparations for Caribbean Slavery and Native Genocide*, Kingston: University of West Indies Press.

Bedi, Rahul (2018), 'India Strips Four Million People of Citizenship in Assam as Modi's BJP "Targets" Muslim Minority', *The Daily Telegraph*, 30 July. Accessed at: www.telegraph.co.uk/news/2018/07/30/india-strips-four-million-people-citizenship-assam-modis-bjp.

Bellrichard, Chantelle (2019), 'Wet'suwet'en Hereditary Leaders Level Human Rights Complaint during Speeches at United Nations Forum', CBC, 26 April. Accessed at: www.cbc.ca/news/indigenous/wet-suwet-en-un-speeches-human-rights-violations-1.5111078.

Bengal, Rebecca (2018), 'What Lies Beneath Lake Oahe: Looking at the Past from the Shores of Standing Rock', *Lapham's Quarterly*, 11 July. Accessed at: www.laphamsquarterly.org/roundtable/what-lies-beneath-lake-oahe.

Benner, Katie (2019), 'Eric Garner's Death Will Not Lead to Federal Charges for N.Y.P.D. Officer', *The New York Times*, 16 July. Accessed at: www.nytimes.com/2019/07/16/nyregion/eric-garner-case-death-daniel-pantaleo.html.

Bennoune, Karima (2018), 'Universality, Diversity and Cultural Rights: In Conversation with Wole Soyinka', YouTube. Accessed at: www.youtube.com/watch?v=ipJwdnF-zxE.

Bennoune, Mahfoud (1988), *The Making of Contemporary Algeria, 1830–1987*, Cambridge University Press.

Bentham, Jeremy (2011) [1975], 'Nonsense upon Stilts (Excluding the Observations on Sieyès)', in Stephen Engelmann (ed.), *Selected Writings: Jeremy Bentham*, New Haven: Yale University Press, 318–94.

Benton, Lauren, and Aaron Slater (2015), 'Constituting the Imperial Community: Rights, Common Good and Authority in Britain's Atlantic Empire, 1607–1815', in Pamela Slotte and Miia Halme-Tuomisaari (eds.), *Revisiting the Origins of Human Rights*, Cambridge University Press, 140–62.

Benton, Ted (2006), 'Do We Need Rights?' in Lydia Morris (ed.), *Rights: Sociological Perspectives*, London: Routledge, 21–36.

Berda, Yael (2017), *Living Emergency: Israel's Permit Regime in the Occupied West Bank*, Stanford University Press.

Berger, John (1972), *Ways of Seeing*, London: Penguin.

Berger, Monroe (1968), *Equality by Statute: The Revolution in Civil Rights*, revised edition, Garden City, NY: Anchor.

Berinzon, Maya, and Ryan Briggs (2016), 'Legal Families Without the Laws: The Fading of Colonial Law in French West Africa', *The American Journal of Comparative Law*, 64, 2: 329–70.

Bidisha (2019), 'Kara Walker: Fons Americanus Review – Monumental Rebuke to the Evils of Empire', *The Guardian*, 5 October. Accessed at: www.theguardian.com/artanddesign/2019/oct/05/kara-walker-fons-americanus-turbine-hall-tate-modern-review-bidisha.

Blagburn, Francis (2019), 'Burkini Ban Women Plan Swimming Pool Protest', *The Independent*, 29 June: 5.

Blidi, Saber (2018), 'Niqab Ban Triggers Reactions from Algerian Salafists', *The Weekly*, 30 September. Accessed at: https://thearabweekly.com/niqab-ban-triggers-reactions-algerian-salafists.

Bloomberg View (2014), 'How Slavery Led to Modern Capitalism', *Huffington Post*, 24 February. Accessed at: www.huffingtonpost.com/2014/02/24/slavery_n_4847105.html?guccounter=1.

Blow, Charles (2015), 'In South Carolina, Shot in the Back as He Ran', *The New York Times*, 8 April. Accessed at: www.nytimes.com/2015/04/09/opinion/charles-blow-walter-scott-video-south-carolina-shooting-michael-slager.html?emc=edit_th_20150409&nl=todaysheadlines&nlid=21277101&_r=0.

Bock, Pauline (2017), 'Macron's Modernism Has Neither Escaped Nor Addressed France's Colonial History in Africa', *New Statesman*, 13 December. Accessed at: www.newstatesman.com/world/europe/2017/12/macron-s-modernism-has-neither-escaped-nor-addressed-france-s-colonial-history.

Boodry, Kathryn (2016), 'August Belmont and the World the Slaves Made', in Sven Beckert and Seth Rockman (eds.), *Slavery's Capitalism: A New History of American Economic Development*, Philadelphia: University of Pennsylvania Press, 163–78.

Borger, Julian (2018), 'US Quits UN Human Rights Council – "a Cesspool of Political Bias"', *The Guardian*, 20 June. Accessed at: www.theguardian.com/world/2018/jun/19/us-quits-un-human-rights-council-cesspool-political-bias.

Borrows, John (2002), *Recovering Canada: The Resurgence of Indigenous Law*, University of Toronto Press.

Borrows, John (2015), 'The Durability of Terra Nullius: Tsilhqot'in Nation v. British Columbia', *University of British Columbia Law Review*, 48, 3: 701–42.

Bowcott, Owen (2019), 'Corbyn Condemns May's Defiance of Chagos Islands Ruling', *The Guardian*, 1 May. Accessed at: www.theguardian.com/world/2019/may/01/corbyn-condemns-mays-defiance-of-chagos-islands-ruling.

Bowcott, Owen, and Julian Borger (2019), 'UK Suffers Crushing Defeat in UN Vote on Chagos Islands', *The Guardian*, 22 May. Accessed at: www.theguardian.com/world/2019/may/22/uk-suffers-crushing-defeat-un-vote-chagos-islands.

Bright, Susan (2018), 'Grenfell: Human Rights and a Ban on Combustible Cladding?' University of Oxford, Faculty of Law, 6 September. Accessed at: www.law.ox.ac.uk/housing-after-grenfell/blog/2018/09/grenfell-human-rights-and-ban-combustible-cladding.

British National Archives (n.d.), 'Commonwealth Immigration'. Accessed at: https://discovery.nationalarchives.gov.uk/results/r?_q=HO%20344&_hb=tna.

Brockell, Gillian (2019), 'Some White People Don't Want to Hear about Slavery at Plantations Built by Slaves', *Washington Post*, 8 August. Accessed at: www. washingtonpost.com/history/2019/08/08/some-white-people-dont-want-hear-about-slavery-plantations-built-by-slaves/?noredirect=on.

Brody, Hugh (1981), *Maps and Dreams*, New York: Pantheon.

Brookings Register (2018), 'Tribes Seek to Challenge Dakota Access Pipeline Study', 11 December. Accessed at: https://brookingsregister.com/article/tribes-seek-to-challenge-dakota-access-pipeline-study.

Brown, Alleen (2017), 'Arrests of Journalists at Standing Rock Test the Boundaries of the First Amendment', *The Intercept*, 27 November. Accessed at: https://theintercept.com/2016/11/27/arrests-of-journalists-at-standing-rock-test-the-boundaries-of-the-first-amendment.

Brown, Alleen, Will Parrish and Alice Speri (2017), 'Leaked Documents Reveal Counterterrorism Tactics used at Standing Rock to "Defeat Pipeline Insurgencies"', *The Intercept*, 17 May. Accessed at: https://theintercept.com/2017/05/27/leaked-documents-reveal-security-firms-counterterrorism-tactics-at-standing-rock-to-defeat-pipeline-insurgencies.

Brown University (2019), 'For Brown's Slavery and Justice Center, a Legacy of Scholarship at the Five-Year Mark', 10 January. Accessed at: https://news. brown.edu/articles/2019/01/cssj.

Brown University (n.d.), *Slavery and Justice: Report to the Steering Committee on Slavery and Justice*. Accessed at: http://brown.edu/Research/Slavery_Justice/documents/SlaveryAndJustice.pdf.

Buchan, Lizzy (2018), 'Schools Should Educate Children about Colonialism and Legacy of Slave Trade, Says Jeremy Corbyn', *The Independent*, 11 October. Accessed at: www.independent.co.uk/news/uk/politics/colonialism-slave-trade-history-school-education-uk-jeremy-corbyn-labour-a8577941.html.

Buck-Morss, Susan (2000), 'Hegel and Haiti', *Critical Inquiry*, 26, 4: 821–65.

Bulman, Mary (2018), 'Theresa May's Cabinet Members Now Five Times More Likely to Be Privately-Educated than British Public', *The Independent*, 10 January. Accessed at: www.independent.co.uk/news/uk/politics/cabinet-ministers-private-education-reshuffle-public-schools-state-educated-uk-public-theresa-may-a8151106.html.

Buncombe, Andrew (2017), 'Allied Forces Knew about Holocaust Two Years Before Discovery of Concentration Camps, Secret Documents Reveal', *The Independent*, 18 April. Accessed at: www.independent.co.uk/news/world/world-history/holocaust-allied-forces-knew-before-concentration-camp-discovery-us-uk-soviets-secret-documents-a7688036.html.

Burke, Jason, and Philip Oltermann (2016), 'Germany Moves to Atone for "Forgotten Genocide" in Namibia', *The Guardian*, 25 December. Accessed at: www.theguardian.com/world/2016/dec/25/germany-moves-to-atone-for-forgotten-genocide-in-namibia.

Buzan, Barry, and George Lawson (2015), *The Global Transformation: History, Modernity and the Making of International Relations*, Cambridge University Press.

Cairo Institute of Human Rights (2017), 'Egypt: Repealed Colonial-Era Law

Used to Sentence 474 Egyptians to Death from 2014–2017', Press Statement. Accessed at: www.adalaheg.org/wp-content/uploads/2018/01/One-year-on-assembly-law-FINAL.pdf.

Calloway, Colin (2013), *Pen and Ink Witchcraft: Treaties and Treaty Making in American Indian History*, Oxford University Press.

Cama, Timothy (2019), 'Court Dismisses Dakota Access Company's Lawsuit against Greens', *The Hill*, 15 February. Accessed at: https://thehill.com/policy/energy-environment/430193-court-dismisses-dakota-access-companys-lawsuit-against-greens.

Camus, Albert (2013), *Algerian Chronicles*, translated by Arthur Goldhammer, Cambridge, MA: Harvard University Press.

Capossela, Peter (2001–2), 'Indian Reserved Water Rights in the Missouri River Basin', *Great Plains Natural Resource Journal*, 6: 131–61.

Carillo, Karen Juanita (2018), 'Spain and Portugal Confront their Dark History of Slavery', *FaceTalk Africa*, 20 October. Accessed at: https://face2faceafrica.com/article/spain-and-portugal-confront-their-dark-history-of-slavery.

Center for Biological Diversity (n.d.), 'America's Dangerous Pipelines'. Accessed at: www.biologicaldiversity.org/campaigns/americas_dangerous_pipelines.

Césaire, Aimé (1955), *Discourse on Colonialism*, translated by James Pinkham, New York: Monthly Review Press.

Chabrol, Denis (2018), 'British Colonial Sedition Law Crushed Free Expression by Blacks; Has No Place in Independent Guyana', *Demerara Waves*, 5 May. Accessed at: http://demerarawaves.com/2018/05/05/british-colonial-sedition-law-crushed-free-expression-by-blacks-has-no-place-in-independent-guyana.

Cheeseman, Nic, and Jonathan Fisher (2019), 'How Colonial Rule Predisposed Africa to Fragile Authoritarianism', *The Conversation*, 31 October. Accessed at: https://theconversation.com/how-colonial-rule-predisposed-africa-to-fragile-authoritarianism-126114.

Chemerinsky, Erwin (2006), 'The Assault on the Constitution: Executive Power and the War on Terrorism', *UC Davis Law Review*, 40, 1: 1–20.

Chikhi, Lamine (2019), 'U.N. Says Algerian Security Move has Stranded Vulnerable Syrians in Desert', Reuters, 3 January. Accessed at: https://af.reuters.com/article/commoditiesNews/idAFL8N1Z34AI.

Chikhi, Lamine and John Irish (2017), 'Time to Move On from Algeria's Colonial Past, Says France's Macron', Reuters, 6 December. Accessed at: https://uk.reuters.com/article/uk-france-algeria/time-to-move-on-from-algerias-colonial-past-says-frances-macron-idUKKBN1E0249.

Chrisafis, Angelique (2018a), 'France Admits Systematic Torture during Algeria War for First Time', *The Guardian*, 13 September. Accessed at: www.theguardian.com/world/2018/sep/13/france-state-responsible-for-1957-death-of-dissident-maurice-audin-in-algeria-says-macron.

Chrisafis, Angelique (2018b), 'Macron Faces Up to France's Colonial Past with €40m "Harkis" Aid', *The Guardian*, 25 September. Accessed at: www.theguardian.com/world/2018/sep/25/macron-faces-up-to-france-algeria-colonial-past-with-40m-euros-harkis-aid.

Clark, Kenneth B. (1965), *Dark Ghetto: Dilemmas of Social Power*, New York: Harper and Row.

Clemmer, Richard (2009), 'Land Rights, Claims, and Western Shoshones: The Ideology of Loss and the Bureaucracy of Enforcement', *Political and Legal Anthropology Review*, 32, 2: 279–311.

Coates, Ta-Nehisi (2014), 'The Case for Reparations', *The Atlantic*, June. Accessed at: www.theatlantic.com/magazine/archive/2014/06/the-case-for-reparations/361631.

Cobain, Ian (2016), *The History Thieves: Secrets, Lies and the Shaping of a Modern Nation*, London: Portobello Books.

Cobain, Ian (2017), 'Government Admits "Losing" Thousands of Papers from National Archives', *The Guardian*, 26 December. Accessed at: www.theguardian.com/uk-news/2017/dec/26/government-admits-losing-thousands-of-papers-from-national-archives.

Cole, David (2016), 'How Voting Rights Are Being Rigged', *New York Review of Books*, 27 October. Accessed at: www.nybooks.com/articles/2016/10/27/how-voting-rights-are-being-rigged.

Cole, David (2017), 'Five Questions for Jeff Sessions', *New York Review of Books*, 8 January. Accessed at: www.nybooks.com/daily/2017/01/08/five-questions-jeff-sessions-confirmation-hearing.

Cole, David (2018), 'Taxing the Poor', *New York Review of Books*, 10 May. Accessed at: www.nybooks.com/articles/2018/05/10/taxing-the-poor.

Cole, Deborah (2018), 'Berlin to Change Street Names over Brutal African Colonial Past', *The Citizen*, 12 April. Accessed at: https://citizen.co.za/news/news-africa/1891941/berlin-to-change-street-names-over-brutal-african-colonial-past.

Cole, Joshua (2010), 'Massacres and Their Historians: Recent Histories of State Violence in France and Algeria in the Twentieth Century', *French Politics, Culture & Society*, 28, 1: 106–26.

Collins, Daniel (2018), 'Georgetown University, Learning from Its Sins', *The New York Times*, 31 August. Accessed at: www.nytimes.com/2016/09/01/opinion/georgetown-university-learning-from-its-sins.html.

Commager, Henry Steele (1978), *The Empire of Reason: How Europe Imagined and America Realized the Enlightenment*, London: Weidenfeld and Nicholson.

Committee to Protect Journalists (2019), 'More Online News Blocked as Algeria Protests Near 6 Month Mark', 14 August. Accessed at: https://cpj.org/2019/08/more-online-news-blocked-as-algeria-protests-near-.php.

Conklin, Alice (1997), *A Mission to Civilize: The Republican Idea of Empire in France and West Africa, 1895–1930*, Stanford University Press.

Conklin, Alice (1998), 'Colonialism and Human Rights, a Contradiction in Terms? The Case of France and West Africa, 1895–1914', *The American Historical Review*, 103, 2: 419–42.

Conrad, Joseph (1994) [1902], *Heart of Darkness*, London: Penguin Popular Classics.

Cooper, Frederick (2018), *Citizenship, Inequality, and Difference: Historical Perspectives*, Princeton University Press.

Coulthard, Glen (2014), *Red Skins, White Masks: Rejecting the Colonial Politics of Recognition*, Minneapolis: University of Minnesota Press.

Crapanzano, Vincent (2011), *The Harkis: The Wound That Never Heals*, University of Chicago Press.

Cronon, William (1983), *Changes in the Land: Indians, Colonists and the Ecology of New England*, New York: Hill and Wang.

Crowell, Maddy (2018), 'The Island Where France's Colonial Legacy Lives On', *The Atlantic*, 21 April. Accessed at: www.theatlantic.com/international/archive/2018/04/france-macron-guadeloupe-slavery-colonialism/557996.

Cruikshank, Julie (1998), *The Social Life of Stories: Narrative and Knowledge in the Yukon Territory*, Lincoln: University of Nebraska Press.

Cuevas, Mayra, and Steve Almasy (2017), 'Keystone Pipeline Leaks 210,000 Gallons of Oil in South Dakota', *CNN*, 17 November. Accessed at: https://edition.cnn.com/2017/11/16/us/keystone-pipeline-leak/index.html.

Cumming-Bruce, Nick (2019), 'Budget Cuts May Undercut the U.N.'s Human Rights Committees', *The New York Times*, 24 May. Accessed at: www.nytimes.com/2019/05/24/world/un-budget-cuts-human-rights.html.

Dahl, Adam (2018), *Empire of the People: Settler Colonialism and the Foundations of Modern Democratic Thought*, Lawrence: University Press of Kansas.

Dahlgreen, Will (2016), 'Rhodes Must Not Fall', YouGov, 18 January. Accessed at: https://yougov.co.uk/topics/politics/articles-reports/2016/01/18/rhodes-must-not-fall.

Dangarembga, Tsitsi (1988), *Nervous Conditions*, Seattle: Seal Press.

Daoud, Kamel (2015), *The Meursault Investigation*, translated by John Cullen, New York: Other Press.

Das, Santanu (2018), 'Presentation Accompanying "Not Yet at Ease" Exhibition by Raqs Media Collective', Firstsite Gallery, Colchester, 28 September.

Daulatzai, Sohail (2016), *Fifty Years of the Battle of Algiers: Past as Prologue*, Minneapolis: University of Minnesota Press.

Davis, David Brion (2014), *The Problem of Slavery in the Age of Emancipation*, New York: Knopf.

Davis, Josh (2019), 'Are Natural History Museums Inherently Racist?' *Science News*, Natural History Museum, 16 July. Accessed at: www.nhm.ac.uk/discover/news/2019/july/are-natural-history-museums-inherently-racist.html.

Dearden, Lizzie (2017), 'Emmanuel Macron Claims Africa Held Back by "Civilisational" Problems and Women Having "Seven or Eight Children"', *The Independent*, 11 July. Accessed at: www.independent.co.uk/news/world/europe/emmanuel-macron-africa-development-civilisation-problems-women-seven-eight-children-colonialism-a7835586.html.

Del Real, Jose (2019), 'No Charges in Sacramento Police Shooting of Stephon Clark', *The New York Times*, 2 March. Accessed at: www.nytimes.com/2019/03/02/us/stephon-clark-police-shooting-sacramento.html.

Deneen, Patrick (2019), *Why Liberalism Failed*, New Haven: Yale University Press.

Denson, Andrew (2017), *Monuments to Absence: Cherokee Removal and the*

*Contest over Southern Memory*, Chapel Hill: University of North Carolina Press.

Dettmer, Jamie (2017), 'Britain Strips More Than 100 Islamic State Fighters of Citizenship', *Voice of America News*, 30 July. Accessed at: www.voanews.com/europe/britain-strips-more-100-islamic-state-fighters-citizenship.

Di Savino, Scott, and Stephanie Kelly (2018), 'Two U.S. Pipelines Rack Up Violations, Threaten Industry Growth', Reuters, 28 November. Accessed at: www.reuters.com/article/us-usa-pipelines-etp-violations-insight/two-u-s-pipelines-rack-up-violations-threaten-industry-growth-idUSKCN1NX1E3.

Dierksheide, Christa (2008), '"The Great Improvement and Civilization of that Race": Jefferson and the "Amelioration" of Slavery, ca. 1770–1826', *Early American Studies*, 6, 1: 165–97.

Diouf, Sylviane (2007), *Dreams of Africa in Alabama: The Slave Ship Clotilda and the Story of the Last Africans Brought to America*, New York: Oxford University Press.

Donnelly, Jack (1998), 'Human Rights: A New Standard of Civilization', *International Affairs*, 74, 1: 1–23.

Douglass, Frederick (1996) [1852], 'What to the Slave is the Fourth of July?' in William Andrews (ed.), *The Oxford Frederick Douglass Reader*, Oxford University Press, 108–30.

Douzinas, Costas (2007), *Human Rights and Empire: The Political Philosophy of Cosmopolitanism*, London: Routledge.

Doward, Jamie (2017), 'British Arms Sales to Repressive Regimes Soar to £5bn since Election', *The Guardian*, 10 September. Accessed at: www.theguardian.com/world/2017/sep/09/arms-sales-repressive-regimes-saudi-arabia.

Doward, Jamie (2018), 'UK "Hides Extent of Arms Sales to Saudi Arabia"', *The Guardian*, 23 June. Accessed at: www.theguardian.com/world/2018/jun/23/uk-hides-arms-trade-saudi-arabia--yemen.

Drake, St Clair, and Horace Cayton (1993) [1945], *Black Metropolis: A Study of Negro Life in a Northern City*, University of Chicago Press.

Draper, Nicholas (2010), *The Price of Emancipation: Slave Ownership, Compensation and British Society at the End of Slavery*, Cambridge University Press.

Draper, Nicholas (2018), 'British Universities and Caribbean Slavery', in Jill Pellew and Lawrence Goldman (eds.), *Dethroning Historical Reputations: Universities, Museums and the Commemoration of Benefactors*, London: School of Advanced Study Press, 93–106.

Draper, Nick (2007), '"Possessing Slaves": Ownership, Compensation and Metropolitan Society in Britain at the Time of Emancipation 1834–40', *History Workshop Journal*, 64, 1: 74–102.

Dresser, Madge (2009), 'Remembering Slavery and Abolition in Bristol', *Slavery and Abolition*, 30, 2: 223–46.

Dresser, Madge (2016), *Slavery Obscured: The Social History of the Slave Trade in an English Provincial Port*, 2nd edition, London: Bloomsbury.

Drif, Zohra (2017), *Inside the Battle of Algiers*, Charlottesville: University of Virginia Press.

Du Bois, W. E. B. (1969a) [1903], *The Souls of Black Folks*, New York: Signet.

Du Bois, W. E. B. (1969b) [1896], *The Suppression of the African Slave Trade to the United States of America 1638–1870*, New York: Schocken.

Du Bois, W. E. B. (1995) [1899], *The Philadelphia Negro: A Social Study*, Philadelphia: University of Pennsylvania Press.

Dubb, Steve (2019), 'American Indian Leaders Call for Congress to End Voter Suppression', *Nonprofit Quarterly*, 22 April. Accessed at: https://nonprofitquarterly.org/2019/04/22/american-indian-leaders-call-for-congress-to-end-voter-suppression.

Dura, Jack (2019), 'North Dakota Lawmakers Bombarded with Emails on "Trespass Bill" Ahead of House Vote', *Jamestown Sun*, 10 April. Accessed at: www.jamestownsun.com/news/government-and-politics/1003021-North-Dakota-lawmakers-bombarded-with-emails-on-trespass-bill-ahead-of-House-vote.

Durkheim, Émile (1973) [1890], 'The Principles of 1789 and Sociology', in Robert Bellah (ed.), *Emile Durkheim on Morality and Society*, translated by Mark Traugott, University of Chicago Press, 34–42.

Echo-Hawk, Walter (2013), *In the Light of Justice: The Rise of Human Rights in Native America and the UN Declaration of the Rights of Indigenous Peoples*, Golden, CO: Fulcrum Publishing.

Edelstein, Dan (2019), *On The Spirit of Rights*, University of Chicago Press.

Egan, Matt (2017), 'Dakota Access Pipeline Suffered a Minor Oil Spill in April', *CNN*. Accessed at: https://money.cnn.com/2017/05/10/investing/dakota-access-pipeline-oil-spill/index.html.

Eichstedt, Jennifer, and Stephen Small (2002), *Representations of Slavery: Race and Ideology in Southern Plantation Museums*, Washington, DC: Smithsonian Institution Press.

Eligon, John, (2015), 'A Year after Ferguson, Housing Segregation Defies Tools to Erase It', *The New York Times*, 8 August. Accessed at www.nytimes.com/2015/08/09/us/a-year-after-ferguson-housing-segregation-defies-tools-to-erase-it.html.

Elkins, Caroline (2005), *Britain's Gulag: The Brutal End of Empire in Kenya*, London: Jonathan Cape.

Eltis, David, and Stanley Engerman (2000), 'The Importance of Slavery and the Slave Trade to Industrializing Britain', *Journal of Economic History*, 60, 1: 123–44.

Eltis, David, and David Richardson (2010), *Atlas of the Transatlantic Slave Trade*, New Haven: Yale University Press.

Emerson, Anne (2019), 'Online Reviews Complain about Focus on Slavery by Charleston Plantation Tour Guides', *ABC4 News*, 13 August. Accessed at: https://abcnews4.com/news/local/online-reviews-complain-about-focus-on-slavery-by-charleston-plantation-tour-guides.

Epstein, Helen (2017), *Another Fine Mess: America, Uganda, and the War on Terror*, New York: Columbia Global Reports.

Epstein, Helen (2018), 'A Deathly Hush', *New York Review of Books*, 28 June: 80–2.

Equality and Human Rights Commission (2018), *The State of Equality and Human Rights 2018*. Accessed at: www.equalityhumanrights.com/sites/default/files/is-britain-fairer-2018-pre-lay.pdf 25 October 2018.

Equality and Human Rights Commission (2019), 'Watchdog Confirms Grenfell Breached Human Rights Laws', Press Release, 13 March. Accessed at: www.equalityhumanrights.com/en/our-work/news/watchdog-confirms-grenfell-breached-human-rights-laws 17 March 2019.

Erakat, Noura (2019), *Justice for Some: Law and the Question of Palestine*, Stanford University Press.

Estes, Nick (2018), *Our History is the Future: Standing Rock versus the Dakota Access Pipeline, and the Long Tradition of Indigenous Resistance*, London: Verso.

Estes, Nick (2019), '"They Took Our Footprint out of the Ground"', in Nick Estes and Jaskiran Dhillon (eds.), *Standing with Standing Rock*, Minneapolis: University of Minnesota Press, 43–55.

Evans, James (2017), *Emigrants: Why the English Sailed to the New World*, London: Weidenfeld and Nicholson.

Evans, Sarah (2018), 'Bristol, the Slave Trade and a Reckoning with the Past', *Financial Times*, 9 August. Accessed at: www.ft.com/content/032fe4a0-9a96-11e8-ab77-f854c65a4465.

Fagan, Andrew (2019), 'The Gentrification of Human Rights', *Human Rights Quarterly*, 41, 2: 283–308.

Faith, Mike (2019), 'Our Fight Against the Dakota Access Pipeline Is Far from Over', *The Guardian*, 15 November. Accessed at: www.theguardian.com/commentisfree/2019/nov/15/dakota-access-pipeline-standing-rock.

Fanon, Frantz (1952), *Black Skin, White Masks*, translated by Charles Lam Markmann, London: Paladin.

Fanon, Frantz (1963), *The Wretched of the Earth*, New York: Grove Press.

Fanon, Frantz (1964), *Toward the African Revolution*, translated by Haakon Chevalier, New York: Grove Press.

Fanon, Frantz (1965), *A Dying Colonialism*, translated by Haakon Chevalier, New York: Grove Press.

Ferguson, Niall (2004), *Empire: How Britain Made the Modern World*, London: Penguin.

Ferguson, Niall (2011), *Civilization: The West and the Rest*, London: Allen Lane.

Fernando, Mayanthi (2014), *The Republic Unsettled: Muslim French and the Contradictions of Secularism*, Durham, NC: Duke University Press.

Fieldhouse, D. K. (1986), *Black Africa 1945–80: Economic Decolonization and Arrested Development*, London: Allen and Unwin.

Finer, Matt, Clinton Jenkins, Stuart Pimm, Brian Keane and Carl Ross (2008), 'Oil and Gas Projects in the Western Amazon: Threats to Wilderness, Biodiversity, and Indigenous Peoples', *PloS one*, 3, 8. Accessed at: https://journals.plos.org/plosone/article?id=10.1371/journal.pone.0002932.

Finkelman, Paul (2015), *Slavery and the Founders: Race and Liberty in the Age of Jefferson*, 3rd edition, New York: Routledge.

Fleming, Fergus (2003), *The Cross and the Sword*, London: Granta Books.

Flynn, Andrea, Susan Holmberg, Dorian Warren and Felicia Wong (2017), *The Hidden Rules of Race: Barriers to an Inclusive Economy*, Cambridge University Press.

Fois, Marisa (2016), 'Identity, Politics and Nation: Algerian Nationalism and the "Berberist Crisis" of 1949', *British Journal of Middle Eastern Studies*, 43, 2: 206–18.

Foreign and Commonwealth Office (2018), 'Lord Ahmad Addresses the 39th Session of the UN Human Rights Council', 17 September. Accessed at: www.gov.uk/government/speeches/lord-ahmad-addresses-the-39th-session-of-the-un-human-rights-council.

Foreign and Commonwealth Office (2019), 'Resolution on the British Indian Ocean Territory', 21 June. Accessed at: www.gov.uk/government/speeches/resolution-on-the-british-indian-ocean-territory.

Forsdick, Charles (2015), 'Compensating for the Past: Debating Reparations for Slavery in Contemporary France', *Contemporary French and Francophone Studies*, 19, 4: 420–9.

Fowler, Loretta (1982), *Arapahoe Politics, 1851–1978*, Lincoln: University of Nebraska Press.

France 24 (2019), 'Algeria Jails 22 Protesters over Berber Flags', 12 November. Accessed at: www.france24.com/en/20191112-algeria-jails-22-protesters-over-berber-flags.

Fredette, Jennifer (2014), *Constructing Muslims in France: Discourse, Public Identity and the Politics of Citizenship*, Philadelphia: Temple University Press.

Freedom House (n.d.), *Policing Belief: A Freedom House Special Report*. Accessed at: https://freedomhouse.org/sites/default/files/PolicingBelief_Algeria.pdf.

Frum, David (2018), *Trumpocracy: The Corruption of the American Republic*, New York: Harper Collins.

Furness, Hannah (2019), 'UK Museums Task Staff with Identifying "Stolen" Colonial Collections', *The Telegraph*, 1 January. Accessed at: www.telegraph.co.uk/news/2019/01/01/uk-museums-task-staff-identifying-stolen-colonial-collections.

Gagarin, Michael (1982), 'The Organization of the Gortyn Law Code', *Greek, Roman, and Byzantine Studies*, 23, 2: 129–46.

Galdos, Guillermo (2018), 'Cambridge Analytica: The Mexico Allegations', Channel 4, 29 March. Accessed at: www.channel4.com/news/cambridge-analytica-the-mexico-allegations.

Garrett, Mitchell Bennett (1970) [1916], *The French Colonial Question, 1789–1791*, New York: Negro Universities Press.

Gassama, Ibrahim (2008), 'Africa and the Politics of Destruction: A Critical Re-examination of Neocolonialism and its Consequences', *Oregon Review of International Law*, 10, 1: 327–60.

Geggus, David (1989), 'Racial Equality, Slavery, and Colonial Secession during the Constituent Assembly', *American Historical Review*, 94, 5: 1290–1308.

Gelder, Sam (2019), 'Hubert Howard: Home Office Says It Will Pay Compensation to Windrush Victim's Family as Funeral Fundraiser Launched',

*Hackney Gazette*, 20 November. Accessed at: www.hackneygazette.co.uk/ news/hubert-howard-family-launch-fundraiser-to-pay-for-funeral-of-lower-clapton-windrush-victim-1-6385358.

Gentleman, Amelia (2018), 'The Week that Took Windrush from Low-Profile Investigation to National Scandal', *The Guardian*, 21 April. Accessed at: www.theguardian.com/uk-news/2018/apr/20/the-week-that-took-windrush-from-low-profile-investigation-to-national-scandal.

Gentleman, Amelia (2019a), 'Windrush Victim Dies with No Apology or Compensation', *The Guardian*, 22 June. Accessed at: www. theguardian.com/uk-news/2019/jun/22/windrush-victim-richard-stewart-dies-with-no-apology-or-compensation.

Gentleman, Amelia (2019b), 'Chased into "Self-deportation": The Most Disturbing Windrush Case So Far', *The Guardian*, 14 September. Accessed at: www.theguardian.com/uk-news/2019/sep/14/scale-misery-devastating-inside-story-reporting-windrush-scandal.

Gerdziunas, Benas (2017), 'Belgium's Genocidal Colonial Legacy Haunts the Country's Future', *The Independent*, 17 October. Accessed at: www. independent.co.uk/news/long_reads/belgiums-genocidal-colonial-legacy-haunts-the-country-s-future-a7984191.html.

Gerster, Jane (2018), 'Is Canada Being Inconsistent about Human Rights Concerns in Saudi Arabia?' *Global News*, 7 August. Accessed at: https:// globalnews.ca/news/4374991/canada-saudi-arabia-human-rights-concerns.

Ghanmi, Lamine (2018), 'Algeria Welcomes Macron's Admission of France's Role in Pro-Algerian Activist's Death', *The Arab Weekly*, 23 September. Accessed at: https://thearabweekly.com/algeria-welcomes-macrons-admission-frances-role-pro-algerian-activists-death.

Ghiles, Francis (2018), 'Being Honest with History Can Help France and Others Build a Better Future', *The Arab Weekly*, 23 September. Accessed at: https://thearabweekly.com/being-honest-history-can-help-france-and-others-build-better-future.

Gibson, Nigel, and Roberto Beneduce (2017), *Frantz Fanon, Psychiatry and Politics*, London: Rowman and Littlefield.

Gifford, Anthony (2000), 'The Legal Basis of the Claim for Slavery Reparations', *Human Rights*, 27: 16–18.

Gildea, Robert (2019), *Empires of the Mind: The Colonial Past and the Politics of the Present*, Cambridge University Press.

Gilroy, Paul (1993), *The Black Atlantic: Modernity and Double Consciousness*, London: Verso.

Goddeeris, Idesbald (2015), 'Postcolonial Belgium: The Memory of the Congo', *Interventions*, 17, 3: 434–51.

Gopal, Priyamvada (2017), 'The British Empire's Hidden History is One of Resistance, Not Pride', *The Guardian*, 28 July. Accessed at: www. theguardian.com/commentisfree/2017/jul/28/british-empire-hidden-history-solidarity-truth-resistance.

Gopal, Priyamvada (2019), *Insurgent Empire: Anticolonial Resistance and British Dissent*, London: Verso.

Gordon, Linda (2017), *The Second Coming of the KKK: The Ku Klux Klan of the 1920s and the American Political Tradition*, New York: Liverlight.

Gosling, W. G. (1910), *Labrador: Its Discovery, Exploration, and Development*, London: Alston Rivers Ltd.

Gotham, Kevin Fox (2000), 'Urban Space, Restrictive Covenants and the Origins of Racial Residential Segregation in a US City, 1900–50', *International Journal of Urban and Regional Research*, 24, 3: 616–33.

Gott, Richard (2011), 'Let's End the Myths of Britain's Imperial Past', *The Guardian*, 19 October. Accessed at: www.theguardian.com/books/2011/oct/19/end-myths-britains-imperial-past.

Grandin, Greg (2006), *Empire's Workshop: Latin America, the United States, and the Rise of the New Imperialism*, New York: Metropolitan Books.

Gray, Nicola (2016), 'Echoes of Empire: Artist and Empire at Tate Britain', *Third Text*. Accessed at: www.thirdtext.org/echoes-of-empire.

Greene, Alan (2019), 'UK Military Amnesty for Historic Prosecutions Could Breach International Human Rights Law', *The Conversation*, 15 May. Accessed at: https://theconversation.com/uk-military-amnesty-for-historic-prosecutions-could-breach-international-human-rights-law-117202.

Grira, Sarra (2019), 'Protestant Church Shut Down in Algeria: "They Came Bearing Truncheons"', *France 24*, 29 October. Accessed at: https://observers.france24.com/en/20191029-latest-protestant-church-shutdowns-algeria-they-came-bearing-truncheons.

Grossman, Zoltán (2017), *Unlikely Alliances: Native Nations and White Communities Join to Defend Rural Lands*, Seattle: University of Washington Press.

Gstalter, Morgan (2018), 'UN Human Rights Experts: Trump Attacks on Media Violate Press Freedom Norms', *The Hill*, 2 August. Accessed at: http://thehill.com/homenews/administration/400216-un-human-rights-experts-trump-attacks-on-media-violate-press-freedom.

Hagen, C. S. (2019), 'More than Two Years Later, Last NoDAPL Trials Finish', *High Plains Reader*, 5 February. Accessed at: https://hpr1.com/index.php/feature/news/more-than-two-years-later-last-nodapl-trials-finish.

Haley, Nikki (2018), 'Letter to Human Rights Watch', 20 June. Accessed at: www.hrw.org/sites/default/files/supporting_resources/un062018_haley_letter.pdf.

Hall, Stuart (2002), 'Democracy, Globalization and Difference', in Okwui Enzewor, Carlos Basualdo, Ute Meta Bauer, et al. (eds.), *Democracy Unrealized*, Ostfildern-Ruit, Germany: Hatje Cantz, 21–36.

Hamilton, Robert (2019), 'Making Space for Indigenous Law in Resource Development Decisions', *OpenCanada*. Accessed at www.opencanada.org/features/making-space-indigenous-law-resource-development-decisions.

Hanchard, Michael (2018), *The Spectre of Race: How Discrimination Haunts Western Democracy*, Princeton University Press.

Hansen, Karen (2013), *Encounter on the Great Plains: Scandinavian Settlers and the Dispossession of Dakota Indians, 1890–1930*, Oxford University Press.

Harjo, Chitto (2015) [1906], 'Keep Our Treaties', in Daniel Cobb (ed.), *Say We*

*Are Nations: Documents of Politics and Protest*, Durham, NC: University of North Carolina Press, 19–23.

Harpin, Lee (2019), 'Exclusive: Jeremy Hunt Announces UK Will Oppose Anti-Israel Measures at the UN Human Rights Council', *Jewish Chronicle*, 21 March. Accessed at: www.thejc.com/news/uk-news/jeremy-hunt-announces-uk-will-oppose-every-uh-human-rights-council-measure-on-israel-1.481834.

Harries, Patrick (2007), 'The Battle of Algiers: Between Fiction, Memory and History', in Vivian Bickford Smith and Richard Mendelsohn, *Black and White in Colour: African History on Screen*, Oxford: James Curry, 203–22.

Hassan, Adeel (2019), 'Georgetown Students Agree to Create Reparations Fund', 12 April. Accessed at: www.nytimes.com/2019/04/12/us/georgetown-reparations.html.

Hasselman, Jan (2018), 'The Renewed Legal Challenge Against the Dakota Access Pipeline', *Earthjustice*, 1 November. Accessed at: https://earthjustice.org/features/explainer-renewed-legal-challenge-dakota-access.

Haydn, Terry (2014), 'How and What Should We Teach about the British Empire in English Schools?' in *Handbook of the International Society of History Didactics*, Schwalbach: Wochenschau Verlag, 23–40.

Heath, Deana (2018), 'British Empire is Still Being Whitewashed by the School Curriculum – Historian on Why This Must Change', *The Conversation*, 2 November. Accessed at: https://theconversation.com/british-empire-is-still-being-whitewashed-by-the-school-curriculum-historian-on-why-this-must-change-105250.

Heggoy, Alf Andrew (1973), 'Education in French Algeria: An Essay on Cultural Conflict', *Comparative Education Review*, 17, 2: 180–97.

Heizer, Robert, and Alan Almquist (1971), *The Other Californians: Prejudice and Discrimination under Spain, Mexico, and the United States to 1920*, Berkeley: University of California Press.

Henley, Jon (2005), 'French Angry at Law to Teach Glory of Colonialism', *The Guardian*, 15 April. Accessed at: www.theguardian.com/world/2005/apr/15/highereducation.artsandhumanities.

Henriksen, Georg (2009), *I Dreamed the Animals. Kaniuekutat: The Life of an Innu Hunter*, Oxford: Berghahn Books.

Higginbotham, F. Michael (2013), *Ghosts of Jim Crow: Ending Racism in Post-racial America*, New York University Press.

High Country News (2017), 'Drop Excessive Charges against Journalist Jenni Monet', 7 February. Accessed at: www.hcn.org/media/2017/drop-charges-against-jenni-monet.

Hill, James (2017), 'Trump Administration Withdrew Legal Memo that Found "Ample Legal Justification" to Halt Dakota Access Pipeline', *ABC News*, 24 February. Accessed at: https://abcnews.go.com/US/trump-administration-withdraws-legal-memo-found-ample-legal/story?id=45696135.

Hill-Martin, Dawn (2008), *The Lubicon Lake Cree: Indigenous Knowledge and Power*, University of Toronto Press.

Hirsch, Afua (2018), *Brit(ish): On Race, Identity and Belonging*, London: Vintage.

Hochschild, Adam (1999), *King Leopold's Ghost*, London: Macmillan.

Hopper, Frank (2019), 'Case Dismissed, Records Unsealed: Iron Eyes Wins Release of NoDAPL Documents', *Indian Country Today*, 16 September. Accessed at: https://newsmaven.io/indiancountrytoday/news/case-dismissed-records-unsealed-iron-eyes-wins-release-of-nodapl-documents-QmTLnDWaPEa9GTdkd0LcGQ.

Horn, Steve (2018), 'TigerSwan, County Sheriff Sued Over Road Blockade During Dakota Access Pipeline Protests', Desmog, 26 October. Accessed at: www.desmogblog.com/2018/10/26/lawsuit-dakota-access-road-blockade.

Horn, Steve (2019), 'Bills Criminalizing Pipeline Protest Arise in Statehouses Nationwide', *Nation of Change*, 23 February. Accessed at: www.nationofchange.org/2019/02/23/bills-criminalizing-pipeline-protest-arise-in-statehouses-nationwide.

Horne, Alistair (2006) [1977], *A Savage War of Peace, Algeria 1954–1962*, New York Review Books.

House, Jim (2001), 'Antiracist Memories: The Case of 17 October 1961 in Historical Perspective', *Modern & Contemporary France*, 9, 3: 355–68.

Hoxie, Frederick (1984), *A Final Promise: The Campaign to Assimilate the Indians, 1820–1920*, Lincoln: University of Nebraska Press.

Hubbard, Tasha (2014), 'Buffalo Genocide in Nineteenth Century North America: "Kill, Skin and Sell"', in Andrew Woolford, Alex Hinton and Jeff Benvenuto (eds.), *Colonial Genocide in North America*, Durham, NC: Duke University Press, 382–416.

Human Rights Watch (2017), 'Burma: Methodical Massacre at Rohingya Village', 19 December. Accessed at: www.hrw.org/news/2017/12/19/burma-methodical-massacre-rohingya-village.

Human Rights Watch (2018), 'Bahrain: Events of 2017'. Accessed at: www.hrw.org/world-report/2018/country-chapters/bahrain.

Human Rights Watch (2019), 'US Stance at UN a Backward Step on Women's Rights', 25 April. Accessed at: www.hrw.org/news/2019/04/25/us-stance-un-backward-step-womens-rights.

Hunt, Jeremy (2019), 'Yemen Crisis Won't Be Solved by UK Arms Exports Halt', *Politico*, 26 March. Accessed at: www.politico.eu/article/conflict-war-un-yemen-crisis-wont-be-solved-by-uk-arms-exports-halt.

Hunt, Lynn (1996), *The French Revolution and Human Rights: A Brief Documentary History*, Boston: Bedford / St. Martin's Press.

Hurston, Zora Neale (2018), *Barracoon: The Story of the Last Slave*, London: HQ Books.

Hussey, Andrew (2014), *The French Intifada: The Long War between France and its Arabs*, London: Granta.

Hussey, Andrew (2018), 'The Return of the Repressed: The Bitter Legacy of the Algerian War', *New Statesman*, 21 November. Accessed at: www.newstatesman.com/world/europe/2018/11/return-repressed-bitter-legacy-algerian-war.

Ibhawoh, Bonny (2014), *Imperial Justice: Africans in Empire's Court*, Oxford University Press.

Ibrahim, Azeem (2016), *The Rohingyas: Inside Myanmar's Hidden Genocide*, London: Hurst.

International Labour Organization (2015), 'ILO Warns of Widespread Insecurity in the Global Labour Market'. Accessed at: www.ilo.org/global/about-the-ilo/newsroom/news/WCMS_368252/lang--en/index.htm.

Ipsos Public Affairs (2018), *Human Rights in 2018: A Global Advisory Survey*. Accessed at: https://rightsinfo.org/britain-split-human-rights-abuse-problem.

Ish-Shalom, Piki (2006) 'Theory Gets Real, and the Case for a Normative Ethic: Rostow, Modernization Theory, and the Alliance for Progress', *International Studies Quarterly*, 50, 2: 287–311.

Jack, Ian (2018), 'The Sun May Never Set on British Misconceptions about Our Empire', *The Guardian*, 6 January. Accessed at: www.theguardian.com/commentisfree/2018/jan/06/british-misconceptions-empire-guilty-colonialism.

Jackson, Helen Hunt (1965) [1881], *A Century of Dishonor: The Early Crusade for Indian Reform*, New York: Harper.

Jackson, Thomas (2007), *From Civil Rights to Human Rights: Martin Luther King, Jr. and the Struggle for Economic Justice*, Philadelphia: University of Pennsylvania Press.

Jacobs, Harriet (1987) [1861], *Incidents in the Life of a Slave Girl*, Cambridge, MA: Harvard University Press.

Jain, Sangaree (2018), 'Theresa May "Deeply Regrets" Colonial Anti-LGBT Laws', Human Rights Watch, 18 April, Accessed at: www.hrw.org/news/2018/04/18/theresa-may-deeply-regrets-colonial-anti-lgbt-laws.

*Jamaica Observer* (2018), 'Clean Up Your Colonial Mess', 1 August. Accessed at: www.jamaicaobserver.com/news/-clean-up-your-colonial-mess-_140184?profile=1373.

Jarvie, Jenny (2018), 'Nikki Haley Calls U.N. Report on Poverty in U.S. "Misleading and Politically Motivated"', *Los Angeles Times*, 21 June. Accessed at: www.latimes.com/world/la-fg-un-us-poverty-20180621-story.html.

Jefferson, Thomas (1975), *The Portable Thomas Jefferson*, edited by Merrill Peterson. New York: Viking Penguin.

Johnson, Ian (2018), 'In Search of the True Dao', *New York Review of Books*, 8 November: 42–4.

*Journal du Cameroun* (2018), 'Macron Unveils Plan to Boost French, "Language of Liberty"', 20 March. Accessed at: www.journalducameroun.com/en/macron-unveils-plan-to-boost-french-language-of-liberty.

Jung, Carl (1965), *Memories, Dreams, Reflections*, recorded and edited by Aniela Jaffé, translated by Richard and Clara Winston, New York: Vintage.

Kaisary, Philip (2012), 'Human Rights and Radical Universalism: Aimé Césaire's and CLR James's Representations of the Haitian Revolution', *Law and Humanities*, 6, 2: 197–216.

Kassam, Ashifa (2017), 'Canada Children's Book Recalled Amid Accusations of Whitewashing History', *The Guardian*, 4 October. Accessed at: www.theguardian.com/world/2017/oct/04/canada-childrens-book-recalled-whitewashing-history.

Keal, Paul (2003), *European Conquest and the Rights of Indigenous Peoples:*

*The Moral Backwardness of International Society*, Cambridge University Press.

Keller, Christian (2000), 'Philanthropy Betrayed: Thomas Jefferson, the Louisiana Purchase, and the Origins of Federal Indian Removal Policy', *Proceedings of the American Philosophical Society*, 144, 1: 39–66.

Kentish, Benjamin (2018), 'Tory Government Votes Not to Retain European Human Rights Charter in UK Law after Brexit', *The Independent*, 16 January. Accessed at: www.independent.co.uk/news/uk/politics/brexit-mps-vote-against-including-european-fundamental-rights-charter-in-uk-law-a8162981.html.

Kessell, John (1981), 'General Sherman and the Navajo Treaty of 1868: A Basic and Expedient Misunderstanding', *The Western Historical Quarterly*, 12, 3: 251–72.

Khadra, Yasmina (2016), *The Angels Die*, translated by Howard Curtis, London: Gallic Books.

Kiernan, Ben (2007), *Blood and Soil: A World History of Genocide and Extermination from Sparta to Darfur*, New Haven: Yale University Press.

Kincaid, Jamaica (2018) [1988], *A Small Place*, London: Daunt Books.

King, Desmond (2007), *Separate and Unequal: Black Americans and the US Federal Government*, New York: Oxford University Press.

Kirby, Phillip (2016), *Leading People: The Educational Backgrounds of the UK Professional Elite*, London: Sutton Trust.

Klose, Fabian (2013) *Human Rights in the Shadow of Colonial Violence*, Philadelphia: University of Pennsylvania Press.

Kobin, Billy (2019), 'Louisville's Southern Baptist Seminary Rejects Call to Make Slavery Reparations', *Courier Journal*, 9 June. Accessed at: https://eu.courier-journal.com/story/news/religion/2019/06/06/louisville-southern-baptist-leaders-reject-slavery-reparations/1350801001.

Koskenniemi, Martti (2011), *The Politics of International Law*, Oxford: Hart.

Kottasová, Ivana (2018), 'The 1% Grabbed 82% of All Wealth Created in 2017', *CNN Money*, 22 January. Accessed at: http://money.cnn.com/2018/01/21/news/economy/davos-oxfam-inequality-wealth/index.html.

Krikler, Jeremy (2012), 'A Chain of Murder in the Slave Trade: A Wider Context of the *Zong* Massacre', *International Review of Social History*, 57: 393–415.

Kunzru, Hari (2019), 'Fool Britannia', *New York Review of Books*, 21 February: 4–6.

Kuo, Lily (2018), 'China "Legalises" Internment Camps for Million Uighurs', *The Guardian*, 11 October. Accessed at: www.theguardian.com/world/2018/oct/11/china-legalises-internment-camps-for-million-uighurs.

Kwibuka, Eugène (2019), 'Rwanda to Repeal All Colonial Laws', *The New Times*, 20 June. Accessed at: www.newtimes.co.rw/news/rwanda-repeal-all-colonial-laws.

la paperson (2017), *A Third University is Possible*, Minneapolis: University of Minnesota Press.

La Pier, Rosalyn (2016), 'Why Understanding Native American Religion Is Important for Resolving the Dakota Access Pipeline Crisis', *The*

*Conversation*, 3 November. Accessed at: https://theconversation.com/why-understanding-native-american-religion-is-important-for-resolving-the-dakota-access-pipeline-crisis-68032.

LaDuke, Winona (2019), 'The Seventh Fire', *Resilience*, 18 July. Accessed at: www.resilience.org/stories/2019-07-18/uncertain-future-forum-winona-laduke-essay.

Ladybud (2017), 'The Aftershocks of the DAPL Standing Rock Protests Are Still Ongoing', 17 September. Accessed at: www.ladybud.com/2018/09/17/the-aftershocks-of-the-dapl-standing-rock-protests-are-still-ongoing.

Lafer, Gordon (2017), *The One Percent Solution: How Corporations Are Remaking America One State at a Time*, Ithaca, NY: ILR / Cornell University Press.

Laing, R. D. (1960), *The Divided Self*, Harmondsworth: Penguin.

Landler, Mark (2018), 'In Extraordinary Statement, Trump Stands with Saudis Despite Khashoggi Killing', *The New York Times*, 20 November. Accessed at: www.nytimes.com/2018/11/20/world/middleeast/trump-saudi-khashoggi.html?emc=edit_th_181121&nl=todaysheadlines&nlid=212771011121.

Langer, William (1969), *Political and Social Upheaval 1832–1852*, New York: Harper.

Lawson, Michael (2009), *Dammed Indians Revisited: The Continuing History of the Pick–Sloan Plan and the Missouri River Sioux*, Pierre: South Dakota Historical Society Press.

Lazaroff, Tovah (2019), 'Netanyahu: U.N. Set New Hypocrisy Record with Israeli War Crimes Allegation', *Jerusalem Post*, 28 February. Accessed at: www.jpost.com/Israel-News/Benjamin-Netanyahu/Netanyahu-UN-set-new-hypocrisy-record-with-Israeli-war-crimes-allegation-582059.

Lazreg, Marnia (2008), *Torture and the Twilight of Empire: From Algiers to Baghdad*, Princeton University Press.

Le Sueur, James (2005), *Uncivil War: Intellectuals and Identity Politics during the Decolonization of Algeria*, Lincoln: University of Nebraska Press.

Legal Information Institute (n.d.), 'Civil Rights Cases'. Accessed at: www.law.cornell.edu/supremecourt/text/109/3.

Lenze, Paul, Jr (2016), *Civil–Military Relations in the Islamic World*, Lanham, MD: Lexington Books.

Lessenich, Stephan (2019), *Living Well at Others' Expense: The Hidden Costs of Western Prosperity*, Cambridge: Polity.

Levin, Sam (2017), 'Revealed: FBI Terrorism Taskforce Investigating Standing Rock Activists', *The Guardian*, 10 February. Accessed at: www.theguardian.com/us-news/2017/feb/10/standing-rock-fbi-investigation-dakota-access.

Levin, Sam, Nicky Woolf and Damian Carrington (2016), 'North Dakota Pipeline: 141 Arrests as Protesters Pushed Back from Site', *The Guardian*, 28 October. Accessed at: www.theguardian.com/us-news/2016/oct/27/north-dakota-access-pipeline-protest-arrests-pepper-spray.

Levitsky, Steven, and Daniel Ziblatt (2018), *How Democracies Die*, New York: Crown.

Lewa, Chris (2009), 'North Arakan: An Open Prison for the Rohingya in Burma', *Forced Migration Review*, 32: 11–13.

Lincoln, Abraham (2001) [1858], 'Fourth Debate with Stephen A. Douglas at Charleston, Illinois', in *Collected Works of Abraham Lincoln*, volume III. Accessed at: https://quod.lib.umich.edu/l/lincoln/lincoln3/1:20.1?rgn=div2;view=fulltext.

Little, Simon (2019), 'Plaque Bearing Name of Controversial British Colonial Icon Covered Up at Vancouver School', *Global News*, 11 June. Accessed at: https://globalnews.ca/news/5379348/ecole-bilingue-cecil-rhodes.

Locke, Attica (2017), *Bluebird, Bluebird*, London: Serpent's Tail.

Locke, John (1965) [1689], *Two Treatises of Government*, revised edition, New York: New American Library.

Loop Jamaica (2019), 'Reparation for Slavery Not a Priority Item for Britain at This Time', 17 May. Accessed at: www.loopjamaica.com/content/reparation-slavery-not-priority-item-britain-time.

Lorcin, Patricia (2014), *Imperial Identities: Stereotyping, Prejudice, and Race in Colonial Algeria*, New Edition, Lincoln: University of Nebraska Press.

Louison, Cole (2019), 'Nothing to See at Belgium's Royal Museum of Central Africa', *The Outline*, 14 May. Accessed at: https://theoutline.com/post/7427/nothing-to-see-at-belgium-s-royal-museum-of-central-africa?zi=xdsqjnfc&zd=2.

Loukaides, Loukes (2007), 'The Concept of "Continuing" Violations of Human Rights', in Loukes Loukaides (ed.), *The European Convention on Human Rights: Collected Essays*, Leiden: Martinus Nijhoff Publishers, 17–33.

Lu, Catherine (2017), *Justice and Reconciliation in World Politics*, Cambridge University Press.

Lundin, Emma (2019), 'There Is No Longer Any Excuse for Not Repatriating Museums' Colonial Art', *Prospect Magazine*, 25 March. Accessed at: www.prospectmagazine.co.uk/arts-and-books/repatriation-museum-colonial-art-parthenon-marbles-easter-island.

MacDougall, James (2006), *History and the Culture of Nationalism in Algeria*, Cambridge University Press.

Macklin, Audrey (2018), 'The Return of Banishment: Do the New Denationalisation Policies Weaken Citizenship?' in R. Bauböck (ed.), *Debating Transformations of National Citizenship*, New York: Springer International Publishing, 163–72.

MacLean, Nancy (2017), *Democracy in Chains: The Deep History of the Radical Right's Stealth Plan for America*, New York: Viking.

MacMaster, Neil (2009), *Burning the Veil: The Algerian War and the 'Emancipation' of Muslim Women, 1954–62*, Manchester University Press.

Madley, Benjamin (2014), 'California and Oregon's Modoc Indians: How Indigenous Resistance Camouflages Genocide in Colonial Histories', in Andrew Woolford, Alex Hinton and Jeff Benvenuto (eds.), *Colonial Genocide in North America*, Durham, NC: Duke University Press, 95–130.

Madley, Benjamin (2016), *An American Genocide: The United States and the California Indian Catastrophe*, New Haven: Yale University Press.

Magdaleno, Johnny (2015), 'Algerians Suffering from French Atomic Legacy, 55 Years after Nuke Tests', Al Jazeera International, 1 March. Accessed at: http://america.aljazeera.com/articles/2015/3/1/algerians-suffering-from-french-atomic-legacy-55-years-after-nuclear-tests.html.

Mamdani, Mahmood (2001), *When Victims Become Killers: Colonialism, Nativism and the Genocide in Rwanda*, Princeton University Press.

Mamdani, Mahmood (2009), *Saviors and Survivors: Darfur, Politics and the War on Terror*, London: Verso.

Mamdani, Mahmood (2012), *Define and Rule: The W. E. B. DuBois Lectures*, Cambridge, MA: Harvard University Press.

Mann, James (2008), *The China Fantasy: Why Capitalism Will Not Bring Democracy to China*, New York: Penguin.

Marsh, Sarah, Haroon Siddique and Caroline Bannock (2018), 'Windrush Generation Tell of Holidays that Led to Exile and Heartbreak', *The Guardian*, 19 April. Accessed at: www.theguardian.com/uk-news/2018/apr/19/windrush-generation-tell-of-holidays-that-led-to-exile-and-heartbreak.

Martens, Kathleen (2018), 'Removing John A. Macdonald's Name "Victory" for Idle-No-More', *APTN News*, 10 January. Accessed at: http://aptnnews.ca/2018/01/10/removing-john-a-macdonalds-name-victory-for-idle-no-more.

Martinez, Luis (2000), *The Algerian Civil War, 1990–1998*, translated by Jonathan Derrick, London: Hurst.

Marx, Karl (1972) [1953], *The Grundrisse*, edited and translated by David McLellan, New York: Harper Torchbooks.

Marx, Karl (1978a) [1843], 'On the Jewish Question', in Robert Tucker (ed.), *The Marx Engels Reader*, 2nd edition, New York: W. W. Norton, 26–52.

Marx, Karl (1978b) [1867], 'Kapital, Volume 1, Chapter XXXI', in Robert Tucker (ed.), *The Marx Engels Reader*, 2nd edition, New York: W.W. Norton, 435–6.

Masalha, Nur (1997), *A Land without a People: Israel, Transfer and the Palestinians 1949–96*, London: Faber and Faber.

Massoud, Mark Fathi (2018), 'How an Islamic State Rejected Islamic Law', *The American Journal of Comparative Law*, 66, 3: 579–602.

Mastracci, Davide (2018), 'Justin Trudeau Doesn't Care about Human Rights', *Huffington Post*, 29 October. Accessed at: www.huffingtonpost.ca/davide-mastracci/saudi-arabia-trudeau-arms-deal_a_23572709.

Matthews-King, Alex (2018), 'Government Announces Jamaican Nurse Recruitment Partnership Amid Windrush Scandal', *The Independent*, 23 April. Accessed at: www.independent.co.uk/news/health/jamaica-nhs-nurse-windrush-theresa-may-amber-rudd-government-india-staff-shortage-a8318121.html.

May, Elaine Tyler (2017), *Fortress America: How We Embraced Fear and Abandoned Democracy*, New York: Basic Books.

Mayblin, Lucy (2014), 'Colonialism, Decolonisation, and the Right to Be Human: Britain and the 1951 Geneva Convention on the Status of Refugees', *Journal of Historical Sociology*, 27, 3: 423–41.

Mayer, Jane (2016), *Dark Money: How a Secretive Group of Billionaires Is Trying to Buy Political Control in the US*, London: Scribe.

Mazower, Mark (2008), *Hitler's Empire: Nazi Rule in Occupied Europe*, London: Allen Lane.

Mazower, Mark (2009), *No Enchanted Palace: The End of Empire and the Ideological Origins of the United Nations*, Princeton University Press.

Mbembe, Achille (2015), 'Decolonizing Knowledge and the Question of the Archive', *Aula Magistral Proferida*. Accessed at: https://wiser.wits.ac.za/system/files/Achille%20Mbembe%20-%20Decolonizing%20Knowledge%20and%20the%20Question%20of%20the%20Archive.pdf.

McArthur, John, and Krista Rasmussen (2017), *Change of Pace: Accelerations and Advances during the Millennium Development Goal Era*. Washington, DC: Brookings Institute. Accessed at: www.brookings.edu/wp-content/uploads/2017/01/global_20170111_change_of_pace.pdf.

McCauley, Lauren (2016), '"Pipelines Leak": Expert Finds Government Downplayed DAPL Impact on Tribe and Water', *Common Dreams*, 4 November. Accessed at: www.commondreams.org/news/2016/11/04/pipelines-leak-expert-finds-government-downplayed-dapl-impact-tribe-and-water.

McCool, Daniel, Susan Olson and Jennifer Robinson (2007), *Native Vote: American Indians, the Voting Rights Act and the Right to Vote*, Cambridge University Press.

McDonnell, Hugh (2018), 'Anything But Pacific', *Jacobin*, 21 November. Accessed at: https://jacobinmag.com/2018/11/new-caledonia-france-independence-colonialism-referendum.

McNeilly, Kathryn (2018), *Human Rights and Radical Social Transformation: Futurity, Alterity, Power*, Abingdon: Routledge.

McVeigh, Karen (2018), 'One-third of UK Arms Sales Go to States on Human Rights Watchlist, Say Analysts', *The Guardian*, 21 December. Accessed at: www.theguardian.com/global-development/2018/dec/21/one-third-of-uk-arms-sales-go-to-states-on-human-rights-watchlist-say-analysts.

Meier, August, and Elliot Rudwick (1966), *From Plantation to Ghetto*, New York: Hill and Wang.

Merriott, Dominic (2017), 'Factors Associated with the Farmer Suicide Crisis in India', *Journal of Epidemiology and Global Health*, 6: 217–27.

*Middle East Eye* (2018), 'The Migrants "Abandoned" in the Desert: Algeria Faces Fresh Scrutiny', 28 June. Accessed at: www.middleeasteye.net/news/algeria-dodges-accusations-after-migrants-abandoned-sahara-1042882803.

*Middle East Monitor* (2018), 'Algeria Abandons 13,000 Migrants in Sahara Desert', 27 June. Accessed at: www.middleeastmonitor.com/20180627-algeria-abandons-13000-migrants-in-sahara-desert.

*Middle East Monitor* (2019a), 'France Agrees to 5th Term for Algeria's Bouteflika', 13 February. Accessed at: www.middleeastmonitor.com/20190213-france-agrees-to-5th-term-for-algerias-bouteflika.

*Middle East Monitor* (2019b), 'Algeria Deports 3,200 Sub-Saharan Africans in One Month', 11 November. Accessed at: www.middleeastmonitor.com/20191111-algeria-deports-3200-sub-saharan-africans-in-one-month.

Miliband, Ralph (1969), *The State in Capitalist Society*, New York: Basic Books.

Mill, John Stuart (1975a) [1859], 'On Liberty', in *Three Essays*, Oxford University Press, 5–141.

Mill, John Stuart (1975b) [1861], 'Considerations on Representative Government', in *Three Essays*, Oxford University Press, 143–423.

Miller, John (1991), *The Wolf by the Ears: Thomas Jefferson and Slavery*, Charlottesville: University of Virginia Press.

Mills, C. Wright (1956), *The Power Elite*, Oxford University Press.

Mills, Charles (1997), *The Racial Contract*, Ithaca, NY: Cornell University Press.

Mills, Charles (2017), *Black Rights / White Wrongs: The Critique of Racial Liberalism*, New York: Oxford University Press.

Millward, James (2019). '"Reeducating" Xinjiang's Muslims', *New York Review of Books*, 7 February. Accessed at: www.nybooks.com/articles/2019/02/07/reeducating-xinjiangs-muslims.

Milmo, Cahal, and Richard Vaughan (2019), 'May to Meet Saudi Ruler Amid Arms Sales Row', *The Independent*, 29 June: 8.

Mirza, Isa, and Helen Clapp (2019), 'Trump Administration's Proposed Prosecution of Pipeline Opponents: Weighing Human Rights Obligations and Congressional Support', *Mondaq*, 16 July. Accessed at: www.mondaq.com/unitedstates/x/826186/Human+Rights/Trump+Administrations+Proposed+Prosecution+of+Pipeline+Opponents+Weighing+Human+Rights+Obligations+and+Congressional+Support.

Mokone, Outsa, Sethunya Tshepho Mosime, Angela Quintal and Vuyisile Hlatshwayo (2019), 'The Colonial-Era Laws that Still Govern African Journalism', *Al Jazeera*, 10 March. Accessed at: www.aljazeera.com/programmes/listeningpost/2019/03/colonial-era-laws-govern-african-journalism-190310080903941.html.

Montemayor, Stephen (2018), 'Dakota Access Pipeline Protester Injured in Blast Sues Government for Return of Evidence', *Minneapolis Star Tribune*, 5 February. Accessed at: www.startribune.com/dakota-access-pipeline-protestor-injured-in-blast-sues-government-for-return-of-evidence/472819363.

Moody, Jessica, and Stephen Small (2019), 'Slavery and Public History at the Big House: Remembering and Forgetting at the American Plantation Museums and British Country Houses', *Journal of Global Slavery*, 4: 34–68.

Moore, Sally Falk (1978), *Law as Progress: An Anthropological Approach*, London: Routledge and Kegan Paul.

Morgan, Edmund, and Marie Morgan (2008), 'Jefferson's Concubine', 9 October. Accessed at: www.nybooks.com/articles/2008/10/09/jeffersons-concubine.

Morris, Lydia (2013), *Human Rights and Social Theory*, London: Palgrave Macmillan.

Morris, Lydia (2015), 'Squaring the Circle: Domestic Welfare, Migrants Rights, and Human Rights', *Citizenship Studies*, 20, 6–7: 1–17.

Morris, Lydia (2016), 'The Moral Economy of Austerity: Analysing UK Welfare Reform', *British Journal of Sociology*, 67, 1: 97–117.

Morrison, Toni (2016), 'Mourning for Whiteness', *New Yorker*, 21 November. Accessed at: www.newyorker.com/magazine/2016/11/21/aftermath-sixteen-writers-on-trumps-america#anchor-morrison.

Mouffe, Chantal (2013), *Agonistics: Thinking the World Politically*, London: Verso.

Moyn, Samuel (2010), *The Last Utopia: Human Rights in History*, Cambridge, MA: Harvard University Press.

Moyn, Samuel (2018), *Not Enough: Human Rights in an Unequal World*, Cambridge, MA: Harvard University Press.

Mubinde, V. Y. (1994), *The Idea of Africa*, Woodbridge: James Currey.

Mumbere, Daniel (2018), 'Photos: Germany Returns Namibia Genocide Skulls', *Africa News*, 29 August. Accessed at: www.africanews.com/2018/08/29/photos-germany-returns-namibia-genocide-skulls.

Napoleon, Val (2015), 'Tsilhqot'in Law of Consent', *University of British Columbia Law Review*, 48, 3: 873–902.

National Enquiry into Missing and Murdered Indigenous Women and Girls (2019), *Executive Summary of the Final Report*. Accessed at: www.mmiwg-ffada.ca/wp-content/uploads/2019/06/Executive_Summary.pdf.

National Museum of African American History and Culture (2019). Accessed at: https://nmaahc.si.edu/explore/initiatives/slaverys-wake.

Native News Network (2016), 'Standing Rock Sioux Tribe Reasserts that DAPL Destroyed Sacred Places', 1 October. Accessed at: https://nativenewsonline.net/currents/standing-rock-sioux-tribe-reasserts-dapl-destroyed-sacred-places.

*Nature* (2018), 'Maths Strikes a Blow for Democracy', 17 January. Accessed at: https://www.nature.com/articles/d41586-018-00661-x.

Ndikumana, Léonce (2015), 'Integrated Yet Marginalized: Implications of Globalization for African Development', *African Studies Review*, 58, 2: 7–28.

Neville, Alan, and Alyssa Kaye Anderson (2013), 'The Diminishment of the Great Sioux Reservation: Treaties, Tricks and Time', *Great Plains Quarterly*, 33, 4: 237–51.

Newcomb, Alyssa, Daniel Medina, Emmanuelle Saliba, Euronews and Chiara A. Sottile (2016), 'Dakota Pipeline, Protesters Questions of Surveillance and "Jamming" Linger', *NBC News*, 31 October. Accessed at: www.nbcnews.com/storyline/dakota-pipeline-protests/dakota-pipeline-protesters-questions-surveillance-jamming-linger-n675866.

Nicholson, Blake (2019), 'Law Officers Respond to Suit over Pipeline Protester Injury', *Minneapolis Star Tribune*, 25 January. Accessed at: www.startribune.com/law-officers-respond-to-suit-over-pipeline-protester-injury/504878852.

Niezen, Ronald (2017), 'Speaking for the Dead: The Memorial Politics of Genocide in Namibia and Germany', *International Journal of Heritage Studies*, 24, 5: 547–67.

Nimako, Kwame, Amy Abdou and Glenn Willemsen (2014), 'Chattel Slavery and Racism: A Reflection on the Dutch Experience', in Philomena Essed and Isabel Hoving (eds.), *Dutch Racism*, Amsterdam and New York: Thamyris, 33–51.

Nolan, Aoife (2019), 'Human Rights and the Grenfell Tower Inquiry', LRB Blog, 4 November. Accessed at: www.lrb.co.uk/blog/2019/november/human-rights-and-the-grenfell-tower-inquiry.

*North Africa Journal* (2019), 'Algeria Police Arrest Dozen Journalists Who Were Protesting against Censorship', 28 February. Accessed at: http://north-africa.

com/algeria-police-arrest-dozen-journalists-who-were-protesting-against-censorship.

*North Africa Post* (2018), 'Algeria: Palestinians, Like Sub-Saharans, Suffer Abuse & Ill-Treatment', 29 November. Accessed at: http://northafricapost.com/26491-algeria-palestinians-like-sub-saharans-suffer-abuse-ill-treatment.html.

Obahopo, Boluwaji (2017) 'Nigeria Must Stop Blaming Colonialism for its Woes – British High Commissioner', *Nigeria Today*, 8 April. Accessed at: www.nigeriatoday.ng/2017/04/nigeria-must-stop-blaming-colonialism-for-its-woes-british-high-commissioner.

Ochoa O'Leary, Anna, Andrea J. Romero, Nolan L. Cabrera and Michelle Rascón (2012), 'Assault on Ethnic Studies', in O. Santa Ana and C. Gonzalez de Bustamante (eds.), *Arizona Firestorm: Global Immigration Realities, National Media, and Provincial Politics*, Lanham, MD: Rowman and Littlefield, 97–120.

Olusoga, David (2019), 'Windrush: The Long Betrayal', *The Observer*, 16 June: 19–21.

Orwell, George (1936), 'Shooting an Elephant,' in *Inside the Whale and Other Essays*, London: Penguin, 91–9.

Orwell, George (1957), 'England Your England', in *Inside the Whale and Other Essays*, London: Penguin, 63–90.

Orwell, George (1988) [1934], *Burmese Days*, Harmondsworth: Penguin.

Osgood-Zimmerman, Aaron, Anoushka Millear, Rebecca W. Stubbs, et al. (2018) 'Mapping Child Growth Failure in Africa between 2000 and 2015', *Nature*, 555, 1 March: 41–7. Accessed at: www.nature.com/articles/nature25760.

Ostler, Jeffrey (2004), *The Plains Sioux and US Colonialism: From Lewis and Clark to Wounded Knee*, Cambridge University Press.

Owen, Jonathan (2016), 'British Empire: Students Should Be Taught Colonialism "Not All Good", Say Historians', *The Independent*, 22 January. Accessed at: www.independent.co.uk/news/education/education-news/british-empire-students-should-be-taught-colonialism-not-all-good-say-historians-a6828266.html.

Paine, Thomas (1987) [1780], 'Public Good', in *The Thomas Paine Reader*, London: Penguin, 124–38.

Parker, Arthur C. (2015) [1918], 'That the Smaller Peoples May Be Safe', in Daniel Cobb (ed.), *Say We Are Nations: Documents of Politics and Protest*, Durham, NC: University of North Carolina Press, 27–31.

Passel, Jeffrey, and D'Vera Cohn (2008), 'U.S. Population Projections: 2005–2050', Pew Research Center, 11 February. Accessed at: www.pewhispanic.org/2008/02/11/us-population-projections-2005-2050.

Passel, Jeffrey, Wendy Wang and Paul Taylor (2010), 'One-in-Seven New U.S. Marriages is Interracial or Interethnic', Pew Research Center, 4 June. Accessed at: www.pewsocialtrends.org/2010/06/04/marrying-out.

Pasternak, Shiri (2017), *Grounded Authority: The Algonquins of Barriere Lake against the State*, Minneapolis: University of Minnesota Press.

Patnaik, Utsa (2007), *The Republic of Hunger and Other Essays*, Monmouth: Merlin Press.

Pérez-Peña, Richard (2015), 'University of Cincinnati Officer Indicted in Shooting Death of Samuel Dubose', *The New York Times*, 29 April. Accessed at www.nytimes.com/2015/07/30/us/university-of-cincinnati-officer-indicted-in-shooting-death-of-motorist.html.

Pilkington, Ed (2019), 'Trump Administration Ignoring Human Rights Monitors, ACLU Tells UN', *The Guardian*, 18 March. Accessed at: www.theguardian.com/law/2019/mar/18/trump-administration-ignoring-human-rights-monitors-aclu.

Pinckney, Darryl (2011), 'Invisible Black America', *New York Review of Books*, 10 March: 33–5.

Polonsky, Naomi (2019), 'Activists Return to the British Museum to Lead Another "Stolen Goods" Tour', *Hyperallergic*, 8 May. Accessed at: https://hyperallergic.com/499433/activists-return-to-the-british-museum-to-lead-another-stolen-goods-tour.

Pompeo, Michael (2019), `Unalienable Rights and U.S. Foreign Policy´, *Wall Street Journal*, 7 July. Accessed at: www.wsj.com/articles/unalienable-rights-and-u-s-foreign-policy-11562526448.

Poniewozik, James (2016), 'A Killing. A Pointed Gun. And Two Black Lives, Witnessing', *The New York Times*, 7 July. Accessed at: www.nytimes.com/2016/07/08/us/philando-castile-facebook-police-shooting-minnesota.html?emc=eta1.

Powers, Stephen (1976) [1877], *Tribes of California*, Berkeley: University of California Press.

Press Association (2013), 'UK to Compensate Kenya's Mau Mau Torture Victims', *The Guardian*, 6 June. Accessed at: www.theguardian.com/world/2013/jun/06/uk-compensate-kenya-mau-mau-torture.

Prucha, Francis Paul (1962), *American Indian Policy in the Formative Years: The Indian Trade and Intercourse Acts, 1790–1834*, Cambridge, MA: Harvard University Press.

Prucha, Francis Paul (ed.) (1975), *Documents of United States Indian Policy*, Lincoln: University of Nebraska Press.

Pueblo of Zuni (1972), *The Zunis: Self Portrayals*, New York: New American Library.

Quinn, Ben (2016), 'French Police Make Woman Remove Clothing on Nice Beach Following Burkini Ban', *The Guardian*, 24 August. Accessed at: www.theguardian.com/world/2016/aug/24/french-police-make-woman-remove-burkini-on-nice-beach.

Rabe, Stephen (2011), *The Killing Zone: The United States Wages Cold War in Latin America*, New York: Oxford University Press.

Radio France Internationale (2017a), 'Africa: Macron Rules Out Reparations for Colonialism', 4 December. Accessed at: https://allafrica.com/stories/201712050362.html.

Radio France Internationale (2017b), 'Macron Ready to Return Algerian Anti-Colonial Fighters' Skulls', 6 December. Accessed at: http://en.rfi.fr/africa/20171206-macron-ready-return-algerian-anti-colonial-fighters-skulls.

Ramdani, Nabila (2018), 'Macron's Acknowledgement of France's History of Brutality against Algerians Is Welcome, But It's Time the Perpetrators Were

Held Accountable', *The Independent*, 16 September. Accessed at: www.independent.co.uk/voices/emmanuel-macron-france-president-algeria-history-brutality-accountable-a8539991.html.

Rankine, Claudia (2019), 'I Wanted to Know What White Men Thought About Their Privilege. So I Asked', *The New York Times*, 17 July. Accessed at: www.nytimes.com/2019/07/17/magazine/white-men-privilege.html.

Ranson, Ian (2018), 'Commonwealth Games: "Stolenwealth" Protesters Disrupt Baton Relay', Reuters, 4 April. Accessed at: https://in.reuters.com/article/games-commonwealth-protests/commonwealth-games-stolenwealth-protesters-disrupt-baton-relay-idINKCN1HB0N7.

Reinbold, Jenna (2017), *Seeing the Myth in Human Rights*, Philadelphia: University of Pennsylvania Press.

Reuters (2018), 'U.N. Rights Boss Bachelet Egypt to Overturn Mass Death Sentences', 9 September. Accessed at: www.reuters.com/article/us-egypt-rights-un/u-n-rights-boss-bachelet-urges-egypt-to-overturn-mass-death-sentences-idUSKCN1LP0BX.

Reuters in Manama (2018), 'Khashoggi Murder Undermines Stability, Mattis Says, as Saudis Bemoan "Hysteria"', *The Guardian*, 27 October. Accessed at: www.theguardian.com/world/2018/oct/27/mattis-jamal-khashoggi-saudi-arabia-bahrain.

Reuters in Montreal (2019), 'Quebec Law Banning Hijab at Work Creates "Politics of Fear", Say Critics', *The Guardian*, 17 June. Accessed at: www.theguardian.com/world/2019/jun/17/quebec-law-hijab-ban-religious-symbols-public-employees.

Riding, Alan (2005), 'Art Show Forces Belgium to Ask Hard Questions about Its Colonial Past', *The New York Times*, 9 February. Accessed at: www.nytimes.com/2005/02/09/arts/design/art-show-forces-belgium-to-ask-hard-questions-about-its.html.

Robertson, Campbell (2018), 'A Lynching Memorial Is Opening: The Country Has Never Seen Anything Like It', *The New York Times*, 25 April. Accessed at: www.nytimes.com/2018/04/25/us/lynching-memorial-alabama.html.

Rogers, Katie, and Sheryl Gay Stolberg (2018), 'Trump Calls for Depriving Immigrants Who Illegally Cross Border of Due Process Rights', 24 June. Accessed at: www.nytimes.com/2018/06/24/us/politics/trump-immigration-judges-due-process.html?emc=edit_th_180625&nl=todaysheadlines&nlid=212771010625.

Romo, Vanessa (2018), 'African-American Senators Introduce Anti-Lynching Bill', National Public Radio, 29 June. Accessed at: www.npr.org/2018/06/29/624847379/african-american-senators-introduce-anti-lynching-bill.

Ross-Tremblay, Pierrot (2019), *Thou Shall Forget: Indigenous Sovereignty, Resistance and the Production of Cultural Oblivion in Canada*, London: School of Advanced Studies Press.

Rothstein, Richard (2017), *The Color of Law: A Forgotten History of How Our Government Segregated America*, New York: Liveright.

Rousseau, Jean-Jacques (1966) [1791], *The Social Contract*, New York: Hafner.

Rowland, Lee, and Vera Eidelman (2017), 'Where Protests Flourish, Anti-Protest Bills Follow', American Civil Liberties Union, 17 February. Accessed at: www.aclu.org/blog/free-speech/rights-protesters/where-protests-flourish-anti-protest-bills-follow?redirect=blog/speak-freely/where-protests-flourish-anti-protest-bills-follow.

Rucker, Patrick (2014), 'Bakken Crude May Be More Flammable than Previously Thought: U.S. Regulator', Reuters, 3 January. Accessed at: www.reuters.com/article/us-usa-energy-bakken-idUSBREA010ZI20140103.

Rutazibwa, Privat (2019), 'The Hypocrisy of Human Rights Discourse of the West on Africa', New Times, 6 July. Accessed at: www.newtimes.co.rw/opinions/hypocrisy-human-rights-discourse-west-africa.

Sabbagh, Dan (2019), 'No 10 Accused of Ignoring Evidence of Russian Interference', The Guardian, 6 November. Accessed at: www.theguardian.com/politics/2019/nov/06/no-10-accused-of-ignoring-evidence-of-russian-interference.

Salandy, Tye (2019), 'Sedition and Other Nonsensical Colonial Laws', Trinidad and Tobago Newsblog, 22 September. Accessed at: www.trinidadandtobagonews.com/blog/?p=11797.

Samson, Colin (2001) 'Sameness as a Requirement for the Recognition of the Rights of the Innu of Canada: The Colonial Context', in Jane Cowan, Marie-Benedicte Dembour and Richard Wilson (eds.), Culture and Rights: Anthropological Perspectives, Cambridge University Press, 226–48.

Samson, Colin (2003), A Way of Life That Does Not Exist: Canada and the Extinguishment of the Innu, St John's: ISER Books; and London: Verso Press.

Samson, Colin (2013), A World You Do Not Know: Settler Societies, Indigenous Peoples and the Attack on Cultural Diversity, London: School of Advanced Studies Press.

Samson, Colin (2014), 'Dispossession and Canadian Land Claims: Genocidal Implications of the Innu Nation Land Claim', in Andrew Woolford, Alex Hinton and Jeff Benvenuto (eds.), Colonial Genocide in North America, Durham, NC: Duke University Press, 246–70.

Samson, Colin (2016), 'A State Strategy of Dispossession: Aboriginal Land and Rights Cessions in Comprehensive Land Claims in Canada', Canadian Journal of Law and Society, 31, 1: 87–110.

Samson, Colin (2018), 'The Idea of Progress, Industrialization, and the Replacement of Indigenous Peoples: The Muskrat Falls Megadam Boondoggle', Social Justice, 44, 4: 1–17.

Samson, Colin (2019), 'Indigenous and European Views of Happiness: An Essay on the Politics of Contentment', in Bryan Turner and Yuri Contreras-Vejar (eds.), Regimes of Happiness: Comparative and Historical Studies, New York: Anthem, 219–34.

Samson, Colin, and Carlos Gigoux (2017), Indigenous Peoples and Colonialism: Global Perspectives, Cambridge: Polity.

Sanford, George (2005), Katyn and the Soviet Massacre of 1940, London: Routledge.

Sarkin, Jeremy (2011), *Germany's Genocide of the Herero: Kaiser Wilhelm II, His General, His Settlers, His Soldiers*, Woodbridge: James Currey.

Sassoon, Siegfried (1997) [1930], *Memoirs of an Infantry Officer*, London: Faber and Faber.

Sato, Shohei (2017), '"Operation Legacy": Britain's Destruction and Concealment of Colonial Records Worldwide', *Journal of Imperial and Commonwealth History*, 45, 4: 697–719.

Save the Children (2018), 'Yemen: 85,000 Children May Have Died from Starvation Since Start of War', Press Release, 20 November. Accessed at: www.savethechildren.org/us/about-us/media-and-news/2018-press-releases/yemen-85000-children-may-have-died-from-starvation.

Schermerhorn, Calvin (2018), *Unrequited Toil: A History of United States Slavery*, Cambridge University Press.

Schmidt, Michael (2018), 'Trump Invited the Russians to Hack Clinton: Were They Listening?' *The New York Times*, 13 July. Accessed at: www.nytimes.com/2018/07/13/us/politics/trump-russia-clinton-emails.html?module=inline.

Schmidt, Michael, and Matt Apuzzo (2015), 'South Carolina Officer Is Charged with Murder of Walter Scott', *The New York Times*, 7 April. Accessed at: www.nytimes.com/2015/04/08/us/south-carolina-officer-is-charged-with-murder-in-black-mans-death.html.

Schmitt, Carl (1996) [1932], *The Concept of the Political*, translated by George Schwab, University of Chicago Press.

Schmitt, Carl (2014), *Dictatorship: From the Origin of the Modern Concept of Sovereignty to Proletarian Class Struggle*, translated by Michael Hoelzl and Graham Ward, Cambridge: Polity.

Scobie, Claire (2019), 'The Long Road Home', *The Guardian*, 28 June. Accessed at: www.theguardian.com/world/2009/jun/28/aborigines-reclaim-ancestors-remains.

Sebald, W. G. (2001), *Austerlitz*, translated by Anthea Bell, New York: Modern Library.

Sen, Asoka Kumar (2012), *From Village Elder to British Judge: Custom, Customary Law and Tribal Society*, Hyderabad: Orient BlackSwan.

Sentencing Project (2013), *Shadow Report to the United Nations on Racial Disparities in the United States Criminal Justice System*, 31 August. Accessed at: www.sentencingproject.org/publications/shadow-report-to-the-united-nations-human-rights-committee-regarding-racial-disparities-in-the-united-states-criminal-justice-system.

Sentencing Project (n.d), '6 Million Lost Voters: State-Level Estimates of Felony Disenfranchisement, 2016'. Accessed at: www.sentencingproject.org/publications/6-million-lost-voters-state-level-estimates-felony-disenfranchisement-2016/.

Sessions, Jennifer (2011), *By Sword and Plow: France and the Conquest of Algeria*, Ithaca, NY: Cornell University Press.

Sessions, Jennifer (2017), 'Why the French Presidential Candidates Are Arguing about Their Colonial History', *The Conversation*, 19 April. Accessed at: https://theconversation.com/why-the-french-presidential-candidates-are-arguing-about-their-colonial-history-75372.

Severson, Kim (2013), 'North Carolina Repeals Law Allowing Racial Bias Claim in Death Penalty Challenges', *The New York Times*, 5 June. Accessed at: www.nytimes.com/2013/06/06/us/racial-justice-act-repealed-in-north-carolina.html.

Shane, Scott, and Sheera Frenkel (2018), 'Russian 2016 Influence Operation Targeted African-Americans on Social Media', *The New York Times*, 17 December. Accessed at: www.nytimes.com/2018/12/17/us/politics/russia-2016-influence-campaign.html.

Shaw, Tamsin (2018), 'Beware the Big Five', *New York Review of Books*, 5 April: 33–5.

Shear, Michael (2018), 'Comey's Memoir Offers Visceral Details on a President "Untethered to Truth"', *The New York Times*, 12 April. Accessed at: www.nytimes.com/2018/04/12/us/politics/trump-comey-book.html?emc=edit_th_18 0413&nl=todaysheadlines&nlid=212771010413.

Shear, Michael (2019), 'Trump Shrugs Off Khashoggi Killing by Ally Saudi Arabia', *The New York Times*, 22 June. Accessed at: www.nytimes.com/2019/06/23/us/politics/trump-khashoggi-killing-saudi-arabia.html.

Shelley, Toby (2004), *Endgame in the Western Sahara: What Future for Africa's Last Colony?* London: Zed Books.

Shepard, Todd (2006), *The Invention of Decolonization: The Algerian War and the Remaking of France*, Ithaca, NY: Cornell University Press.

Shepherd, Verene (2018), 'Past Imperfect, Future Perfect? Reparations, Rehabilitation, Reconciliation', *Journal of African American History*, 103, 12: 19–43.

Short, Damien (2016), *Redefining Genocide: Settler Colonialism, Social Death and Ecocide*, London: Zed Books.

Siddique, Harroon (2018), '"Not Everything Was Looted": British Museum to Fight Critics', *The Guardian*, 12 October. Accessed at: www.theguardian.com/culture/2018/oct/12/collected-histories-not-everything-was-looted-british-museum-defends-collections.

Sikkink, Kathryn (2017), *Evidence for Hope: Making Human Rights Work in the 21st Century*, Princeton University Press.

Singer, Joseph William (2002), '*Lone Wolf*, or How to Take Property by Calling It a Mere Change in the Form of Investment', *Tulsa Law Review*, 38: 37–48.

Sitaraman, Ganesh (2017), *The Crisis of the Middle-Class Constitution: Why Economic Inequality Threatens our Republic*, New York: Knopf.

Slotkin, Richard (1998), *The Fatal Environment: The Myth of The Frontier in the Age of Industrialization, 1800–1890*, Norman: University of Oklahoma Press.

Small, Stephen (2015), 'Social Mobilization and Public History of Slavery in the United States', in Marta Araújo and Silvia Rodríguez Maeso (eds.), *Eurocentrism, Racism and Knowledge: Debates on History and Power in Europe and the Americas*, Basingstoke: Palgrave Macmillan, 229–46.

Small, Stephen (2017), *20 Questions and Answers on Black Europe*, The Hague: Amrit.

Smart, Amy (2018), 'John A. Macdonald Statue "Painful Reminder" of Colonialism: Victoria Mayor', 8 August. Accessed at: https://theprovince.com/pmn/news-pmn/canada-news-pmn/john-a-macdonald-statue-painful-reminder-of-colonialism-victoria-b-c-mayor/wcm/c5d280d4-83a4-4952-96cf-0422923ed357.

Smith, Lydia (2017), 'Emmanuel Macron Vows to Make French the World's First Language', *The Independent*, 30 November. Accessed at: www.independent.co.uk/news/world/europe/emmanuel-macron-french-language-france-president-world-first-africa-burkina-faso-a8084586.html.

Smith, Mitch, and John Swartz (2019), '"Breaches Everywhere": Flooding Bursts Midwest Levees, and Tough Questions Follow', *The New York Times*, 31 March. Accessed at: www.nytimes.com/2019/03/31/us/midwest-floods-levees.html?emc=edit_th_190401&nl=todaysheadlines&nlid=212771010401.

Snyder, Timothy (2009), 'Holocaust: The Ignored Reality', *New York Review of Books*, 16 July: 14–16.

Sogolo, Godwin (1998), 'Logic and Rationality', in P. H. Coetzee and A. P. J. Roux (eds.), *Philosophy from Africa: A Text with Readings*, Johannesburg: International Thomson Publishers, 217–33.

Sontag, Susan (2004), *Regarding the Pain of Others*, London: Penguin.

Spencer, Michael (2019), 'Shamima Begum: Is Stripping Her of Her Citizenship the Right Response?' UK Human Rights Blog, 1 March. Accessed at: https://ukhumanrightsblog.com/2019/03/01/shamina-begum-is-stripping-her-of-her-citizenship-the-right-response.

Spohn, Cassia (2015) 'Race, Crime, and Punishment in the Twentieth and Twenty-First Centuries', *Crime & Justice*, 44: 49–98.

Stack, Liam (2019), 'Tulsa Police Officer Who Killed Unarmed Black Man Won't Face Civil Rights Charges', *The New York Times*, 1 March. Accessed at: www.nytimes.com/2019/03/01/us/betty-shelby-terence-crutcher-tulsa.html.

Staples, Louis (2019), 'Trump Says He Handled Charlottesville "Very Fine People" Question "Perfectly", Praises General Who Fought to Preserve Slavery', 27 April. Accessed at: www.indy100.com/article/trump-charlottesville-very-fine-people-white-supremacy-joe-biden-8889121.

Steiker, Carol, and Jordan Steiker (2015), 'The American Death Penalty and the (In)Visibility of Race', *The University of Chicago Law Review*, 82: 243–94.

Stein, Sharon (2017), 'A Colonial History of the Higher Education Present: Rethinking Land-Grant Institutions through Processes of Accumulation and Relations of Conquest', *Critical Studies in Education*, December: 1–17.

Stockel, H. Henrietta (2006), *Shame and Endurance: The Untold Story of the Chiricahua Apache Prisoners of War*. Tucson: University of Arizona Press.

Stokes, Eric (1959), *The English Utilitarians and India*, Oxford: Clarendon Press.

Stolberg, Sheryl Gay (2015), 'Baltimore Enlists National Guard and a Curfew to Fight Riots and Looting', *The New York Times*, 27 April. Accessed at: www.nytimes.com/2015/04/28/us/baltimore-freddie-gray.html?emc=edit_th_20150428&nl=todaysheadlines&nlid=21277101&_r=0.

Stoler, Ann Laura (2016), *Duress: Imperial Durabilities in our Time*, Durham, NC: Duke University Press.

Stora, Benjamin (2001), *Algeria, 1830–2000: A Short History*, translated by Jane Marie Todd, Ithaca, NY: Cornell University Press.

Stuart, David E. (2000), *Anasazi America*, Albuquerque: University of New Mexico Press.

Stuntz, William (2011), *The Collapse of American Criminal Justice*, Cambridge, MA: Belknap, Harvard University Press.

Suleiman, Susan Rubin (2002), 'History, Memory, and Moral Judgment in Documentary Film: On Marcel Ophuls's "Hotel Terminus: The Life and Times of Klaus Barbie"', *Critical Inquiry*, 28, 2: 509–41.

Sumich, Jason (2018), *The Middle Class in Mozambique: The State and the Politics of Transformation in Southern Africa*, Cambridge University Press.

Surkis, Judith (2010), 'Ethics and Violence: Simone de Beauvoir, Djamila Boupacha, and the Algerian War', *French Politics, Culture & Society*, 28, 2: 38–55.

Swart, Mia (2008), 'Name Change as Symbolic Reparation after Transition: The Example of Germany and South Africa', *German Law Journal*, 9, 2: 105–21.

Sweeney, James (2018), 'Massacre in Malaysia: Why the Quest for an Investigation into Alleged UK Colonial Crimes Faltered', *The Conversation*, 23 October. Accessed at: https://theconversation.com/massacre-in-malaysia-why-the-quest-for-an-investigation-into-alleged-uk-colonial-crimes-faltered-104602.

Syal, Rajeev (2018), 'Donors Fork Out £7m to Have Dinner with PM, Records Show', *The Guardian*, 21 July: 15.

Sykes, Emerson (2019), 'The Government Is Hiding Its Plans for Anti-Pipeline Protests', American Civil Liberties Union, 20 March. Accessed at: www.aclu.org/blog/free-speech/rights-protesters/government-hiding-its-plans-anti-pipeline-protests.

Taussig, Michael (1987), *Shamanism, Colonialism and the Wild Man: A Study in Terror and Healing*, University of Chicago Press.

Taylor, Diane (2018), 'Appeal Court Rules that Ministerial Code Does Not Dilute Human Rights', *The Guardian*, 1 August. Accessed at: www.theguardian.com/law/2018/aug/01/appeal-court-rules-that-ministerial-code-does-not-dilute-human-rights.

Tehranian, John (2000), 'Performing Whiteness: Naturalization Litigation and the Construction of Racial Identity in America', *Yale Law Journal*, 109, 4: 817–48.

Texas State Library and Archives Commission (n.d.), *DECLARATION OF CAUSES: February 2, 1861: A declaration of the causes which impel the State of Texas to secede from the Federal Union*. Accessed at: www.tsl.texas.gov/ref/abouttx/secession/2feb1861.html.

Tharoor, Shashi (2016), *Inglorious Empire: What the British Did to India*, London: Hurst and Co.

*The Gleaner* (2019), '"Clean Up The Mess You Left" – Shepherd Says Former Colonial Powers Have a Duty to Pay Reparations', 17 May. Accessed at: http://jamaica-gleaner.com/article/lead-stories/20190517/clean-mess-you-left-shepherd-says-former-colonial-powers-have-duty-pay.

*The New Arab* (2018), 'Thousands of Algeria Ex-soldiers March on Capital,

Demanding Government Benefits', 24 September. Accessed at: www.alaraby. co.uk/english/news/2018/9/24/thousands-of-algeria-ex-soldiers-march-on-capital-after-clashes#collapsedComments.

*The New York Times* (2017), 'Confederate Monuments Are Coming Down Across the US: Here's the List', 28 August. Accessed at: www.nytimes.com/interactive/2017/08/16/us/confederate-monuments-removed.html.

Tilianaki, Myrto (2018), 'Britain Should Stand Up for Saudi Women Activists', *Human Rights Watch*, 19 December. Accessed at: www.hrw.org/news/2018/12/19/britain-should-stand-saudi-women-activists.

Tocqueville, Alexis de (1945), *Democracy in America*, volume I, translated by Philips Bradley, New York: Vintage Books.

Tocqueville, Alexis de (2001a) [1837], 'Second Letter on Algeria (22 August 1837)', in Jennifer Pitts (ed. and trans.), *Writings on Empire and Slavery*, Baltimore: Johns Hopkins University Press, 14–26.

Tocqueville, Alexis de (2001b) [1841], 'Essay on Algeria (October 1841)', in Jennifer Pitts (ed. and trans.), *Writings on Empire and Slavery*, Baltimore: Johns Hopkins University Press, 59–116.

Todorov, Tzetvan (2009), *In Defence of the Enlightenment*, London: Atlantic Books.

Toh, Amos (2019), 'The Disastrous Roll-out of the UK's Digital Welfare System Is Harming Those Most in Need', *Human Rights Watch*, 10 June. Accessed at: www.hrw.org/news/2019/06/10/disastrous-roll-out-uks-digital-welfare-system-harming-those-most-need.

Tomasky, Michael (2018), 'Fighting to Vote', *New York Review of Books*, 8 November. Accessed at: www.nybooks.com/articles/2018/11/08/fighting-to-vote.

Trahant, Mark (2019), 'Muscogee (Creek) Nation: "Dust Will Settle" after Supreme Court Pass on Treaty Case', *Indian Country Today*, 27 June. Accessed at: https://newsmaven.io/indiancountrytoday/news/muscogee-creek-nation-dust-will-settle-after-supreme-court-pass-on-treaty-case-JgTcRnrTok-ntgn3-ac6bw.

Truth and Reconciliation Commission of Canada (2015), *Calls to Action.* Accessed at: http://trc.ca/assets/pdf/Calls_to_Action_English2.pdf.

Tsang, Steve (2018), 'Is China's Africa Investment More Than a "New Version of Colonialism"?', *Arab News*, 18 September. Accessed at: www.arabnews.com/node/1373416.

Tully, James (2012), 'Rethinking Human Rights and Enlightenment: A View from the Twenty-First Century', in Kate Tunstall (ed.), *Self-Evident Truths? Human Rights and the Enlightenment*, London: Bloomsbury, 3–34.

Turner, Frederick Jackson (1961), *Frontier and Section: Selected Essays of Frederick Jackson Turner*, Englewood Cliffs, NJ: Prentice-Hall.

Uddin, Tasnima (2017), 'What Created the Blueprint for Rohingya Genocide in Myanmar? Western Colonialism', *The Independent*, 6 September. Accessed at: www.independent.co.uk/voices/rohingya-genocide-myanmar-aung-sun-suu-kyi-colonialism-bangladesh-a7932876.html.

United Kingdom Government (2018), 'UK Marks 70th Anniversary of UN Declaration of Human Rights', Foreign and Commonwealth

Office, 11 December. Accessed at: www.gov.uk/government/news/uk-marks-70th-anniversary-of-un-declaration-of-human-rights.

United Kingdom Government (2019), 'UK to Stand for Re-election to Human Rights Council', Press Release, 25 February. Accessed at: www.gov.uk/government/news/uk-to-stand-for-re-election-to-human-rights-council.

United Kingdom Mission to Human Rights Council Geneva (2018), 'Human Rights Council 39: UK Statement for the Item 2 General Debate'. Accessed at: www.gov.uk/government/news/human-rights-council-39-uk-statement-for-the-item-2-general-debate.

United Nations (1960), *Declaration on the Granting of Independence to Colonial Countries and Peoples*, General Assembly. Accessed at: www.un.org/en/decolonization/declaration.shtml.

United Nations (2006), Committee for the Elimination of Racial Discrimination Decision 1 (68) United States of America, Sixty-eighth session, Geneva, 20 February – 10 March 2006. Accessed at: www.refworld.org/pdfid/45c30ba90.pdf.

United Nations (2018), 'With 22 Million People across Yemen Suffering, $2.96 Billion Humanitarian Response Must Be Fully, Rapidly Funded, Secretary-General Tells Pledging Conference', Press Release, 3 April. Accessed at: https://www.un.org/press/en/2018/sgsm18968.doc.htm.

United Nations (n.d.), 'Vulnerable People: People of African Descent'. Accessed at: www.un.org/en/letsfightracism/africandescent.shtml.

United Nations, Department of Economic and Social Affairs (UN DESA) (2009) *State of the World's Indigenous Peoples*. New York: United Nations.

United Nations High Commission on Refugees (2019), 'News Comment – UNHCR Appeals for Access to Refugees on Algeria–Niger Border', 3 January. Accessed at: www.unhcr.org/uk/news/press/2019/1/5c2e35b94/news-comment-unhcr-appeals-access-refugees-algeria-niger-border.html.

United Nations, Human Rights, Office of the High Commissioner (2016), 'Statement by the United Nations Special Rapporteur on the Rights to Freedom of Peaceful Assembly and of Association at the Conclusion of his Visit to the United States of America'. Accessed at: www.ohchr.org/EN/NewsEvents/Pages/DisplayNews.aspx?NewsID=20317&LangID=E.

United Nations, Human Rights, Office of the High Commissioner (2017), 'Statement on Visit to the USA, by Professor Philip Alston, United Nations Special Rapporteur on Extreme Poverty and Human Rights', 15 December. Accessed at: www.ohchr.org/EN/NewsEvents/Pages/DisplayNews.aspx?NewsID=22533&LangID=E.

United Nations, Human Rights, Office of the High Commissioner (2018a), 'Statement on Visit to the United Kingdom, by Professor Philip Alston, United Nations Special Rapporteur on Extreme Poverty and Human Rights', 16 November. Accessed at: www.ohchr.org/Documents/Issues/Poverty/EOM_GB_16Nov2018.pdf.

United Nations, Human Rights, Office of the High Commissioner (2018b), 'France: Banning the Niqab Violated Two Muslim Women's Freedom of

Religion – UN Experts', 23 October. Accessed at: www.ohchr.org/EN/NewsEvents/Pages/DisplayNews.aspx?NewsID=23750&LangID=E.

United Nations, Human Rights, Office of the High Commissioner (2019), 'UN Human Rights Chief Deeply Concerned by Mass Terrorism Convictions in Bahrain', 18 April. Accessed at: www.ohchr.org/EN/NewsEvents/Pages/DisplayNews.aspx?NewsID=24502&LangID=E.

United Nations, Human Rights Council (2016), *Report of the Working Group of Experts on People of African Descent on its Mission to the United States of America*. Accessed at: https://documents-dds-ny.un.org/doc/UNDOC/GEN/G16/183/30/PDF/G1618330.pdf?OpenElement.

United Nations, Human Rights Council (2018), *Report to Human Rights Council – 2018. Attacks against and Criminalization of Indigenous Peoples Defending Their Rights*, Thirty-ninth session, 10–28 September 2018, Agenda item 3. Accessed at: http://unsr.vtaulicorpuz.org/site/index.php?option=com_content&view=article&id=251%3Areport-hrc2018&catid=11%3Aannual-reports&Itemid=40&lang=en.

United Nations, Human Rights Council (2019), *Annex to the Report of the Special Rapporteur on Extrajudicial, Summary or Arbitrary Executions: Investigation into the Unlawful Death of Mr. Jamal Khashoggi*, Forty-first session, 24 June – 12 July 2019. Accessed at: https://digitallibrary.un.org/record/842553?ln=en.

United States Department of State (2019), 'Mike Pompeo: Remarks to the Press', 26 March. Accessed at: www.state.gov/secretary/remarks/2019/03/290669.htm.

University College London (n.d.), *Legacies of British Slave-Ownership*. Accessed at: www.ucl.ac.uk/lbs/project.

University of Bristol (n.d.), 'Past Matters: The University of Bristol and Transatlantic Slavery'. Accessed at: www.bristol.ac.uk/university/history/past-matters.

Utley, Robert (1963), *The Last Days of the Sioux Nation*, New Haven: Yale University Press.

Van der Schyff, Dylan (2010), 'The Algerian Harkis: témoignages d'une histoire cachée', *International Journal of the Humanities*, 8, 1: 147–55.

Van der Wetering, Simone Antonia Lucia (2017), 'Stigmatization and the Social Construction of a Normal Identity in the Parisian Banlieues', *Geoforum*. Accessed at: www.sciencedirect.com./science/article/pii/S0016718517301276?via%3Dihub.

Vestal, Stanley (1932), *Sitting Bull: Champion of the Sioux*, Norman: University of Oklahoma Press.

Vestal, Stanley (1934), *New Sources of Indian History 1850–1891*, Norman: University of Oklahoma Press.

Vidal-Naquet, Pierre (1963), *Torture: Cancer of Democracy – France and Algeria 1954–1962*, Baltimore: Penguin.

Vine, David (2011), 'From the Birth of the Ilois to the "Footprint of Freedom": A History of Chagos and the Chagossians', in Sandra Evers and Marry Kooy (eds.), *Eviction from the Chagos Islands: Displacement and Struggle for Identity against Two World Powers*, Leiden: Brill, 11–36.

Vinik, Danny (2014), 'The Economics of Reparations: Why Congress Should Meet Ta-Nehisi Coates's Modest Demand', *New Republic*, 22 May. Accessed at: https://newrepublic.com/article/117856/academic-evidence-reparations-costs-are-limited.

Viscusi, Gregory, and Simon Gongo (2017), 'Macron Says He Aims to Leave France's Colonial Past in Africa Behind', *Bloomberg News*, 28 November. Accessed at: www.bloomberg.com/news/articles/2017-11-28/macron-tells-african-crowd-he-aims-to-leave-colonial-past-behind.

Vizenor, Gerald, and Jill Doerfler (2012), *The White Earth Nation: Ratification of a Native Democratic Constitution*, Lincoln: University of Nebraska Press.

Von Bernuth, Lauren (2019), 'Bill to Protect Pipelines from Public Records Requests Moves Forward in North Dakota', *Citizen Truth*, 20 March. Accessed at: https://citizentruth.org/bill-to-protect-pipelines-from-public-records-requests-moves-forward-in-north-dakota.

Wagner, Adam (2019), 'After Brexit They Will Come for Human Rights – and This Time the Public Debate Must Be Won', *Prospect*, 9 June. Accessed at: www.prospectmagazine.co.uk/politics/after-brexit-they-will-come-for-human-rights-and-this-time-the-public-debate-must-be-won.

Walker, Peter (2018), 'Amber Rudd Condemns UN Poverty Report in Combative Return to Frontline Politics', *The Guardian*, 19 November. Accessed at www.theguardian.com/politics/2018/nov/19/amber-rudd-un-poverty-report-return-frontline-politics.

Walker, Samuel, Cassia Spohn and Miriam DeLone (2000), *The Color of Justice: Race, Ethnicity and Crime in America*, Belmont, CA: Wadsworth.

Walter, Natasha (2017), 'Heimat', *New York Review of Books*, 23 November: 10–12.

Wang, Tova Andrea (2012), *The Politics of Voter Suppression: Defending and Expanding Americans' Right to Vote*, Ithaca, NY: Cornell University Press.

Watters, Shane (2016), 'Old Boy Networks: The Relationship between Elite Schooling, Social Capital, and Positions of Power in British Society', in Aaron Koh and Jane Kenway (eds.), *Elite Schools: Multiple Geographies of Privilege*, London: Routledge, 101–16.

Weale, Sally (2016), 'Michael Gove's Claims about History Teaching Are False, Says Research', *The Guardian*, 13 September. Accessed at: www.theguardian.com/world/2016/sep/13/michael-goves-claims-about-history-teaching-are-false-says-research.

Weaver, John (2003), *The Great Land Rush and the Making of the Modern World, 1650–1900*, Montreal and Kingston: McGill-Queen's University Press.

Weber, Max (1958) [1919], 'Politics as a Vocation', in H. H. Gerth and C. Wright Mills (eds.), *From Max Weber: Essays in Sociology*, New York: Oxford University Press, 77–128.

Weissbrodt, David, and Amy Bergquist (2006), 'Extraordinary Rendition: A Human Rights Analysis', *Harvard Human Rights Journal*, 19: 123–60.

Weizman, Eyal (2007), *Hollow Land: Israel's Architecture of Occupation*, London: Verso.

Welch, James, with Paul Stekler (1994), *Killing Custer: The Battle of Little Bighorn and the Fate of the Plains Indians*, New York: Penguin.

Wilkinson, Bert (2018), 'Guyana Scrubs Witchcraft, Colonial Laws', *Caribbean Life*, 13 October. Accessed at: www.caribbeanlifenews.com/stories/2018/10/2018-10-12-bw-guyana-scrubs-witchcraft-laws-cl.html.

Williams, Timothy, and Mitch Smith (2015), 'Cleveland Officer Will Not Face Charges in Tamir Rice Shooting Death', *The New York Times*, 28 December. Accessed at: www.nytimes.com/2015/12/29/us/tamir-rice-police-shootiing-cleveland.html.

Wines, Michael, and Richard Fausset (2018), 'Federal Court Throws Out North Carolina's Congressional Districts, Again', *The New York Times*, 27 August. Accessed at: www.nytimes.com/2018/08/27/us/north-carolina-congressional-districts.html?emc=edit_th_180828&nl=todaysheadlines&nlid=212771010828.

Winston, Ali (2019), '"Not a Big Deal", Police Commander Said as Eric Garner Died', *The New York Times*, 16 May. Accessed at: www.nytimes.com/2019/05/16/nyregion/eric-garner-pantaleo-trial.html?nl=todaysheadlines&emc=edit_th_190517.

Withnall, Adam (2014), 'How Much for Dinner with David Cameron? Tories Reveal List of "Mega-Rich Donors" Who Spend £50,000 to Dine with the PM', *The Independent*, 13 November. Accessed at: www.independent.co.uk/news/uk/politics/how-much-for-dinner-with-david-cameron-tories-reveal-list-of-mega-rich-donors-who-spend-50000-to-9858102.html.

Wong, Edward, Eric Schmidt and Eileen Sullivan (2018), 'Trump Calls Relations with Saudi Arabia "Excellent", While Congress Is Incensed', *The New York Times*, 11 October. Accessed at: www.nytimes.com/2018/10/11/us/politics/trump-jamal-khashoggi-turkey-saudi.html.

Woodward, C. Vann (1966), *The Strange Career of Jim Crow*, 2nd edition, New York: Oxford University Press.

Wootliff, Raoul (2018), 'Final Text of Jewish Nation-State Law, Approved by the Knesset Early on July 19', *Times of Israel*, 18 July. Accessed at: www.timesofisrael.com/final-text-of-jewish-nation-state-bill-set-to-become-law.

Worley, Will (2017), '"Stunning" Gaffe: Appalled Ambassador Stops Boris Johnson Reciting Colonial Poem in Burma's Holiest Site', *The Independent*, 30 September. Accessed at: www.independent.co.uk/news/world/asia/boris-johnson-poem-burma-rudyard-kipling-mandalay-a7975246.html.

Worth, Robert (2019), 'Yemen under Siege', *New York Review of Books*, 21 February. Accessed at: www.nybooks.com/articles/2019/02/21/yemen-under-siege.

Wunder, John (1994), *'Retained by the People': A History of American Indians and the Bill of Rights*, New York: Oxford University Press.

YouGov (2014), 'The British Empire Is "Something to Be Proud of"'. Accessed at: https://yougov.co.uk/news/2014/07/26/britain-proud-its-empire.

Younge, Gary (2018), 'Britain's Imperial Fantasies Have Given Us Brexit', *The Guardian*, 3 February. Accessed at: www.theguardian.com/commentisfree/2018/feb/03/imperial-fantasies-brexit-theresa-may.

Zandonini, Giacomo (2018), '"Your Skin Colour Was a Crime": African Migrants in Algeria', Al Jazeera, 24 December. Accessed at: www. aljazeera.com/indepth/features/skin-colour-crime-african-migrants-algeria-181222084531701.html.

Zanolli, Lauren (2018), '"They're Billin' Us for Killin' Us": Activists Fight Dakota Pipeline's Final Stretch', *The Guardian*, 17 October. Accessed at: www.theguardian.com/environment/2018/oct/16/dakota-access-pipeline-bayou-bridge-protest-activism.

Zimring, Franklin (2017), *When Police Kill*, Cambridge, MA: Harvard University Press.

Zitkala-Ša (2003), *American Indian Stories, Legends and Other Writings*, Harmondsworth: Penguin.

Zotigh, Dennis (2018), 'The 1868 Treaty of Fort Laramie, Never Honored by the United States, Goes on Public View', *Smithsonian Magazine*, 30 October. Accessed at: www.smithsonianmag.com/blogs/national-museum-american-indian/2018/10/31/treaty-fort-laramie/#ZJOhhbIzqoyTm2jc.99.

# Index